𝕿𝖍𝖊 𝕯𝖆𝖎𝖑𝖞 𝕿
GARDENER'S GUIDE
TO BRITAIN

PATRICK TAYLOR

The Daily Telegraph
GARDENER'S GUIDE
TO BRITAIN

PAVILION

DEDICATION
For Laura, with much love

First published 1992 by
PAVILION BOOKS LIMITED
26 Upper Ground, London SE1 9PD

Reprinted 1993, 1994, 1995 and 1996

Text copyright © 1996 Patrick Taylor

Illustrations © Open Books Publishing Ltd
except pages 36 (© Robin Loder) and 279 (© Faith Raven)

This book was devised and produced by
Open Books Publishing Ltd, Beaumont House,
Wells BA5 2LD, Somerset, UK

Designer: Andrew Barron

Maps: John Gilkes

Computer Consultant: Mike Mepham

All rights reserved. No part of this publication may be
reproduced, stored in a retrieval system, or transmitted in
any form or by any means, electronic, mechanical,
photocopying, recording or otherwise, without the prior
permission of the copyright holders.

A CIP catalogue record for this book is available from the
British Library

ISBN: 1-85793-771-6

Printed and Bound in Hong Kong by
Mandarin Offset

CONTENTS

7 INTRODUCTION

9 SOUTH-EAST ENGLAND
Kent, London, Surrey, Sussex

59 SOUTH-CENTRAL ENGLAND
Berkshire, Buckinghamshire, Hampshire,
Oxfordshire, Wiltshire

95 SOUTH-WEST ENGLAND
Cornwall, Devon, Dorset, Somerset

143 WALES AND WEST-CENTRAL ENGLAND
Cheshire, Gloucestershire, Hereford and Worcester,
Shropshire

183 THE HEART OF ENGLAND
Derbyshire, Leicestershire, Northamptonshire,
Nottinghamshire, Staffordshire, Warwickshire,
West Midlands

211 THE EAST OF ENGLAND
Bedfordshire, Cambridgeshire, Essex, Hertfordshire,
Lincolnshire, Norfolk, Suffolk

249 THE NORTH OF ENGLAND
Cumbria, County Durham, Humberside, Lancashire,
Northumberland, Yorkshire

275 SCOTLAND

307 NORTHERN IRELAND

311 APPENDICES
Types of Gardens and Garden Features; Nurseries for
Specific Kinds of Plants; Gardens by Famous
Designers; National Collections of Plants

317 INDEX

INTRODUCTION & ACKNOWLEDGEMENTS

This is the fifth edition of *The Gardener's Guide to Britain*. All details of every place in the book have been checked and, where necessary, revised. This, of course, includes opening times, telephone numbers and other practicalities of this sort. In addition I have noted any major changes in the gardens and described shifts of direction in the nurseries. For the first time one or two places are included which open by appointment only. In these cases I know that the owners truly welcome visitors.

I should like to spell out once again the principles that lie behind the book. It describes, region by region, places of special interest to gardeners that are open regularly to the public. Uniquely, it includes nurseries and shops for pots and ornaments, as well as gardens of every kind. It is a *personal* choice but occasionally I have included some historic garden, not much to my taste, because its renown has conferred upon it almost holy status and it cannot be ignored. For this new edition I have added many new gardens. Some of these (such as the marvellous Wollerton Old Hall) are fairly recently made and others (like the exquisite Renishaw Hall) now open sufficiently frequently to be included.

Opening times, and other practical details, have been checked to the very last moment. But these may change and it is always worth checking by phone before setting out on a long special journey. Dates shown are inclusive – Mar to Sept means from the 1st March to the 30th September. One or two places had not fixed their opening times when we went to press. I have left these in, giving the phone number so that visits can be made. Most gardens will not welcome you less than 45 minutes before closing time. I have indicated those places where the house is also open but I do not give opening times for it. While it is often possible, by prior appointment, to make visits at other times than those shown, it is absolutely essential to give plenty of notice. It is not wise, or courteous, to assume that you can just turn

*Illustration opposite:
The garden at Tresco*

up – no garden welcomes last minute intrusions.

Many of the best nurseries are very small and the proprietor has from time to time to desert his or her post. For these, it is especially important to check by phone beforehand. Some of the nurseries produce catalogues, many of which are precious reference books. I have included the price of them where appropriate.

I should like to thank The National Trust, and The National Trust for Scotland, both of which gave me much vital help. Private owners have also been extremely helpful and I am truly grateful to them. My wife Caroline has become an even more essential contributor than before and I am very deeply in her debt. The designer, Andrew Barron of Andrew Barron and Collis Clements Associates, has continued to weave his magic spell over the appearance of the book, for which I thank him most warmly.

Colin Webb and his colleagues at Pavilion Books have been the ideal publishers – most grateful thanks to them for all their friendly advice and help.

Patrick Taylor
Wells, Somerset

SOUTH-EAST ENGLAND
Kent
London
Surrey
Sussex

ALFRISTON CLERGY HOUSE
East Sussex

The Tye, Alfriston,
Polegate BN26 5TL
4m NE of Seaford by
B2108
Tel: 01323 870001

Owner:
The National Trust

Open: 30 Mar to 2 Nov,
daily 10.30-5 or sunset if
earlier. 1/2 acre. House
open

ALTHOUGH THE garden surrounding this beautiful medieval hall house is quite small it has all sorts of virtues and many ideas for owners of gardens with limited space. It has a wide range of different styles – from brick-edged borders of cottage-garden exuberance to a charmingly austere parterre of standard box trees clipped into umbrellas and underplanted with pinks. A herb garden has square beds with low hedges of santolina and there is a proper kitchen garden. A trickling stream runs along one side of the garden and beyond there are views of the countryside and the downs.

JACQUES AMAND LTD
Middlesex

Illustration: Fritillaria
michailovsky

The Nurseries, 146 Clamp
Hill, Stanmore HA7 3JS
NW of London off the
Uxbridge Road (A410)
Tel: 0181 954 8138
Fax: 0181 954 6784

Open: Mon to Fri 9–5, Sat
9–4, Sun 9–1.30 (closed Sun
in Dec and Jan)

JACQUES AMAND specialises in bulbs of which he sells one of the best selections in the country, and regularly wins medals at RHS shows and elsewhere. Although he also carries a few shrubs such as dwarf rhododendrons and some herbaceous perennials, especially those that are suitable for woodland gardens, like *Jeffersonia diphylla* and *Mertensia virginica*, it is the bulbs that are the great glory of the place – very many alliums, fritillaries, lilies and narcissi are stocked, and less usual plants such as trilliums of which an exceptional range is listed. Well illustrated complimentary catalogues, full of useful advice on cultivation, are produced in spring and autumn from which orders by post may be made. There is a special spring display area.

ARCHITECTURAL PLANTS
West Sussex

Cooks Farm, Nuthurst,
Horsham RH13 6LH
2m S of Horsham by A281
and minor roads
Tel: 01403 891772
Fax: 01403 891056

Open: Mon to Sat 9–5

ARCHITECTURAL PLANTS has a completely distinctive house style. It sells plants that have strong architectural shapes and contribute to the structure of the garden. Angus White, the founder, described his garden in winter as being as fascinating to look at as 'a wet breeze block'; he wanted to find exotic, preferably evergreen plants to give winter liveliness. This nursery is his answer. His elegant list (free) is colour coded – green means that a plant is perfectly hardy, orange that a plant will survive in the right site in the southern counties, and red that a plant will survive only on the Atlantic coast or the privileged islands. The list is full of rarities – like the cartwheel tree, *Trochodendron aralioides*, or the Mexican strawberry tree (*Arbutus glandulosa*) – and packed with information. A mail order service is provided but it is much better to go to Cooks Farm and see the exotics in splendid action.

BATEMAN'S
East Sussex

Burwash,
Etchingham TN19 7DS
1/2 m S of Burwash by A265
Tel: 01435 882302

Owner:
The National Trust

Open: 30 Mar to 2 Nov, daily except Thur and Fri (open Good Fri) 11–5.30. 10 acres. House open

RUDYARD KIPLING lived here, in the handsome early 17th-century house, from 1902 to 1936 and himself designed many of the existing features of the elegant garden. The site is flat but it is animated by attractive decorative ingredients and a strongly designed layout. Above the house a beautiful tunnel of pears and clematis trained over broad arches is underplanted with bergenias, spring bulbs, geraniums and Corsican hellebores. A path leads down one side of the house and occasional 'windows' cut in a yew hedge give glimpses of the country beyond. In the formal garden a curved seat in a bower of clipped yew overlooks a long rectangular pool. At the end of the pool there is a rose garden with flagged paths and beds of floribunda roses, and to one side of it a shady double pleached lime walk. The whole place has the air of the quintessential English garden of the Edwardian period; the sort of thing dreamed of by homesick men in Poona.

BEDGEBURY NATIONAL PINETUM
Kent

nr Goudhurst, TN17 2SL
4 1/2 m S of Goudhurst by B2079
Tel: 01580 211044
Fax: 01580 212423

Owner:
The Forestry Commission

Open: Daily 10–dusk.
160 acres

BEDGEBURY PINETUM lies in a splendid site in a broad and deep valley. An ornamental lake at the bottom provides the right conditions for moisture-loving plants such as swamp cypresses, of which there are some handsome specimens, and on the slopes of the valley conifers are grouped either by kind – cypressess, junipers, spruces and so on – or by place of origin – the Chinese glade, the American glade or the Japanese glade. Conifers are obviously the main meal here but the menu is varied with some deciduous trees and many rhododendrons. The appearance of evergreens varies subtly through the growing year – the changing colour of foliage and fruit – and a visit is rewarding in any season. Bedgebury holds National Collections of junipers, of Lawson cypress cultivars and of yews. In the autumn an added interest is the outstanding range of mushrooms that flourishes here. Open throughout the year, there is always something to admire.

BORDE HILL
West Sussex

Haywards Heath
RH16 1XP
1 1/2m N of Haywards Heath by minor roads
Tel: 01444 450326

Owner:
Borde Hill Gardens Ltd

Open: 17 Mar to 29 Sept, daily 10–6. 40 acres

BORDE HILL is famous for trees and shrubs but near the house there are handsome flower gardens and formal planting: a pair of ebullient borders leads towards the house and, on the west terrace, a mysterious marble statue of a veiled lady emerges from clumps of euphorbia. That is all very decorative but the serious matter at Borde Hill is the splendid collection of ornamental woody plants. It was started in 1892 by Colonel Stephenson Clarke who was one of the sponsors of the great plant-hunting expeditions to the Chinese Himalayas between the wars. Thus, the garden is wonderfully rich in magnolias and rhododendrons (particularly species) which relish the light, slightly acid soil. But the collection is wide-ranging and there are also very good conifers in Warren Wood and rare deciduous trees, particularly American species, in Little Bentley Wood. The agreeably undulating site makes it a most attractive place in which to admire some marvellous plants.

BROGDALE HORTICULTURAL TRUST

Kent

Brogdale Road, Faversham
ME13 8XZ
1m SE of Faversham
Tel: 01795 535286

Owner: The Brogdale Horticultural Trust

Open: Apr to Dec, Wed to Sun (and Bank Hol Mon) 11-5. 150 acres

BROGDALE HAS the national collection of fruit with over 4,000 varieties disposed in 30 acres of orchards. It is a marvellous enterprise, preserving, for example, 2,300 old cultivars of apples alone. Guided tours of the orchards are offered and fruit is for sale in season. Special events of a fruity kind are organised throughout the year, reaching their climax with the great Apple Celebration held in October. There are plants for sale, including a collection of citrus fruit and other tender kinds displayed by Read's, the Norfolk specialist (see p. 241).

CAPEL MANOR

Middlesex

DISPLAY GARDENS such as this can be both entertaining and instructive. On this substantial site surrounding the 18th-century manor house are many different thematic and demonstration gardens.

Bullsmoor Lane,
Enfield EN1 4RQ
14m N of Central London
by A10. Off M25 by
Jnct 25
Tel: 01992 763849
Fax: 01992 717544

Owner: Capel Manor
Horticultural and
Environmental Centre

Open: Daily 10–5.30 (last
ticket 4.30, dusk in winter).
30 acres

A series of historical gardens includes a Tudor-style knot, a formal 17th-century garden and a recently planted prickly maze of holly taken from William Nesfield's design for the great exhibition in 1851. A garden for the physically disabled is full of ideas and a 'Sensory Garden' rich with the scent of herbs and the sounds of water is designed for the visually impaired. Demonstration gardens – woodland, water and courtyard – give ideas for design and planting. Recently opened are a beautifully laid out Japanese garden displaying all the essential features of that tradition of gardening; and a wildlife garden. Capel Manor is a satisfying mixture of both useful practical information and inspiration.

CHARLESTON FARMHOUSE
East Sussex

nr Firle, Lewes BN8 6LL
6m E of Lewes by A27
Tel: 01323 811265 (visitors)
01323 811626
(administration)
Fax: 01323 811628

Owner:
The Charleston Trust

Open: Apr to Oct, Wed to
Sun and Bank Hol Mon
2–6 (12 Jul to 3 Sept 11–6);
last admission 5pm. 1 acre.
House open

CHARLESTON FARMHOUSE may fairly be described as the country seat of the Bloomsbury set. Vanessa and Clive Bell, and Duncan Grant, lived here, and the whole place, now most sympathetically restored, is redolent of Bloomsbury. In the walled garden, with gravel paths and narrow borders, the planting is cheerfully colourful – the horticultural equivalent of Omega workshop textiles. Old apple trees erupt from borders and a long box hedge has been clipped into undulating waves. Everywhere there are decorative touches – a pottery mask overlooking a little pool, mosaics of broken china (Bloomsbury and older) on a terrace, amusing busts dotted along a wall. Outside the walled garden, by a wild orchard, Ophelia floats on the edge of a pool and Venus lurks in a grove of cow parsley. All this gives a vivid picture of one of the most attractive aspects of Bloomsbury life.

CHELSEA PHYSIC GARDEN
London

Illustration opposite: Venus
among cow parsley at
Charleston Farmhouse

A 4-ACRE WALLED GARDEN – with full Secret Garden character – in the middle of London is a marvel. Founded as a garden of medicinal herbs in 1673 it became, especially under the directorship of Philip Miller in the 18th century, an important botanic

66 Royal Hospital Road,
SW3 4HS
Tube: Sloane Square
Tel: 0171 352 5646

Owner: Trustees of Chelsea Physic Garden

Open: Apr to Oct, Sun 2–6 and Wed 2–5; also during Chelsea Flower Show week and Chelsea Festival week. 4 acres

garden. It still possesses a large collection of herbs, a range of 'order' beds and a research area. But there are magnificent trees including male and female *Ginkgo biloba*, a cork oak (*Quercus suber*) and a splendid olive tree (which in fine years produces big crops) and all sorts of other tender things relishing the protection of the old walls. The garden holds the National Collection of cistus and has some good plants for sale.

CHILSTONE GARDEN ORNAMENTS
Kent

Victoria Park Farm,
Fordcombe Road, Langton Green, Tunbridge Wells
TNB3 0RE
3m W of Tunbridge Wells on A264
Tel: 01892 740110

Open: Mon to Fri, 9–5, Sun 10–4.30

CHILSTONE make high-quality composition stone garden ornaments and architectural pieces, many meticulous copies of fine originals. The firm has recently moved to these new quarters at Victoria Park where the ornaments are handsomely arranged in woodland. In the display garden is arranged a lovely profusion of the stock – colonnades, sprinkling fountains, impassive sphinxes, stately urns and the busts of emperors.

CHISWICK HOUSE
London

Burlington Lane,
Chiswick W4 2RP
4m SW of Central London
by A4 and A316
Tel: 0181 742 1225

Owner: London Borough of Hounslow

Open: Daily 7.30–dusk.
62 acres. House open

L ORD BURLINGTON built Chiswick House as a pleasure dome in 1723-9 and surrounded it with appropriate gardens. The house itself, domed and portico'd, dominates the formal garden with its avenue of cypresses interspersed with grand urns. To one side, slightly hidden, a circular sunken pool is surrounded by orange trees in pots and overlooked by a temple. At a little distance from the house a Victorian garden has a dazzling conservatory and a parterre of arabesques of clipped box, lush bedding schemes and an avenue of mop-headed acacias.

CHURCH HILL COTTAGE GARDENS
Kent

Charing Heath, Ashford
TN27 0BU
8m NW of Ashford by A20; 400 yds from Red Lion pub towards Charing Heath church
Tel: 01233 712522

Open: Feb to Nov, Tue to Sun (and Bank Hol Mon) 10–5

A N ATTRACTIVE development in recent years is that of the small nursery alongside the owners' private garden where the plants can be seen in cultivation. The nursery here specialises in herbaceous perennials with excellent collections of penstemons, named varieties of pinks, herbaceous sages, unusual verbenas and violas. The garden next door to the nursery permits the distinctive virtues of these and other plants to be seen and savoured. A winding stream is edged with waterside plants, and herbaceous beds are given an occasional note of emphasis by some well-placed ornamental tree – a golden acacia or a variegated maple, for example. An immense number of plants is grown, some of them very unfamiliar.

CLANDON PARK
Surrey

West Clandon GU4 7RQ
3m E of Guildford off A25
Tel: 01483 222482
Fax: 01483 223479

Owner:
The National Trust

Open: Mar, Sat and Sun 12–5.30; 30 Mar to 30 Oct, daily except Thur and Fri (open Good Fri) 1.30–5.30; Sat 12–4; Bank Hol Mon 11–5.30. 8 acres.

THE MANSION at Clandon Park, built of brick and stone in about 1730, dominates the garden. Under its south façade a neat parterre of box hedges, topiary box cones and summer bedding is flanked by raised hedges of clipped hornbeam. Across the lawn, a damp and ferny flint grotto houses a cluster of shivering nymphs, almost certainly dating from the late 18th-century landscaping of the garden. To one side of this, in the shade of an immense oak, there is a charming oddity, a carved and painted Maori house brought here in the 1890s by the 4th Earl of Onslow who had served as Governor of New Zealand. Half-way up the drive, rather tucked away and easy to miss, is a Dutch garden enclosed in tall yew hedges and laid out in a geometric pattern of hedges of box, lavender and variegated euonymus, with pyramids of white roses rising above.

CLAREMONT LANDSCAPE GARDEN
Surrey

Portsmouth Road,
Esher KT10 9JG
14m SW of Central London by A3
Tel: 01372 469421

Owner:
The National Trust

Open: Jan to Mar, daily except Mon 10–5 (or sunset if earlier); Apr to Oct, Mon to Fri 10–6, Sat, Sun and Bank Hol Mon 10–7 (10 Jul closed; 12–16 Jul closes 2); Nov to March, daily except Mon 10–5 or sunset if earlier (closed 25 Dec). 49 acres

THE LANDSCAPE GARDEN at Claremont had virtually disappeared from view, drowned in a sea of rhododendrons and laurels, until the National Trust took it in hand in 1975. Some of the greatest figures in landscape design worked here from 1720 onwards – Sir John Vanbrugh, Charles Bridgeman, William Kent and 'Capability' Brown. What has now been restored is chiefly the work of the first three and what the visitor may see, never mind garden history, is an enchanting garden of woodland, beech alleys rising steeply uphill, a vast turf amphitheatre which looks down on a lake with an island temple designed by Kent, and beautiful stands of sweet chestnuts.

This is not a garden for those who love only flower power. At summer weekends it fills with people picnicking and savouring the delights of an Elysian oasis threatened on all sides by suburbia.

COGHURST NURSERY
East Sussex

Illustration: Camellia
'Jury's Yellow'

Ivy House Lane, nr Three Oaks, Hastings TN35 4NP
3 1/2m NE of Hastings by A259 and minor roads
Tel: 01424 756228

Open: Mon to Fri 12–4.30, Sun 10–4.30

CAMELLIAS ARE the main thing at Coghurst and they have one of the best collections in the country, including many that are available commercially nowhere else. They grow well over 300 varieties including a particularly choice range of cultivars of the autumn-flowering *C. sasanqua* and the tender *C. reticulata*. Even if you do not not have acid soil camellias are among the most marvellous of plants for pots, making marvellous winter ornaments. Coghurst also sell a good range of rhododendrons – including many evergreen azaleas – mostly cultivars but with a choice handful of species. Catalogues are issued (two 2nd-class stamps) and smaller specimens may be sent by post.

CROWTHER OF SYON LODGE
Middlesex

CROWTHER PIONEERED dealing in antique garden ornaments and architectural fragments and their premises at Syon Lodge are a treasure trove of wonderful things. Here, displayed in a crowded garden is a bewildering and constantly changing profusion of temples, seats, statues, urns and fountains. All are decorative and some are distinguished – and expensive – works of art. Many

Busch Corner, London
Road, Isleworth TW7 5BH
3 1/2m SW of central
London by A315
Tel: 0181 560 7978
Fax: 0181 568 7572

Open: Mon to Fri 9–5, Sat
to Sun 11–4.30 and at other
times by appointment

of them have grand provenances and are the sort of thing about which a new garden may be designed. There are very few places anywhere in the world where such a range of garden ornaments of this quality may be found for sale. Displayed all together in such profusion the ever-changing stock gives the place a dream-like quality, like a scene from an elegant surrealistic film.

DENMANS
West Sussex

Fontwell,
nr Arundel BN18 0SU
5m E of Chichester on A27
Tel: 01243 542808
Fax: 01243544064

Owner: Mrs J.H. Robinson
(with John Brookes)

Open: Daily 9–5 (closed 25
Dec and 1 Jan).
3 1/2 acres

THIS UNUSUAL GARDEN was started in 1946 by Mrs J.H. Robinson and for the last thirteen years has been run by the well-known garden designer and writer, John Brookes. The entrance is through a huge glasshouse, which houses a large collection of tender plants. Gravel paths meander across a walled garden in which profuse herbaceous planting is given structure by huge clipped mounds of variegated box, a handsome strawberry tree and the bold foliage of rhus and rheum. Beyond, in the main garden, sweeping beds have mixed plantings and there is repeated use of yellow foliage, particularly of golden yew and *Robinia pseudoacacia* 'Frisia'. There are many unusual plants here, and an attractively bold sense of design with the creative use of interesting foliage. A small nursery sells some good plants, mostly herbaceous but with a carefully chosen selection of shrub roses. An excellent catalogue (£2.50) is produced but there is no mail order. The potential of most of the plants may be seen handsomely displayed in the adjacent garden, so a visit will be doubly rewarded.

EMMETTS GARDEN
Kent

Ide Hill,
Sevenoaks TN14 6AY
1 1/2m N of Ide Hill by
B2042
Tel: 01732 750367/750429

Owner:
The National Trust

Open: Mar, Sat and Sun
2–5; 30 Mar to 2 Nov,
Wed to Sun and Bank Hol
Mon 1–6. 6 acres

THIS IS THE highest point in Kent and the garden has splendid views of the North Downs. Many of the best plants date from the sale of stock from Veitch's famous nursery in 1907 when Frederick Lubbock, a friend of William Robinson, lived here. He put into practice Robinson's idea of arranging hardy exotic plants in a naturalistic setting. A formal rose garden is hedged in thuja, and a rock garden added by a later owner, are the only tamed parts of what is essentially an informal garden of wild character which merges imperceptibly with the surrounding woodland and scrub. The soil is acid and there are many azaleas, camellias, eucryphias rhododendrons, stewartias and other ericaceous plants. Excellent trees and shrubs are to be seen everywhere – *Kalmia latifolia*, magnolias, maples, dogwoods – and there are also real rarities, such as the charming American fringe tree, *Chionanthus virginicus*. The slopes of the densely wooded valley are carpeted with bluebells. The two best seasons are spring for the profusion of flowering shrubs and bulbs, and autumn when there is a wonderful display of colour from azaleas, cercidiphyllums, maples and other deciduous trees and shrubs. The fine undulating site and profusion of good plants make it a wonderful place to explore.

FENTON HOUSE
London

Windmill Hill,
Hampstead NW3 6RT
In Hampstead village.
Tube: Hampstead
Tel: 0171 435 3471

Owner:
The National Trust

Open: Mar, Sat and Sun
2–5; Apr to Oct, Sat, Sun
and Bank Hol Mon
11–5.30, Wed, Thur and
Fri 1–5.30. 1 acre. House
open

A COMPLETE COUNTRY garden in the middle of Hampstead village reminds the visitor of the former rural character of this part of London. Fenton House, a suave Georgian house of brick, looks out over a formal garden in which a gravel path is edged with standard-trained Portugal laurels in tubs, and borders are given formality with rhythmic plantings of clipped lavender or Irish yews. At the far end, yew hedges conceal hidden borders and elegant benches. At a lower level, parallel to this, an orchard bursts into life in spring, with fruit blossom and many bulbs naturalised in the long grass – anemones, narcissi and snake's head fritillaries.

FISHBOURNE ROMAN PALACE GARDEN
West Sussex

Salthill Road,
Fishbourne PO19 3QR
1 1/2m W of Chichester by A259
Tel: 01243 785859
Fax: 01243 539266

Owner: Sussex Archaeological Society

Open: Mar, Apr, Oct, daily 10–5; May to Sept, daily 10–6; 14 to 28 Feb, Nov, 1 to 16 Dec, daily 10–4; remainder of year, Sun 10–4. 2 acres

THIS IS an unusual attempt to show what an aristocratic Roman garden would have looked like, based on archaeological examination of the site, and Roman gardening practice. The garden was originally entirely surrounded by a verandah with a colonnade; in this area a low box hedge is shaped into a geometric pattern and some of the characteristic Roman plants (such as acanthus) are used. A new development is a representative collection of plants grown by the Romans culled from classical sources and a display area shows typical features of gardens of the period – such as an out-of-doors dining room. In the adjoining museum are mosaics of exquisite beauty and a detailed model of the palace and the garden, showing how it appeared in its original state.

GODINTON PARK
Kent

Ashford TN23 3BW
1 1/2m W of Ashford at Potter's Corner on A20
Tel: 01233 620773

Owner: The Godinton House Preservation Trust

Open: Easter weekend, Jun to Sept, Sun 2–5. 12 acres. House open

NOTHING COULD BE a greater contrast to the creeping urbanism of Ashford than the exceptional park, dotted with wonderful oaks and Spanish chestnuts, through which one drives to Godinton. The gabled brick house is Jacobean and in 1902 Sir Reginal Blomfield added an appropriately

gabled garden – superb yew hedges clipped into gables surround the forecourt – deploying the full, delightful repertoire of the architectural garden. A figure of Pan lies at the heart of an intricate box parterre, Venus stands among purple cotinus at the head of a canal, a wisteria-hung white marble colonnade decorated with fine statues leads to a little Italian garden with a formal pool and loggia.

GOODNESTONE PARK
Kent

nr Wingham, Canterbury
CT3 1PL
7m E of Canterbury by A257 and minor roads; signposted from Wingham
Tel: 01304 840107

Owner: Lord and Lady FitzWalter

Open: Apr to Oct, Mon, Wed and Fri 11–5; Sun 12–6. 6 acres

THE CHARMS of this garden are revealed only gradually, but they are real and the place has memorable character. At first glance the visitor may think – 'oh dear, another old country house garden about to go to seed'. The entrance to the garden takes the visitor past the 18th-century mansion with traces of an old formal garden and specimen trees. A stupendous ancient sweet chestnut is suddenly revealed – and behind the house are equally ancient but rather battered cedars of Lebanon of tremendous presence. The trump card of the place is the series of exuberantly planted walled gardens between house and church which borrow the church tower as an eyecatcher for their central vista. Apart from excellent mixed borders here is a splendid kitchen garden with a central walk flanked by beds of old roses, peonies and delphinums. Some of the planting shows crafty colour planning – in one corner there is a sprightly arrangement of yellows and apricots includes asphodels, yellow daylilies, Moroccan broom, *Fremontodendron californicum*, orange pokers, the rose 'Buff Beauty' and a pale orange honeysuckle.

GRAVETYE MANOR
West Sussex

nr East Grinstead
RH19 4LJ
4m SW of East Grinstead
by B2110
Tel: 01342 810567
Fax: 01342 810080

Owner: Peter Herbert

Open: Perimeter walk only, Tue and Fri 10–5; private gardens by house, for use of hotel and restaurant customers *only*. 30 acres

THIS WAS the house and garden of William Robinson, the greatest and most influential of late-Victorian gardeners. Thanks to a brilliant restoration carried out by the present owner, visitors may now see a properly Robinsonian garden in all its splendour. The gabled 17th-century manor house, now an unashamedly comfortable hotel with one of the best restaurants in England, looks south across a valley. South and west of the house are formal gardens with many of the plants that Robinson loved. On the northern wooded slopes things become wilder, with azaleas, camellias and magnolias planted among the trees. South of the house, sweeping down to a lake made by Robinson, is a meadow dazzling in spring with naturalised bulbs where in summer the grass is allowed to grow long. Although in a densely populated part of England, Gravetye is at the heart of a large Forestry Commission wood and has preserved to a remarkable degree the authentically wild atmosphere that Robinson cherished.

GREAT COMP
Kent

Comp Lane, St Mary's Platt, nr Borough Green
TN15 8QS
7m E of Sevenoaks off A25; signposted on B2016, off A20/A25 between Sevenoaks and Maidstone
Tel: 01732 882669

Owner: Great Comp Charitable Trust

Open: Apr to Oct, daily 11–6. 7 acres

THERE IS something enticing about the design of the garden at Great Comp – paths lead the visitor on, curving out of sight round bold plantings. The atmosphere is essentially informal, an impression which is only sharpened by the occasional straight line and touch of formality. Against a background of deciduous woodland a very wide range of ornamental trees and shrubs relishes the acid loam. Spreading out south of the house a generous apron of impeccable lawn is fringed with tall conifers, oaks and willows and, as it reaches the woodland, bordered with beds of heathers. Paths lead off into the wilder woodland (and a temple lost in the woods) and thence back towards the house. Everywhere there are excellent trees and shrubs set off by well chosen underplanting – the larger campanulas, geraniums, hostas, lilies and violas. This is not a garden which depends on superficial fripperies – but capitalises on the very skilful use of carefully chosen ornaments and plants;

GREAT DIXTER
East Sussex

Northiam, Rye TN31 6PH
11m N of Hastings off A28
Tel: 01797 253107
Fax: 01797 252879

Owner: Christopher Lloyd

Open: Apr to mid-Oct, daily except Mon (but open Bank Hol Mon) 2–5. 5 acres. House open

THE DISTINGUISHED gardener/writer Christopher Lloyd is the genius of this place, with its timbered 15th-century house restored by Edwin Lutyens who also planned the garden upon which Mr Lloyd has put his lively stamp. Billowing yew topiary and cunning vistas date from Lutyens's time but most of the planting is of more recent date. Here is Christopher Lloyd's virtuoso mixed border which he constantly improves; sheets of spring flowers in the orchard; a meadow garden; and, wherever you look, fastidiously chosen plants of all kinds planted with a crafty eye for colour. A recent experiment is a late-summer 'tropical garden' rich in bold shapes and brilliant colours. No gardener could visit Great Dixter without making discoveries and rekindling the zest for gardening. There are good plants for sale of which there is a catalogue (75p), and they are sold by mail order.

GROOMBRIDGE PLACE GARDENS
Kent

Groombridge, Tunbridge Wells, Kent TN3 9QG
4m SW of Tunbridge Wells by A264 and B2110

Tel: 01892 861444
Fax: 01892 863996

Owner: Blenheim Asset Management

Open: Apr to Oct, daily 10–6. 164 acres

THE HOUSE at Groombridge is a wildly romantic and slightly gloomy brick 17th-century mansion suspended ethereally on a moat. Behind the house are gardens of formal inspiration with a parterre, an avenue of yews clipped into pillars, an oriental garden and a mysterious 'drunken garden' of misshapen yew and juniper topiary. At some distance from all this, across a field, is the 'Enchanted Forest' which is not a California-style cemetery but an ambitious and beautifully executed woodland garden packed with ideas. It is a place worth watching to see if this early promise is maintained.

HAM HOUSE
Surrey

THE EARLY 17th-century brick house was modernised in the smartest taste in the 1670s by the Duke and Duchess of Lauderdale who took as much interest in the garden as they did in the house. The garden decayed until in 1976 work was started

Ham, Richmond
TW10 7RS
Off A307 at Petersham,
SW of Central London
Tel: 0181 940 1950

Owner:
The National Trust

Open: Daily except Fri
(open Good Fri) 10.30–6 or
dusk if earlier, closed 25
and 26 Dec and 1 Jan.
18 acres. House open

by the National Trust on its restoration. This was helped by the survival of late 17th-century documentation – plans and plant lists – which enabled an authentic reconstruction. The formal walled garden south of the house is divided into spacious grass plats with a maze-like wilderness of hornbeam, winding paths and hidden pavilions. To one side a further walled garden has a large orangery (now a tea-room) with, sprawling in front of it, a vast *Paliurus spina-christi*, the thorned tree from which Christ's crown of thorns was supposed to have been made. In the east court on the other side of the house a parterre of gravel paths and box hedges is arranged in racy lozenges of lavender and santolina and overlooked by shady tunnels of yew and pleached hornbeam.

HAMPTON COURT
Surrey

East Molesey KT8 9AU
At Hampton Wick where
A308 and A309 meet,
6m SW of Central
London
Tel: 0181 781 9500
Fax: 0181 781 9509

Owner:
Historic Royal Palaces

Open: Daily, dawn–dusk.
30 acres. Palace open

THIS IS ONE of the most famous places in England and has much to interest the gardener. It was started by Thomas Wolsey in the early 16th century and became a royal palace, which it remains. In the late 17th century Sir Christopher Wren added grandiose extensions to the Tudor palace and was involved in the design of a new garden of which part of his 'wilderness' survives: a yew maze – the earliest known hedge maze in England. South of the palace the original royal privy garden, has been

THE SOUTH-EAST OF ENGLAND · 29

Illustration opposite: 17th-century avenue at Hampton Court

triumphantly restored showing exactly what King William III would have seen in the late 17th century. Views of the Thames are framed by Jean Tijou's exquisite late 17th-century wrought-iron screen. Nearer the palace there is a colourful (some say *too* colourful) sunken pond garden and a reconstructed Tudor knot. In the vinery is a 'Black Hamburgh' grape-vine planted in 1768 and still productive. To the east of the palace old topiary of yew and holly rise above spring and summer bedding schemes, and three noble lime avenues radiate from a semi-circle of clipped yew and holly.

HAZELDENE NURSERY
Kent

Dean Street, East Farleigh, Maidstone ME15 0PS
3m SW of Maidstone by B2010
Tel: 01622 726248

Open: Mar to Sept, by appointment

VIOLETS AND VIOLAS are the speciality of this nursery which has won Gold Medals at Chelsea for its excellent plants. An immense range is sold of winter- and summer-flowering pansies, violas, violettas and species violets. Many varieties are propagated by cuttings to preserve their identity. An informative list is produced (s.a.e.), with valuable information on cultivation, and a mail order service is provided both for growing plants and for seeds of those varieties that come true from seed; the catalogue includes invaluable advice on germination.

HEVER CASTLE
Kent

nr Edenbridge TN8 7NG
3m SE of Edenbridge by minor roads
Tel: 01732 865224
Fax: 01732 866796

Owner:
Broadland Properties Ltd

Open: 14 Mar to 5 Nov, daily 11–6. 50 acres. Castle open

HEVER HAS everything a castle should have – a romantic moat, whimsical topiary, an infuriating maze and an excellent garden. The setting of old woodland is very fine and in spring there are some excellent rhododendrons and azaleas. The enormous Italian garden was designed chiefly to show off the collection of classical statuary collected by William Waldorf Astor who bought the estate in 1903. Much of the statuary is artfully arranged in enclosures running along the Pompeian Wall which is planted to great decorative effect. Facing it, on the shady north-facing side, is an immense pergola draped with vines, clematis and roses, and behind which there is a

series of grotto-like niches, dripping with water, where ferns, hostas and other moisture-loving plants thrive. Much of the garden is flamboyantly grand – a swashbuckling Italianate loggia with fountains and naked nymphs, for example – but there are more intimate moments and much attractive planting.

THE HIGH BEECHES
West Sussex

Handcross RH17 6HQ
1m E of Handcross off B2110
Tel: 01444 400589

Owner: High Beeches Gardens Conservation Trust

Open: Easter Mon to Jun, 3 Sept to Oct, daily except Wed 1–5. 20 acres

AFTER WALKING round this exquisite woodland garden it is hard to believe that it is only 20 acres in area. Winding paths, shifting views and the subtle lie of the gently undulating land give such a rich diversity of scenery. The High Beeches formerly belonged to the Loder family of Leonardslee and Wakehurst; the Hon. Edward and Mrs Boscawen came here in 1966 and have added immensely to it. The emphasis is as much on the quality of the landscape as on the distinction of the planting. There are marvellous camellias, magnolias, maples and rhododendrons and many other groups of woody plants, including a National Collection of stewartias. But there are many herbaceous plants – drifts of naturalised willow gentian, irises and primulas – and a 4-acre meadow, unploughed in living memory, with 15 species of grass, many cowslips and orchids.

HIGHDOWN
West Sussex

Littlehampton Road,
Goring-by-Sea BN12 6NY
3m W of Worthing by A259
Tel: 01903 501054

Owner:
Worthing Borough Council

Open: Apr to Sept, Mon to Fri 10–6; Sat, Sun and Bank Hol Mon 10–8. Oct to Mar, Mon to Fri 10–4. 9 1/2 acres

SIR FREDERICK STERN, who died in 1967, was a banker whose passionate hobby was gardening. He lived at Highdown and the making of the garden here is vividly described in his book *A Chalk Garden*, a 20th-century gardening classic. On his death it was left to Worthing Borough Council and there is still much to admire; the site is a steep, south-facing slope and the layout is informal with occasional formality such as the avenue of *Prunus serrula*, with its glistening, peeling bark, at the entrance. The garden is of particular interest to gardeners who want to know more about the splendours and miseries of gardening on chalk. Stern was able to discover here exactly what flourished in chalk; for example, maples from China and Europe did very well but those from Japan and the U.S.A. did not. Although the garden is particularly rich in woody plants there are marvellous groups of herbaceous perennials and bulbs – agapanthus, anemones, hellebores, irises, narcissi and peonies – which provide floriferous underplanting.

HILEY NURSERY
Surrey

25 Little Woodcote Estate,
Wallington SM5 4AU
Off Woodmansterne Lane
Tel: 0181 647 9679

Open: Wed to Sat 9–5

BRIAN HILEY SPECIALISES in rare perennials and tender plants and has an excellent eye for a good plant. Some groups are very deeply represented; he has a particularly good collection of penstemons – species and cultivars – and an exceptional list of sages, woody and herbaceous. But throughout his list there are unusual and well chosen things, not all of them herbaceous. He sells the tender yellow *Bidens ferulifolia*, felicias, the mysterious *Hieracium candidum*, a creeping loosestrife

Illustration: Bidens
ferulifolia

Lysimachia henryi, several kinds of phygelius and of polemonium. A catalogue is issued (three 1st-class stamps) and there is a mail order but plants are often propagated in numbers too small to allow them to be listed. Brian Hiley's own 1-acre garden next door, stuffed with excellent plants, is open on Wednesday and Saturday and by appointment.

IDEN CROFT HERBS
Kent

Frittenden Road,
Staplehurst TN12 0DH
In the village of Staplehurst
8m S of Maidstone by
A229
Tel: 01580 891432
Fax: 01580 892416

Open: Feb to Sept, Mon to
Sat 9–5, Sun and Bank Hol
Mon 11–5; Oct to Jan,
daily except Sun 9–5

IDEN CROFT supplies culinary herbs on a massive scale to the catering trade, and this is a full-scale working herb farm. There are also well planted herbaceous beds, a garden designed for the blind, partially sighted or disabled – with plenty to feel and smell – and a walled garden. Iden Croft holds National Collections of mint and origanums, and has large collections of lavender, sedums and thymes. Many other culinary herbs are sold as well as a selection of other herbaceous perennials. There is a mail order service (catalogue £2.50; plant list, s.a.e.).

W.E.Th. INGWERSEN LTD
West Sussex

ANYONE WHO HAS not heard of Ingwersen has probably not heard of alpine plants either. Will Ingwersen, who died in 1990, was one of the great plantsmen and nurserymen of his time. His half brother Paul carries on the business and offers 1,800 different types of plants for sale, grown to exemplary standards and often rare. The elegantly produced list

Birch Farm Nursery,
Gravetye,
East Grinstead RH19 4LE
2 1/2m SW of East
Grinstead by B2110 and
minor roads
Tel: 01342 810236

Open: Mar to Sept, daily
9–1, 1.30–4; Oct to Feb,
Mon to Fri 9–1, 1.30–4

(£1 stamps) has wonderful groups of alliums, campanulas, dianthus, primulas, dwarf rhododendrons, saxifrages and violas. Among bulbs are excellent colchicums, crocuses, fritillaries, narcissi, and species tulips. The nursery presents a mouth-watering sight, with endless neat rows of plants. It is on sacred ground, too, for this was formerly part of William Robinson's Gravetye estate.

KYOTO GARDEN
London

Holland Park W14
W of the centre of London
in the middle of Holland
Park
Tube: Holland Park

Owner: The Royal
Borough of Kensington and
Chelsea

Open: Daily 8–sunset.
1 acre

INTO THE SEDATE and splendid setting of Holland Park the Kyoto Garden made an exotic arrival in 1991. Largely financed by Japanese firms, and designed by Japanese garden designers, it is of the type known as a 'tour garden', with all the ingredients one expects – a pool fed by a rocky cascade, stepping stones, Japanese maples, raked gravel, snow lanterns and an atmosphere pregnant with meaning even if one cannot understand it. At all events, on its sloping site and backed by fine old trees, it is a welcome and exhilarating presence – a refreshing oddity in urban conservatism.

THE SOUTH-EAST OF ENGLAND • 35

LEEDS CASTLE
Kent

nr Maidstone ME17 1PL
4m E of Maidstone by A20
and B2163. Jnct 8 of M20
Tel: 01622 765400
Fax: 01622 735616

Owner:
Leeds Castle Foundation

Open: Daily: Mar to Oct,
10–5; Nov to Feb, 10–3.
500 acres. Castle open

DISTANT VIEWS of Leeds Castle are enchanting – the silvery 12th-century castle wildly romantic, apparently floating on its vast moat. The gardens are modern and there are two features of special interest. The Culpeper Garden, designed by Russell Page, is a series of box-edged beds overflowing with herbaceous plants underplanted among shrub roses. Farther from the castle a yew maze, finished in 1988, was designed by Randall Coate and Adrian Fisher, its shape echoing the medieval architecture of the castle. The elusive goal at its centre is the entrance to an extraordinary grotto lined with tufa embellished by Diana Rennell and Simon Verity with statues, rare stones and shells, the cave-like gloom occasionally pierced by circular skylights.

LEONARDSLEE GARDENS
West Sussex

Lower Beeding,
nr Horsham RH13 6PP
4m SW of Handcross
(bottom of M23) by A279
Tel: 01403 891212

Owner: The Loder Family

Open: Apr to Oct, daily
10–6 (closes at 8 in May).
200 acres

SIR EDMUND LODER bought the estate of Leonardslee in 1889 and started to make his great woodland garden. The spectacular site – a shallow valley with a series of linked lakes running along the bottom – makes a superb place to grow ornamental trees and shrubs. The soil is a slightly acid moisture-retentive silt; the densely clothed sides of the valley give protection from the wind, and there is excellent frost drainage. Rhododendrons were Sir Edmund's first love and he raised the hybrid *R.* 'Loderi' which has produced some of the best garden varieties. But there are also especially choice collections of camellias and magnolias, including some of the largest specimens in the country. Large numbers of evergreens – wellingtonias, Douglas firs, deodars and spruce – make a fine background for spring flowering and the explosion of autumn colour. A bonsai display and alpine house have recently been added, and a summer wildflower walk opens this year.

MERRIMENTS GARDENS
East Sussex

Illustration: Gaura lindheimeri

Hawkhurst Road, Hurst Green TN19 7RA
12m SE of Tunbridge Wells by A21
Tel: 01580 860666

Open: Daily 10–5.30

THIS FAMILY NURSERY was started in 1988 and a splendid 4-acre garden alongside was subsequently added to display its wares. The nursery carries a general stock of shrubs, trees and climbers but of special interest to gardeners, is the wide range of herbaceous perennials: named cultivars of dianthus, euphorbias, geraniums, excellent lobelias, many penstemons, poppies, sages and violas. These are very well chosen and, in addition, there is a choice selection of ferns. A useful catalogue is published (£1.00) but there is no mail order. The well planned and richly planted garden – which covers an area of 4 acres – is beginning to show its paces, and forms an attractive display ground for the wide range of plants that the nursery sells.

Illustration opposite: The terraced gardens at Northbourne Court

MUSEUM OF GARDEN HISTORY
London

Lambeth Palace Road,
SE1 7LB
Immediately S of Lambeth Bridge. *Tube*: Victoria or Waterloo
Tel: 0171 261 1891

Owner:
The Tradescant Trust

Open: Mon to Fri 11–3, Sun 10.30–5

JOHN TRADESCANT, father and son, immensely influential gardeners and collectors of exotic plants in the 17th century, lived and died in Lambeth where they are buried in a magnificent tomb. In the disused church an excellent museum of garden history has been formed, containing a permanent collection and a small gallery devoted to Gertrude Jekyll, and presenting temporary exhibitions, courses and lectures. In the old churchyard a charming replica 17th-century garden has been made, with a knot of box hedges designed by the Marchioness of Salisbury and containing plants of a Tradescantian flavour.

NORTHBOURNE COURT
Kent

Northbourne,
Deal CT14 0LW
2m W of Deal, in the village of Northbourne near the church
Tel: 01304 611281
Fax: 01304 614512

Owner: The Hon. Charles James

Open: Jun to Aug, Sun 2–6. 2 acres

HISTORIC GARDENS that yield their secrets only to the cognoscenti are pretty boring to most garden visitors. The great early 17th-century terraces at Northbourne Court, however, make an immediate and delightful impression. They were built by Sir Edwin Sandys to be seen from his mansion, which was destroyed by fire in 1750. The terraces and garden walls, of fine brick, survive and there is much lively recent planting, some of it carefully planned to take advantage of sharp drainage and a southern

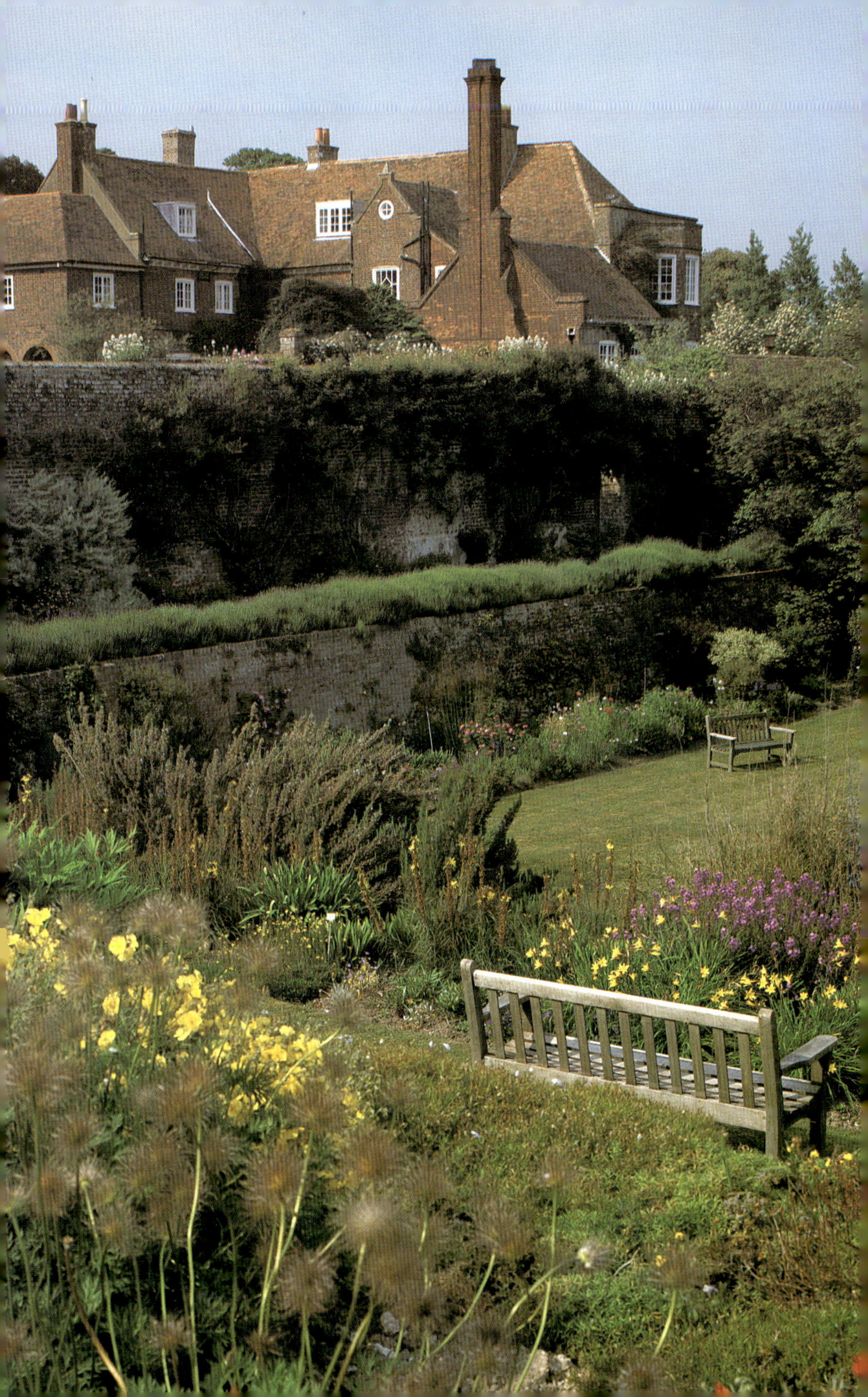

exposure. An avenue of peonies ornaments the kitchen garden where there is a virtuoso arrangement of purple cotinus, purple sage and purple-headed artichokes, and everywhere there are old roses. This is not a place for great rarities – the irresistible character of the ancient garden layout is the rare pleasure here.

NYMANS GARDEN
West Sussex

Handcross, nr Haywards Heath RH17 6EB
7m NW of Haywards Heath by A272 and B2114
Tel: 01444 400321/400777

Owner:
The National Trust

Open: Mar to Oct, daily except Mon and Tue (open Bank Hol Mon) 11–7 or sunset if earlier). 30 acres

THERE ARE FEW gardens anywhere in England where rare and beautiful plants are grown in such an attractive setting, in which formality and informality are subtly interwoven. Nymans was acquired by Leonard Messel in 1890 when he began introducing a wide range of plants. He made a woodland garden in which magnificent trees and flowering shrubs – particularly camellias, eucryphias, magnolias and rhododendrons – are seen to great advantage. One of the best hybrid eucryphias, *E.* × *nymansensis*, had its origins here. In an irregularly shaped walled garden Messel laid out a pair of spectacular herbaceous borders, whose design was influenced by William Robinson. These are wonderful today, and in late summer their flowering season is prolonged by the subtle use of annuals. Surrounding the borders are choice ornamental trees, such as dogwoods, *Koelreuteria paniculata* and styrax. There is much topiary of yew and box – geometric shapes and plump birds – and romantic ruins. A great number of trees were lost in the great storm of October 1987 but the rose garden containing many old roses – in whose use Mrs Messel was a pioneer – has been restored.

OSTERLEY PARK
Middlesex

Isleworth TW7 4RB
5m W of Central London by A4
Tube: Osterley
Tel: 0181 560 3918

Owner:
The National Trust

Open: Daily 9–7.30 or sunset if earlier. 140 acres. House open

THE PARK AT Osterley survives only in part, but there are some good remaining garden buildings and some marvellous trees decorate the landscape. Block your ears to the roar of the Great West Road and something of the Elysian atmosphere of the past can be brought to life. The late Elizabethan mansion was rebuilt after 1761 by Robert Adam who also designed the semi-circular conservatory against the old kitchen garden wall. A series of lakes to the south and east of the house glitter among splendid trees – old cedars of Lebanon, oaks, limes and London planes. The lake nearest the house has an octagonal Chinese pavilion on an island. The pleasure gardens have been undergoing their long-awaited restoration which is beginning to show its paces.

PAINSHILL PARK
Surrey

Portsmouth Road, Cobham KT11 1JE
1m W of Cobham by A245
Tel: 01932 868113
Fax: 01932 868001

Owner:
Painshill Park Trust

Open: Mid Apr to mid Oct, Sun 11–6. Further openings in 1996 are possible; telephone 01932 864674 for details. 158 acres

THIS EXTRAORDINARY landscape garden is being restored by a private trust and it is one of the most worthwhile of all recent garden restorations. The garden was made by the Hon. Charles Hamilton between 1738 and 1773, when he ran out of money. It is an intensely original example of the large-scale creation of ornamental landscape. At the heart of the garden a long curvaceous lake with islands is overlooked by decorative buildings – an airy ten-sided gothic pavilion, a fake ruined abbey and a ruined Roman arch. One of the islands has the remains of a dazzling grotto and is linked to the mainland by an elegant Chinese bridge. Paths wind through woods and across meadows about the shores

of the lake. In the westernmost part of the park a
huge water wheel is revealed, and on the wooded
slopes high above, a castellated gothic tower
commanding immense views over the landscape and
the country beyond. The vineyard below the gothic
temple has recently been replanted and the elaborate
Turkish tent is once more in place. Everywhere the
landscape composes itself into delicious views and the
place has an unforgettable exhilaration.

PANTILES NURSERIES LTD
Surrey

Almners Road, Lyne,
Chertsey KT16 0BJ
1 1/2m W of Chertsey, Jnct
11 of M25
Tel: 01932 872195
Fax: 0932 874030

Open: Daily 9–5.30
(Sun 9–5)

MANY PEOPLE WILLINGLY spend thousands of pounds on a new kitchen but might never think of buying expensive large trees and shrubs which will give instant character to a new garden. At Pantiles there is a wide selection of woody plants in whopping sizes: a 20ft-high *Magnolia grandiflora* 'Galissonière' (not the commonest tree in the world) will cost over £3,000 but it will last your lifetime, getting lovelier all the time, which is more than you can say of a new kitchen. A new line of Tasmanian tree ferns, *Dicksonia antarctica*, which will stand up to −13°C in their native habitat, will make this lovely

PARHAM HOUSE
West Sussex

Pulborough RH20 4HS
4m S of Pulborough by
A283
Tel: 01903 744888
Fax: 01903 746557

Owner: Parham Park Ltd

Open: Easter Sun to 1st
Sun in Oct, Sun, Wed,
Thur and Bank Hol Mon
1–6. 11 acres. House open

plant more available to a much wider range of gardeners. A catalogue is produced, and delivery and planting – a tricky business with a very large tree – can be arranged by the nursery.

PARHAM, a grand Elizabethan house, is splendidly situated in an atmospheric old deer park dotted with ancient oaks. The chief ornamental part of the garden lies in the walled former kitchen garden, divided by gravel paths. Here are some very effective herbaceous borders with carefully controlled colour schemes: a pair of blue borders enlivened with dashes of magenta, pink diascias and purple penstemons; a gold border, given structure by repeated plantings of yellow potentilla, a golden elder and juniper, yellow loosestrife and achilleas; and a long border, facing west, of hot, bright colours. It is very much a working kitchen garden, providing cut flowers, fruit and vegetables for the house. To the west, a lake is overlooked by a pavilion and, to one side, there is a fiendish maze with infuriatingly complicated rules.

PASHLEY MANOR
East Sussex

nr Ticehurst TN5 7HE
1 1/2m SE of Ticehurst by
B2099
Tel: 01580 200692
Fax: 01580 200102

Owner:
Mr and Mrs James Sellick

Open: mid Apr to mid Oct,
Tue, Wed, Thur and Sat
and Bank Hol Mon 11–5.
8 acres

THE APPROACH TO Pashley manor lies through beautiful parkland and the house, mid 16th-century half-timbered on one façade and Queen Anne on another, sits well in its setting. The gardens have recently been revived with the help of the garden designer Anthony du Gard Pasley who has contrived elegant formal plantings near the house, with carefully judged colour associations, and a wilder garden of woodland character behind it. The kitchen garden has recently been redesigned, many new old roses added and improvements have been made to the water-side planting in the wild garden. All this is impeccably well maintained. The Sellicks have by no means completed their ambitious garden schemes and this will be a place to watch keenly in the future.

PENSHURST PLACE
Kent

Penshurst,
nr Tonbridge TN11 8DG
In Penshurst village
Tel: 01892 870307
Fax: 01892 870866

Owner: The Rt Hon.
Viscount De L'Isle

Open: 30 Mar to 29 Sept,
daily 11–6; and weekends
in Mar and Oct 11–6. 10
acres. House open

THE SIDNEY FAMILY have been here since the 16th century but the house is much older and magnificently dominates the huge walled gardens that surround it. Although the planting is modern in this enclosure, with its lovely Tudor bricks, the present pattern of beds, pools and walks closely resembles that shown in Kip's engraving of around 1700. Very few gardens preserve their essential layout from such an early time as Penshurst does. The entrance leads past a border planted as a dazzling Union Jack, with the colours picked out in spring and summer bedding. Beyond it all sorts of ornamental schemes spread out: a charming orchard of apples and Kentish cobs; a garden of magnolias and golden Irish yews; a pair of herbaceous borders; a rose garden; a spring garden; and a pair of handsome borders designed by Lanning Roper.

PERRYHILL NURSERIES
East Sussex

Illustration:
Rosa '*Gertrude Jekyll*'

Hartfield TN7 4JP
8m W of Tunbridge Wells
by A264 and B2026, 1m N
of Hartfield
Tel: 01892 770377
Fax: 01892 770929

Open: Daily 9–5 (closes
4.30 in winter)

A MARVELLOUS GARDEN could be made using Perryhill as your only source of plants. They have well chosen representatives of the most valuable ornamental plants, both woody and herbaceous, and there is a small selection of fruit. With some plants, such as roses, they have an exceptional choice of the best kinds. In other groups – species peonies, for example – you will find things which you would not see in the average garden centre. A useful catalogue is produced (£1.65), but there is no mail order.

PETWORTH HOUSE

West Sussex

Petworth GU28 0AE
In Petworth village
Tel: 01798 342207/343929
Fax: 01798 342963

Owner:
The National Trust

Open: Pleasure grounds: 23
Mar 2–4; 30 Mar to Oct,
daily except Mon and Fri
(open Good Fri and Bank
Hol Mon, closed Tue
following) 12–6. *Park:*
Daily 8–sunset (except
28–30 Jun 8–12)). 700
acres. House open

PETWORTH HAS an ancient gardening history: Elizabethan gardens had a fountain and roses, and in the late 17th century formal gardens were made for the newly built house. Today the park is the thing at Petworth and it is best appreciated by taking a long walk in it (for this, go to the Park, rather than the House, car park). It was laid out from 1752 for the 2nd Earl of Egremont by 'Capability' Brown and is one of the best of all his surviving landscapes. It is big enough to reduce the very large mansion, seen from a distance framed in trees, to the stature of a garden ornament. Brown placed a Doric temple to the north of the house and an Ionic rotunda beyond it on an eminence. Marvellous limes, oaks, sweet chestnuts and planes survive from Brown's time.

POLESDEN LACEY

Surrey

THE DAPPER early 19th-century house was owned by the great Edwardian political hostess, the Hon. Mrs Ronald Greville, and the garden has much of the blowsy charm of the age. A beech avenue leads up the hill and wonderful views of the valley are revealed from the house at the top. Beyond the house a very large formal rose garden, with such distinctive

nr Dorking RH5 6BD
5m NW of Dorking by A246
Tel: 01372 458203/452048

Owner:
The National Trust

Open: Daily 11–6 or sunset if earlier. 30 acres. House open

Edwardian varieties as 'Dorothy Perkins' and 'American Pillar', has at its centre a white marble well-head. South of the rose garden a magnificent herbaceous border, backed by a wall festooned with climbing plants, is an object lesson in bold but disciplined planting.

PORT LYMPNE GARDENS
Kent

Lympne, Hythe CT21 4PD
3m W of Hythe by A20 and B2067; Jnct 11 of M20
Tel: 01303 264647
Fax: 01303 264944

Owner: John Aspinall

Open: Daily 10–5 (or 1 hour before dusk in winter). 15 acres

HIGH ABOVE Romney Marsh the gabled brick house was built by Sir Philip Sassoon to designs by Sir Herbert Baker before World War I, and completed after the war by Philip Tilden who, in collaboration with his patron, laid out the garden. Sassoon died in 1939 and subsequently the place deteriorated until John Aspinall bought it in 1973 and commissioned a complete restoration with advice from Russell Page. The garden is formal in spirit and decorative in execution, making full use of the lovely position. Compartments are hedged in yew or Leyland cypress and the chess-board garden and the striped garden present dazzling geometric patterns in bedding schemes. Beautiful herbaceous borders, a fig garden, vineyard, and terraces of roses and dahlias decorate the slopes. Within its carefully designed architectural setting the garden at Port Lympne has a brilliantly festive air.

POTS AND PITHOI
West Sussex

The Barns, East Street,
Turners Hill RH10 4QQ
E of Turners Hill on
B2110, 5m E of Crawley by
A264 and B2028
Tel: 01342 714793

Open: Daily 10–5 (4 in
winter) including Bank Hol
Mon (closed 24 Dec–2 Jan
and Sat and Sun in Jan)

MOST GARDEN POTS are mass produced to fairly commonplace designs but Pots and Pithoi sell a unique range of hand-made Cretan pots in many different designs and sizes. They are fired at a very high temperature and are therefore resistant to frost. The great attraction is their beautiful patina and the liveliness of their design and decoration, with patterns that are either incised or applied in delicate ribbons of clay. These are the kind of pots that, without being in the slightest pretentious, have tremendous garden presence. There is a good catalogue and delivery can be arranged. But a visit is really essential to appreciate these rare pots.

G. REUTHE LTD
Kent

Illustration: Rhododendron campylocarpum

Crown Point Nursery,
Sevenoaks Road, Ightham,
nr Sevenoaks TN15 0HB
4m E of Sevenoaks by A25
Tel: 01732 810694
Fax: 01732 862166

Open: Mon to Sat 9.30–4.30

REUTHE IS FAMOUS for rhododendrons. Here is an exceptionally wide range of species and hybrids and a choice collection of evergreen and deciduous azaleas – the catalogue runs to well over 30 pages of them. The nursery sells other things, particularly woody plants, but its real distinction lies in its rhododendrons. It is essential to buy the informative list (£1.50); mail order is available. The nursery is now part of Starborough Nursery (see p. 54) to whom all correspondence should be sent.

THE ROOF GARDENS
London

99 Kensington High Street,
W8 5ED
Central London.
Tube: High Street,
Kensington
Tel: 0171 937 7994
Fax: 0171 9382774

Open: Daily 9–5 but
telephone beforehand as
sometimes closed for
private functions.
1 1/2 acres

THESE ARE THE largest roof gardens open to the public in London. On the top of the old Derry & Toms department store, they are one of the most unexpected horticultural sights that the capital has to offer. This extraordinary place, complete with pink flamingoes, is delightful. It has well tended borders with substantial shrubs, secluded sitting places, thoughtfully planted pots, attractive paths of old York stone and herring-bone laid brick, and a knock-out Moorish extravanganza with more than a whiff of the Alhambra – old coloured tiles, and a scalloped canal with fountains and palm trees.

ROYAL BOTANIC GARDENS, KEW
Surrey

Kew, Richmond TW9 3AB
7m SW of Central London.
Tube: Kew Gardens
Tel: 0181 940 1171
Fax: 0181 3325610

Owner: Trustees of the
Royal Botanic Gardens

Open: Daily 9.30–4 (6.30
on summer weekdays; 7.30
on Sun and Bank Hol Mon
in high summer). 300 acres

IT IS NOT THE PURPOSE of Kew to be interesting to gardeners but this, despite itself, it effortlessly is. The landscape park with its great Chinoiserie pagoda (designed by Sir William Chambers in 1761) and many specimen trees going back to the 18th century is exquisite; its setting on the Thames wonderful. Most of the plants are wild species rather than garden varieties but it is a perfect place to come on any day of the year and discover new plants, impeccably labelled and well grown. The various glasshouses are immensely rich in non-hardy plants: the Palm House designed by Richard Turner and

Illustration: Erythronium californicum

Decimus Burton; the Temperate House; and the Princess of Wales Conservatory with tender plants of different climates arranged in naturalistic settings. Among the hardy plants there are several reference collections of great interest to gardeners – they include heathers, bulbs, bamboos and grasses, and several others. A new glasshouse showing the evolution of plants has recently opened. The atmosphere of Kew is livelier than it has been for many years and it is now one of the most attractive places in the country for gardeners to visit.

THE SAVILL AND VALLEY GARDENS
Surrey

The Great Park, Windsor
SL4 2HT
3m W of Egham by A30
and Wick Road
Tel: 01753 860222
Fax: 01753 859617

Owner: Crown Property

Open: Savill Garden: daily 10–6 (closed for Christmas period). 35 acres. *Valley Garden:* daily sunrise–sunset. 400 acres

SOME GARDENS set a style and affect the future style of gardening. The Savill Garden has had a strong influence on the tradition of woodland gardening. It was started in 1932 by E.H. (later Sir Eric) Savill who was Deputy Ranger of Windsor Great Park. He invented a natural style of woodland gardening which gave the plants appropriate habitats and made something that was beautiful. The well-watered site with many old trees – especially marvellous beeches and oaks – was an excellent place for such a garden. He planted large numbers of ornamental trees and shrubs – azaleas, camellias, dogwoods, magnolias, rhododendrons – and about the streams moisture-loving plants such as ferns, lysichiton, primulas and rheums. In addition to this there are handsome formal gardens – herbaceous borders, a dry garden and rose gardens – which are maintained to wonderful old-fashioned standards. In 1947 Sir Eric turned his attention to the nearby Valley Garden, on a wonderful undulating site on the north bank of Virginia Water. Here the planting is of a similar style but, on an immensely larger site, the variety is much greater. You'll find here National Collections of dwarf conifers, hollies, magnolias, mahonias, pernettyas, pieris and species rhododendrons.

SCOTNEY CASTLE
Kent

Lamberhurst, Tunbridge Wells TN3 8JN
1m S of Lamberhurst by A21
Tel: 01892 890651

Owner:
The National Trust

Open: 30 Mar to 2 Nov, Wed to Fri 11–6 or sunset if earlier (closed Good Fri), Sat and Sun 2–6 or sunset if earlier, Bank Hol Mon 12–6. 19 acres

THE GARDENS AT Scotney Castle are a piece of irresistibly romantic picturesque landscape gardening made in the middle of the 19th century by Edward Hussey, with advice from William Sawrey Gilpin. At the same time Hussey built a new house high on a hill, benefitting from wonderful views down towards the moated medieval castle which became an exotic eye-catcher for his landscaping schemes. Walks descend the precipitous and rocky hill with superb trees and shrubs; the flowers of azaleas and rhododendrons, and the new foliage of maples, are dazzling in spring. In the castle forecourt there is a pretty herb garden designed by Lanning Roper and, nearby on an island, a bronze by Henry Moore seems strangely at home in the wild planting.

SHEFFIELD PARK

East Sussex

Uckfield TN22 3QX
Midway between East
Grinstead and Lewes off
A275
Tel: 01825 790655

Owner:
The National Trust

Open: Mar, Sat and Sun
11–4; 30 Mar to 10 Nov,
Tue to Sun and Bank Hol
Mon 11–6 or sunset if
earlier; 13 Nov to 22 Dec,
Wed to Sat 11–4. 100 acres.

THERE IS SOMETHING dream-like about Sheffield Park. Both 'Capability' Brown and Humphry Repton had a hand in the design but the present appearance of the gardens is due chiefly to Arthur Soames who bought the estate in 1905. James Wyatt's gothic palace of 1775–8, sits on an eminence at the head of a broad valley, with a series of four descending lakes extending far into the distance. On the banks trees and shrubs are arranged in bold groups with subtle contrasts, conifers and deciduous trees artfully mingled. The hinterland surrounding the lakes is laced with paths and full of marvellous trees and shrubs, with the occasional dazzling piece of herbaceous planting such as a path fringed with gentians. The garden is exquisitely laid out and a slow walk at any time during the long opening season offers some of the most beautiful garden scenes the visitor may ever see.

SISSINGHURST CASTLE GARDEN

Kent

THE HISTORY OF this garden is quickly told – it was made by Vita Sackville-West and Harold Nicolson from 1930 onwards, and became the most admired English garden of its time. Few great gardens live up to their reputation so effortlessly as this. Whatever superlatives have been heaped on it,

Sissinghurst,
nr Cranbrook TN17 2AB
2m NE of Cranbrook off
A262
Tel: 01580 712850

Owner:
The National Trust

Open: 2 Apr to 15 Oct,
Tue to Fri 1–6.30, Sat, Sun
and Good Fri 10–5.30. 10
acres. House open

Sissinghurst never disappoints and each visit will reveal new pleasures. The National Trust was fortunate to inherit two gardeners, Pamela Schwerdt and Sibylle Kreutzberger, who had worked with Vita Sackville-West before her death in 1963. They maintained the garden to perfectionist standards until their recent retirement and their successor seems every bit as good. Within the disciplined enclosures of old brick walls, cool hedges of yew, and linking paths and vistas, here is a profusion of fastidiously chosen plants in which an immense collection of old roses provides a recurring theme. One of the many refreshing things about Sissinghurst is the way in which virtuoso changes in mood are effortlessly achieved – from the hot oranges and reds of the Cottage Garden, for example, to the austere yew alley that separates the formal gardens from the orchard. Despite Vita Sackville-West's aristocratic spirit, it would be wrong to think of Sissinghurst as far from the interests of everyday gardeners. In terms of practical gardening – the pruning, training and feeding of plants, for example – the highest standards were maintained and are still a delight to observe. Certainly Sissinghurst has the power to enchant but it is also an unending source of practical inspiration for all gardeners.

STANDEN

West Sussex

East Grinstead RH19 4NE
2m S of East Grinstead off
B2110
Tel: 01342 323029

Owner:
The National Trust

Open: 23, 24, 30, 31 Mar,
1.30–4.30; Apr to Oct, Wed
to Sun and Bank Hol Mon
12.30–6. 10 acres. House
open

Illustration opposite:
Sissinghurst Castle Garden

STANDEN HAS a memorable position, high on an eminence with views across the Medway Valley to Crowborough Beacon. Below the house, which was designed by Philip Webb, the land falls away on south-facing slopes. An enclosed formal garden is hedged in beech and yew and has square beds edged in catmint with an Irish juniper at each corner and a crab apple at each centre, surrounded by rugosa roses. The rest of the garden consists of terraced lawns and paths that amble through groups of shrubs and trees – azaleas and rhododendrons with maples rising above. In the quarry garden above the house there is a collection of ferns. A wonderful tulip tree and a very large Scots pine at the foot of a sloping lawn frame distant views of cornfields surrounded by woodland – a marvellous scene.

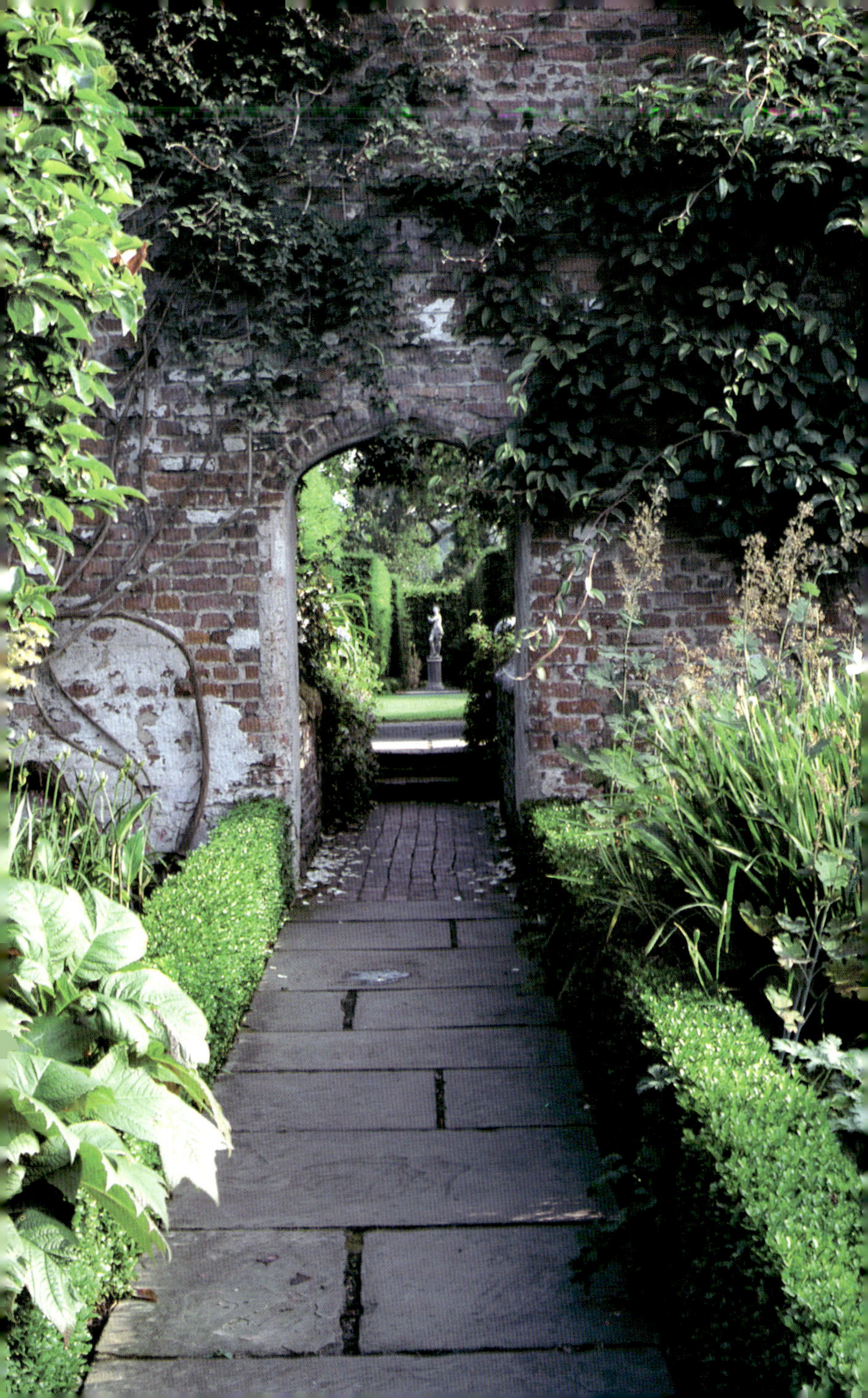

STARBOROUGH NURSERY
Kent

Illustration: Styrax japonica

Marsh Green,
Edenbridge TN8 5RB
Tel: 01732 865614
Fax: 01732 862166

Open: Daily except Tue
and Wed 10–4; closed all
Jan and Jul

STARBOROUGH SPECIALISES in acid-loving woody plants – many of them rarely seen in nurseries. There are also good selections of acers, camellias, daphnes, magnolias, pieris, rhododendrons, stewartias, styrax, viburnums and a choice selection of climbing plants; among all these are many rare and lovely things. A catalogue is published (£1.50) and mail orders are fulfilled. The nursery is in the same ownership as G. Reuthe (see p. 47).

SYON PARK AND GARDENS
Middlesex

Brentford TW8 8JF
On the N bank of the
Thames between Brentford
and Isleworth
Tel: 0181 560 0881
Fax: 0181 5680936

Owner: The Duke of
Northumberland

Open: Mar to Oct, daily
10–6; Nov to Feb, daily
10–sunset. 55 acres. House
open

IT IS SURPRISING to find a complete great country estate so near to the centre of London. It has been owned by the Percy family, later Dukes of Northumberland, since 1594 and the approach to the house runs through classic ancient parkland. The house, with grand rooms by Robert Adam, faces a wide avenue of limes. The chief pleasure gardens lie on one side of the house and are dominated by one of the finest conservatories you will see anywhere, built by Charles Fowler in 1827 in beautiful golden stone. There is an excellent collection of trees – acacias, catalpas, holm oaks and sweet chestnuts, and rarer things such as sweet buckeye (*Aesculus flava*). A long narrow lake is edged with trees including some good swamp cypresses. A very large garden centre has a good stock in all departments, and a fine selection of garden pots.

TILE BARN NURSERY
Kent

Illustration:
Cyclamen repandum

Standen Street, Iden Green,
Benenden TN17 4LB
In the hamlet of Standen
Street 1/2m S of Benenden
Tel: 01580 240221

Open: Wed to Sat 9–5

THIS IS THE kind of nursery that makes converts of even the most unyielding. It specialises in cyclamen and stocks all the most garden-worthy species and varieties of these charmingly seductive plants, several of which are very hard to come by. An excellent list is produced (s.a.e.), giving valuable information on their cultivation – indeed it constitutes a perfect guide to the subject. Plants are sold by mail but visitors are welcomed and a few additional bulbous plants are available to callers only.

WAKEHURST PLACE GARDEN
West Sussex

nr Ardingly, Haywards
Heath RH17 6TN
1 1/2m NW of Ardingly on
B2028
Tel: 01444 892701

Owner:
The National Trust

Open: Daily except 25 Dec
and 1 Jan; Nov to Jan
10–4; Feb, Oct 10–5; Mar
10–6; Apr to Sept 10–7.
170 acres

ALTHOUGH THERE IS an attractively planted walled garden and some good borders (albeit with a botanical slant – one is devoted to monocotyledons) Wakehurst Place is really about trees and shrubs. It is the country department of the Royal Botanic Gardens at Kew and it is full of wonderful things. By the house the site is relatively flat and the house looks out onto pools and a water garden fringed with maples and moisture-loving plants. Farther from the house the ground sweeps down into the Himalayan Glade and the precipitous ravine of Westwood Valley and its lake, and beyond that, to more woodland. There are wonderful collections of azaleas, magnolias and rhododendrons in the Himalayan Glade and the Westwood Valley, and particularly fine groups of conifers in the Pinetum. The lie of the land adds immensely to the beauty of the trees and this is a wonderful place in which to spend a few hours walking, looking and learning.

WASHFIELD NURSERY
Kent

Illustration:
Helleborus orientalis

Hawkhurst TN18 4QU
1m SW of Hawkhurst by
A229
Tel: 01580 752522

Open: Wed to Sat 10–5

WONDERFUL HERBACEOUS PERENNIALS are the strongest point of this exceptional nursery. The presiding genius behind it, Elizabeth Strangman, is an authority on hellebores and has bred some exquisite hybrids of *Helleborus orientalis* in which she aims for 'purity of colour and full rounded flower'. But throughout the list there are great treasures – epimediums, hardy geraniums, kniphofias, pulmonarias – all chosen in the very best species and cultivars. Some of these are from seed collected in the wild by the nursery's botanist friends, and thus the true, unadulterated form. A very good catalogue is produced but there is no mail order.

WEST DEAN GARDENS
West Sussex

West Dean,
Chichester PO18 0QZ
6m N of Chichester by
A286
Tel: 01243 811303
Fax: 01243 811342

Owner: The Edward James
Foundation

Open: Mar to Oct, daily
11–6. 90 acres

THE FLINT AND STONE early 19th-century gothic house by James Wyatt belonged to Edward James, patron of surrealism, though the only surrealistic touch in his garden is a curious fibreglass truncated beech-tree. The garden is set in a beautiful valley and at its heart is an immense pergola designed by Harold Peto, draped in clematis, roses and wisteria and underplanted with agapanthus, daylilies, ferns, geraniums and lamium. This, and the fine beds on its southern side, have recently been superbly restored and replanted. Marking one end of it is a pretty gothic flint summer house whose floor is

curiously paved in horse's teeth, and at the other end
a sunken garden has a pool, ornamental grasses, a
sea of *Alchemilla mollis*, ferns and roses. Half way
down the pergola the tunnel of foliage is interrupted
by a long rectangular lily pond. The magnificent
walled kitchen garden, with Edwardian glasshouses,
has recently been restored to perfectionist standards.
The glasshouses brim with melons, tender foliage
plants and all the exotic produce of the Edwardian
age. Beyond the garden, handsome parkland with
some outstanding old trees, especially conifers, in St
Roche's Arboretum, spreads across folds in the South
Downs, of which there are fine views from the circuit
walk. Always interesting, West Dean in the hands of
dynamic new gardeners has become outstanding.

WISLEY GARDEN

Surrey

WISLEY IS WHERE the Royal Horticultural Society
shows the gardening public how it should be
done. Here are the highest standards of practical
horticulture deployed over an immense range of
different kinds of gardening, in the setting of a
splendid old site rich in fine trees and a very large

nr Ripley, Woking
GU23 6QB
6m NE of Guildford by
A3; S of Jnct 10 of the M25
Tel: 01483 224234
Fax: 01483 211750

Owner: The Royal
Horticultural Society

Open: Daily 10–7 (Sun for
RHS Members only).
250 acres

number of other plants all impeccably labelled. There is a pinetum, an alpine house, a vast and beautifully kept rock garden, trial grounds of various kinds, and practical display areas. A huge shop contains the biggest selection of new gardening books in Britain (and a valuable mail order service is provided for books), and a large nursery sells plants of high quality, many unusual, but there is no catalogue and no mail order. Changes are afoot in the garden, with a master-plan devised by the landscape architect Hal Moggridge – let us hope it will lead to more distinguished planting.

YALDING ORGANIC GARDENS
Kent

Benover Road, Yalding, nr
Maidstone ME18 6EX
5m SW of Maidstone on
B2010
Tel: 01622 814650
Fax: 01622 814650

Owner: Henry Doubleday
Research Association

Open: May to Sept, Wed to Sun and Bank Hol Mon 10–5; October, Sat and Sun 10–5. 10 acres

NOTHING HELPS the organic gardening movement so effectively as a good display garden. The Henry Doubleday Research Association, which also owns the garden at Ryton in the Midlands (see page 206) has now expanded in the south east with this ambitious new place. A series of recreated historic gardens shows the distinctive styles of gardening of their time: from medieval plots to such distinctively 20th-century types as the organic allotment, the wildlife garden and a garden planned to withstand drought. This is a garden of ideas and the philosophy is one of the proper stewardship of resources and respect for the ecology. Many gardeners have been won over to organic methods and Yalding will make more converts.

SOUTH-CENTRAL ENGLAND

Berkshire
Buckinghamshire
Hampshire
Oxfordshire
Wiltshire

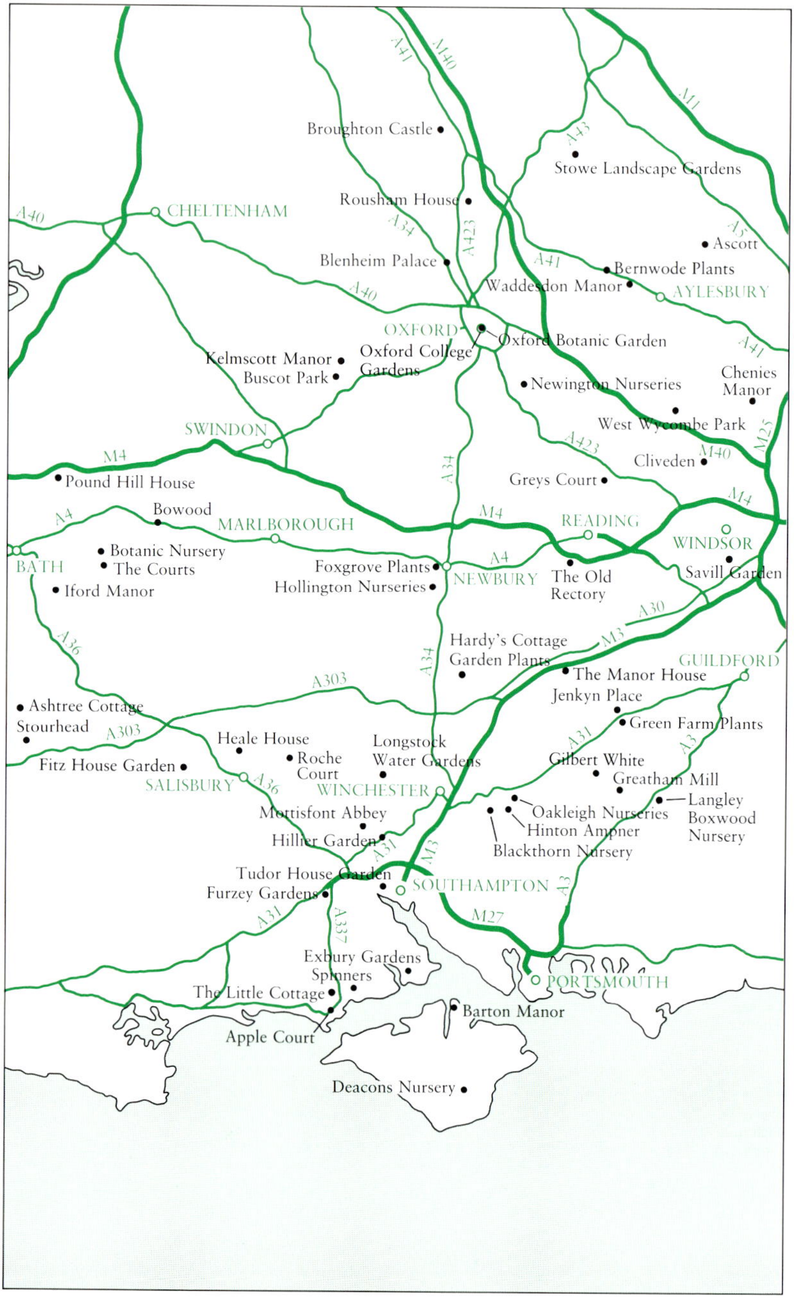

A41
M40
M1
Broughton Castle
A43
Stowe Landscape Gardens
Rousham House
A40
CHELTENHAM
A34
A423
A5
Ascott
Blenheim Palace
A41
Bernwode Plants
Waddesdon Manor
A40
AYLESBURY
OXFORD
Oxford Botanic Garden
A41
Kelmscott Manor
Oxford College Gardens
Chenies Manor
Buscot Park
Newington Nurseries
West Wycombe Park
SWINDON
M25
A423
M40
M4
Cliveden
Pound Hill House
A34
Greys Court
Bowood
M4
A4
M4
MARLBOROUGH
READING
WINDSOR
Botanic Nursery
A4
BATH
The Courts
Foxgrove Plants
NEWBURY
The Old Rectory
Savill Garden
Iford Manor
Hollington Nurseries
A30
A36
Hardy's Cottage Garden Plants
M3
A34
GUILDFORD
The Manor House
A303
Jenkyn Place
Ashtree Cottage
Green Farm Plants
Stourhead
A303
Heale House
Longstock Water Gardens
A31
A3
Roche Court
Gilbert White
Fitz House Garden
Greatham Mill
SALISBURY
A36
WINCHESTER
Langley Boxwood Nursery
Oakleigh Nurseries
Mottisfont Abbey
Hinton Ampner
Hillier Garden
A31
Blackthorn Nursery
M3
Tudor House Garden
SOUTHAMPTON
A3
Furzey Gardens
A337
M27
A31
Exbury Gardens
Spinners
PORTSMOUTH
The Little Cottage
Barton Manor
Apple Court
Deacons Nursery

APPLE COURT

Hampshire

Hordle Lane, Lymington
SO41 0HU
3 1/2m W of Lymington by
A337
Tel: 01590 642130
Fax: 01950 644220

Open: Feb to Nov, daily
except Tue and Wed
9.30–1, 2–5; every day Jul
to second week in Aug

THIS VERY attractive nursery and garden have some outstandingly good plants – hostas (over 80 varieties), daylilies, ferns and ornamental grasses. In the charming, recently completed garden, which is now really beginning to show its paces, there is a splendid hosta walk where many different kinds may be seen performing. Many of the other specialities of the nursery are displayed in excellent borders. A catalogue is produced (three 1st-class stamps) and a mail order service is provided but a visit to the garden where many of the plants sold are displayed so handsomely is particularly worthwhile.

ASCOTT

Buckinghamshire

Wing, nr Leighton Buzzard
LU7 0PS
2m SW of Leighton
Buzzard by A418
Tel: 01296 688242

Owner:
The National Trust

Open: 2 Apr to 5 May and
3 to 29 Sept, Tue to Sun
2–6; 8 May to 28 Aug,
every Wed and last Sun in
each month 2–6. 39 acres.
House open

THIS IS a rare garden, in which the distinctive late Victorian character is cherished and made into something special. The house was a hunting box on the Rothschilds' Mentmore estate, and the gardens were made at the end of the 19th century. Behind the house, lawns are terraced down towards a long double herbaceous border hedged with variegated holly and golden yew. From the middle of these borders a path leads to rose beds and a splashing fountain of Venus designed by Ralph Waldo Story. To the east there are great topiary pieces in golden and common yew, and a unique topiary sundial. From the terraces marvellous views of the Vale of Aylesbury are seen in the distance.

ASHTREE COTTAGE
Wiltshire

Ashtree Cottage,
Kilmington Common,
Warminster BA12 6QY
On Kilmington Common
5m S of Frome by B3092
Tel: 01985 844740

Owner: Mr and Mrs L.J. Lauderdale

Open: By appointment. 1 acre

Illustration opposite: The pool garden at Ashtree Cottage

I'M NOT SURE how useful it would be to call this a cottage garden. It certainly surrounds a cottage but its spirit is very far from the hectic jumble usually associated with the term. Wendy Lauderdale is a fastidious gardener and you will soon notice that her garden is flawlessly kept, full of marvellous and healthy plants and craftily laid out in all respects. In ten years she has fashioned a work of art which gives more pleasure than places twenty times larger. There are brilliant effects – a pool of pale blue *Corydalis flexuosa* lapping at the trunk of a *Cornus controversa* 'Variegata'; or a hummock of blood red *Dicentra* 'Bacchanal' in the shade of a rich purple Japanese maple. A long pergola leads from the entrance to the front door, garlanded with roses and clematis and with mounds of catmint billowing at your feet. There will be something to enjoy in any season and if you are lucky the gardener herself will show you round, brimming over with a wonderful knowledge of plants that only years of practical experience can give. There are a few excellent plants for sale.

BARTON MANOR
Isle of Wight

Whippingham, East Cowes
PO32 6LB
1m SE of Cowes by A3021
next to Osborne House
Tel: 01983 292835
Fax: 01983 293923

Owner:
Mr Robert Stigwood

Open: Apr to second Sun in Oct, daily 10.30–5.30. 20 acres

FORMERLY PART of the Osborne House estate, the Barton estate, with its gabled stone manor house, was a particular interest of Prince Albert who laid out the gardens and planted the splendid grove of cork oaks (*Quercus suber*) at the entrance. Today a large part of it is run as a commercial vineyard but since 1976 the gardens have been very well restored to preserve their Victorian character. By the house there are herbaceous borders and a secret garden of roses and winding paths. An avenue of bushes of St John's Wort leads down to a lake with a romantic 19th-century thatched boat house. Here are many good trees (especially willows relishing the moist ground) and the banks are brilliant with daffodils in spring. In summer a National Collection (over 100 species and cultivars) of red hot pokers (*Kniphofia*) may be seen doing its dazzling stuff. A new rose hedge maze was added in 1993.

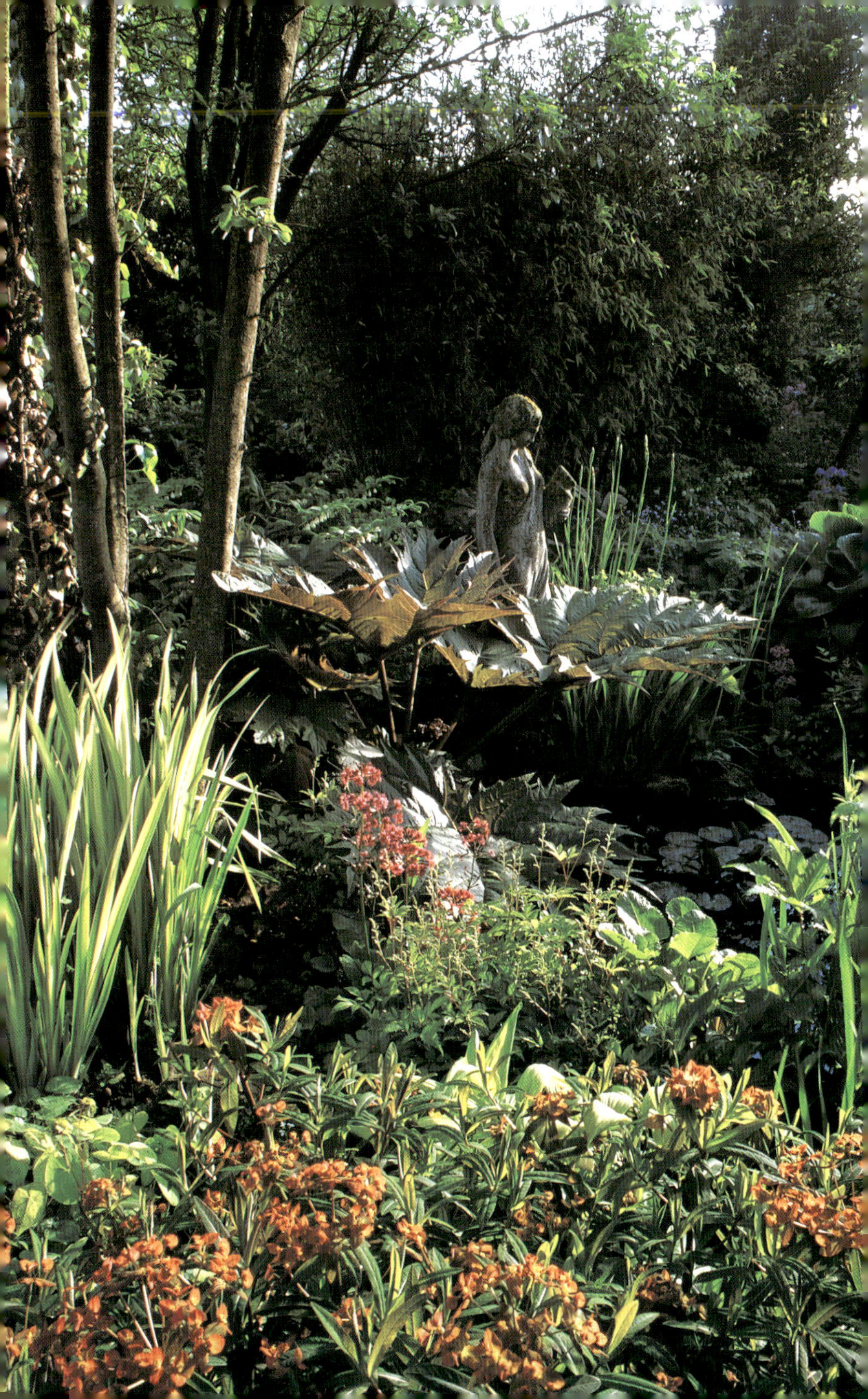

BERNWODE PLANTS
Buckinghamshire

Wotton Road, Ludgershall, nr Aylesbury HP18 9NZ
1m SE of Ludgershall on Wotton Road; 11m W of Aylesbury by A41
Tel: 0378 625266
Fax: 01844 237415 (and answerphone)

Open: Mar to Oct, Wed to Sun and Bank Hol Mon 10–6

BERNWODE PLANTS used to be called 'Plants from a Country Garden' and the lovely plants sold by Derek and Judy Tolman remain 'rare, old-fashioned and desirable'. The emphasis is on herbaceous plants, and the selections of many groups of plants are among the best you will find. There are several achilleas, aquilegias, campanulas, euphorbias (probably the largest collection for sale in the country) hardy geraniums, a marvellous range of Michaelmas daisies, mints, a selection of old cultivars of pinks, a wide range of primulas, very many violas and several perennial wall-flowers. No gardener could visit this nursery and come away empty-handed. A new selection of old apple cultivars is now stocked. An excellent catalogue (£1.50) is available and orders are fulfilled by cheap courier.

BLACKTHORN NURSERY
Hampshire

Illustration:
Helleborus × ericsmithii

Kilmeston, nr Alresford
SO24 0NL
6 1/2m SE of Winchester by A272
Tel: 01962 771796

Open: Mar to 29 Jun, Fri and Sat 9–5

THERE ARE SOME very rare and desirable plants at the Blackthorn Nursery, which you will not often see offered for sale. The nursery specialises in herbaceous perennials and alpines but among a short list of woody plants is an excellent selection of daphnes. Among the herbaceous plants are a magnificent range of epimediums (about which an excellent leaflet is available), several euphorbias, marvellous hellebores and ferns. There is no mail order but a good catalogue is produced (three 1st-class stamps).

BLENHEIM PALACE
Oxfordshire

Woodstock OX20 1PX
In Woodstock, 8m N of
Oxford by A44
Tel: 01993 811091
Fax: 01993 813527

Owner: The Duke of
Marlborough

Open: Park daily 9–4.45;
formal gardens at palace,
mid Mar to Oct, daily
10.30–4.45. 2,000 acres
(including parkland). Palace
open

THE PARK AT Blenheim has an immensely long history: in the 12th century it was the site of Henry II's Rosamond's Bower – and her well still exists; the gardens were originally laid out by Henry Wise in the early 18th century, and Sir John Vanbrugh who designed the immense palace also had a hand in them; in the 1760s the park was landscaped by 'Capability' Brown; and in the early 20th century new parterres by the palace were laid out by the French designer Achille Duchêne – fortissimo exercises in the grand formal manner. The water parterre has arabesques of box outlining pools and classical statuary; the Italian parterre has a magnificent central fountain, topiary of golden yew and pots of oranges and agapanthus. Everywhere ingredients from different periods are harmoniously interwoven with, at their heart, the palace and its vista leading north across Vanbrugh's bridge to the immense Column of Victory surmounted by a statue of the Duke of Marlborough clasping a winged victory 'as an ordinary man might hold a bird'. Brown's park, disposed on gently undulating land about the vast serpentine lake that he made by damming the River Glyme, is one of his masterpieces – a subtle and satisfyingly rural contrast to the extravagant architecture of the palace.

THE BOTANIC NURSERY
Wiltshire

Atworth,
nr Melksham SN12 8NU
9m E of Bath by A4 and
A365
Tel: 0850 328756 (mobile)
01225 706597 (office)
Fax: 01225 700953

Open: Daily except Tue
10–1, 2–5

TERENCE AND MARY Baker's nursery specialises in lime tolerant plants of which it has an excellently chosen range. Those who garden on alkaline soil will find a wide selection that will flourish in their gardens. The nursery concentrates on no particular groups of plants but what it has is carefully selected – for example a list of species foxgloves of which it holds the National Collection. Although their catalogue (£1.50) is full of good, and unusual, plants the Bakers are always on the look out for something new, and many items available are too few to be listed. In addition, many plants are too large or too fragile to be posted, so a visit is essential.

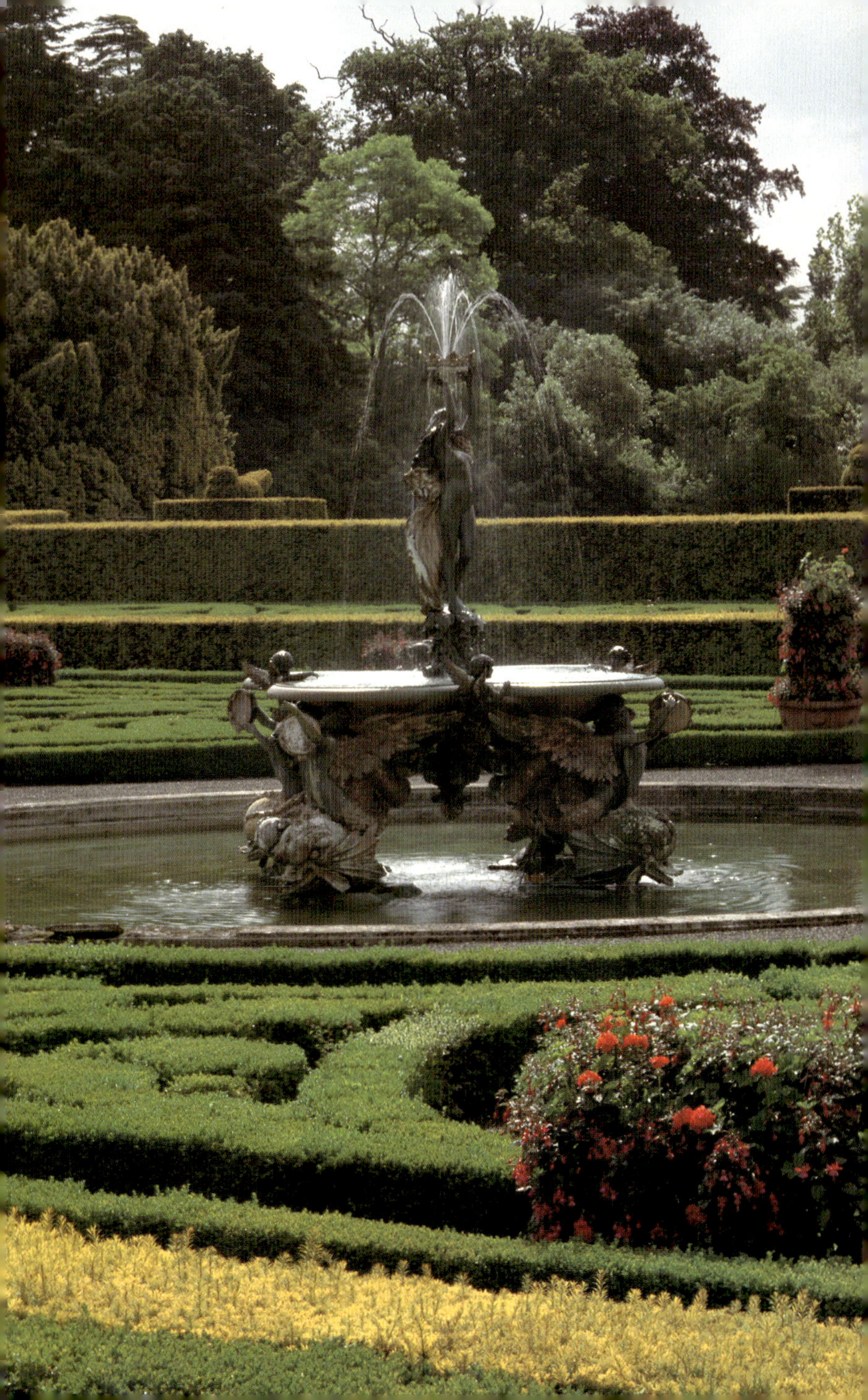

BOWOOD
Wiltshire

Calne SN11 0LZ
2 1/2m W of Calne by A4
Tel: 01249 812102

Owner: Earl and Countess of Shelburne

Open: Apr to Oct, daily 11–6. Garden centre: daily 10–5. 100 acres. House open

Illustration opposite: The Mermaid Fountain by Ralph Waldo Story in the Italian Garden at Blenheim

THE HOUSE – partly designed by Robert Adam – is a splendid 18th-century confection and very much in keeping with the park which is chiefly of the same period. The park, with its great serpentine lake, spreads out below the house and is enlivened by a wonderfully picturesque cascade concealed in the woods, a hermit's cave and an elegant pillared temple; all this is at some distance from the house but there is no point in going to Bowood if you cannot be bothered to walk as far as this. This is the work partly of 'Capability' Brown and, later, of Humphry Repton, and it is one of the very best of its kind. There are marvellous trees at Bowood and the mid 19th-century pinetum is exceptionally good, with some of the finest specimens of conifers in the country – magnificent cedars of Lebanon, pines, firs and giant redwoods. Immediately alongside the house there are 19th-century formal gardens with beds of roses, balustrades, vases and clipped Irish yews. The particularly good garden centre concentrates on woody plants and also has Haddonstone ornaments and terracotta pots. A mail order service is available.

BROUGHTON CASTLE
Oxfordshire

Broughton Castle, nr
Banbury OX15 5EB
2m SW of Banbury by
B4035
Tel: 01295 262624/720041

Owner: Lord Saye and Sele

Open: 18 May to 14 Sept,
Wed and Sun 2–5; Jul and
Aug, also Thur 2–5; also
Bank Hol Mon and
preceding Sun 2–5. 3 acres.
Castle open

THIS SPECTACULAR castle is really a 14th-century moated and fortified manor house, set in exquisite parkland, and occupying a beautiful site next to the church. Within the castle walls there are very distinguished borders showing a fastidious sense of colour harmony. Running along a wall overlooking the moat a mixed border is planted in yellow, cream and blue with much grey and variegated foliage. My Lady's Garden has a pattern of *fleur de lis* clipped in box and a Victorian centrepiece well planted with trailing *Convolvulus sabatius*, pelargoniums and ivy. Disposed around the walls, overflowing mixed borders are planted with many shrub roses in a colour scheme of pink, mauve and white. They look superb against the grey stone and are an object lesson in charming, and appropriate, design and planting – generous abundance softening the stern castle walls. Visitors to the castle may go out onto the roof, from which there is a bird's eye view of this garden and the surrounding parkland; it is one of loveliest views you will ever see and should certainly not be missed – unforgettable in June but marvellous in any season.

BUSCOT PARK
Oxfordshire

Faringdon SN7 8BU
3m NW of Faringdon on A417
Tel: 01367 242094 (not weekends)

Owner:
The National Trust

Open: Apr to Sept, Mon to Fri (closed Bank Hol Mon) and every 2nd and 4th Sat and Sun (including Easter) 2–6 . 20 acres. House open

EAST OF THE HOUSE, running through woodland towards a lake, is a water garden you will never forget. Designed by Harold Peto before World War I it is in the form of a canal that drops down the incline in gentle steps, dips under occasional little bridges, widens and contracts, and from time to time bursts forth in exuberant fountains. The water garden is edged with stately clipped hedges of box, and the flanking path is punctuated by Irish yews, statues and urns. Approaching the lake the visitor sees on its far bank a gleaming temple and an ornamental bridge. To one side of the water garden a pattern of exhilarating avenues is punctuated by handsome eyecatchers. On the far side of the house, by the kitchen garden, there is a recent development of strongly designed borders in yellow and blue by the late Peter Coats; and, within the walls, Tim Rees has made tunnels of pleached hop hornbeam and Judas trees underplanted with spring bulbs followed by waves of many different daylilies – an admirable and instructive piece of modern design.

CHENIES MANOR
Buckinghamshire

Chenies WD3 6ER
4m E of Amersham on A404
Tel: 01494 762888

Owner: Lt. Col. and Mrs MacLeod Matthews

Open: Apr to Oct, Wed, Thur 2–5, also Bank Hol Mon 2–5. 3 acres. House open

THE MANOR is an early Tudor brick house of tremendous character, and the recently made garden is an excellent setting for it. The formal gardens are chiefly behind the house, with a white garden in which a figure of Cupid takes pot shots at plump topiary birds of yew, a cool tunnel of pleached lime, and a virtuoso little sunken garden, intricately planted, in which spring tulips are followed by an elaborate summer bedding scheme. Beyond this, a physic garden has beds of medicinal and culinary herbs laid out round a decorative old octagonal well-house. To one side of the house an ornamental kitchen garden has gravel paths edged with catmint or box, currants and gooseberries grown in cordons, beautifully tended vegetables and a turf maze in an orchard. The whole garden is impeccably well kept and gives the impression of bursting with horticultural endeavour.

CLIVEDEN
Buckinghamshire

Taplow, Maidenhead
SL6 0JA
2m N of Taplow on B476,
near Jnct 7 of M4 and Jnct
4 of M40
Tel: 01628 605069

Owner:
The National Trust

Open: Daily: Mar to Oct
11–6; Nov and Dec 11–4.
375 acres. House open

THE MANSION at Cliveden, built in the 17th century and rebuilt twice in the 19th century, commands a spectacular site on a bluff overlooking the snaking Thames. A giant balustraded terrace looks south to a vast parterre of box and santolina, first laid out for the Duke of Sutherland in the 1850s. At its far end the land falls away in wooded slopes that run down to the river below. The pleasure gardens lie chiefly to the north of the house. In the forecourt are excellent herbaceous borders and, beyond the walls, a hidden rose garden designed by Geoffrey Jellicoe. A lime avenue leads to the eye-stopping Fountain of Love commissioned by Lord Astor from the American Ralph Waldo Story at the turn of the century. To one side is the magical Long Garden with serpentine box hedges, whimsical topiary and mysterious stone figures from the Commedia dell'Arte. Farther up the drive, the water garden has a pagoda overlooking a lake fringed with maples and Japanese cherries. In the woods that surround the house, and by the house itself, there are many exceptional garden ornaments – exquisite statues, urns and garden buildings.

THE COURTS
Wiltshire

Holt, nr Trowbridge
BA14 6RR
In Holt village, 3m SW of
Melksham by B3107
Tel: 01225 782340

Owner:
The National Trust

Open: Apr to Oct, daily
except Sat 2–5. Also by
appointment out of season.
7 acres

CONCEALED BEHIND village walls a pleached lime alley leads up to an ornate Bath stone 18th-century house at the heart of a highly decorative garden in which yew topiary and Irish yews give firm structure. Good shrubs and ornamental trees half conceal an ornamental pool smothered in season with water-lilies, and a billowing hedge of two varieties of holly forms the eastern boundary to a meadow garden. This is a vision of a cottage garden seen through aristocratic eyes. The whole garden has recently been given a good wash and brush-up.

DEACONS NURSERY
Isle of Wight

Godshill, Isle of Wight,
PO38 3HW
In village of Godshill 9m
S of Cowes by A3020
Tel: 01983 840750/522243

Open: Daily except Sun 8–4

DEACONS NURSERY specialises in fruit trees and bushes, of which it has an immense collection – around 250 varieties of apples alone, for example, which may be ordered on a choice of five rootstocks. There is virtually no fruit that is hardy in Britain which is not stocked, and many of the varieties, especially the old kinds, are very difficult to find elsewhere. Although visitors are welcome, virtually all the business of this nursery is conducted by mail order, and an exceptionally informative catalogue is produced (29p stamp).

EXBURY GARDENS
Hampshire

nr Southampton SO4 1AZ
From Totton (W of
Southampton) 14m to
Exbury village by A326 and
B3054
Tel: 01703 891203
Fax: 01703 243380

Owner: E.L. de Rothschild

Open: Mar to Oct 10–5.30
or sunset if earlier.
250 acres

THE CLIMATE is particularly mild at Exbury. Lionel de Rothschild came here in 1919 and started to build up the collection of rhododendrons, many bred by him, which was to make the garden famous. His son has continued the tradition and has added many new varieties which may be seen growing in this huge garden. But even for those not interested in rhododendrons there is much to see throughout the season, especially superb old specimens of ornamental trees. There is an excellent plant centre; a catalogue is available (s.a.e.) and a mail order service.

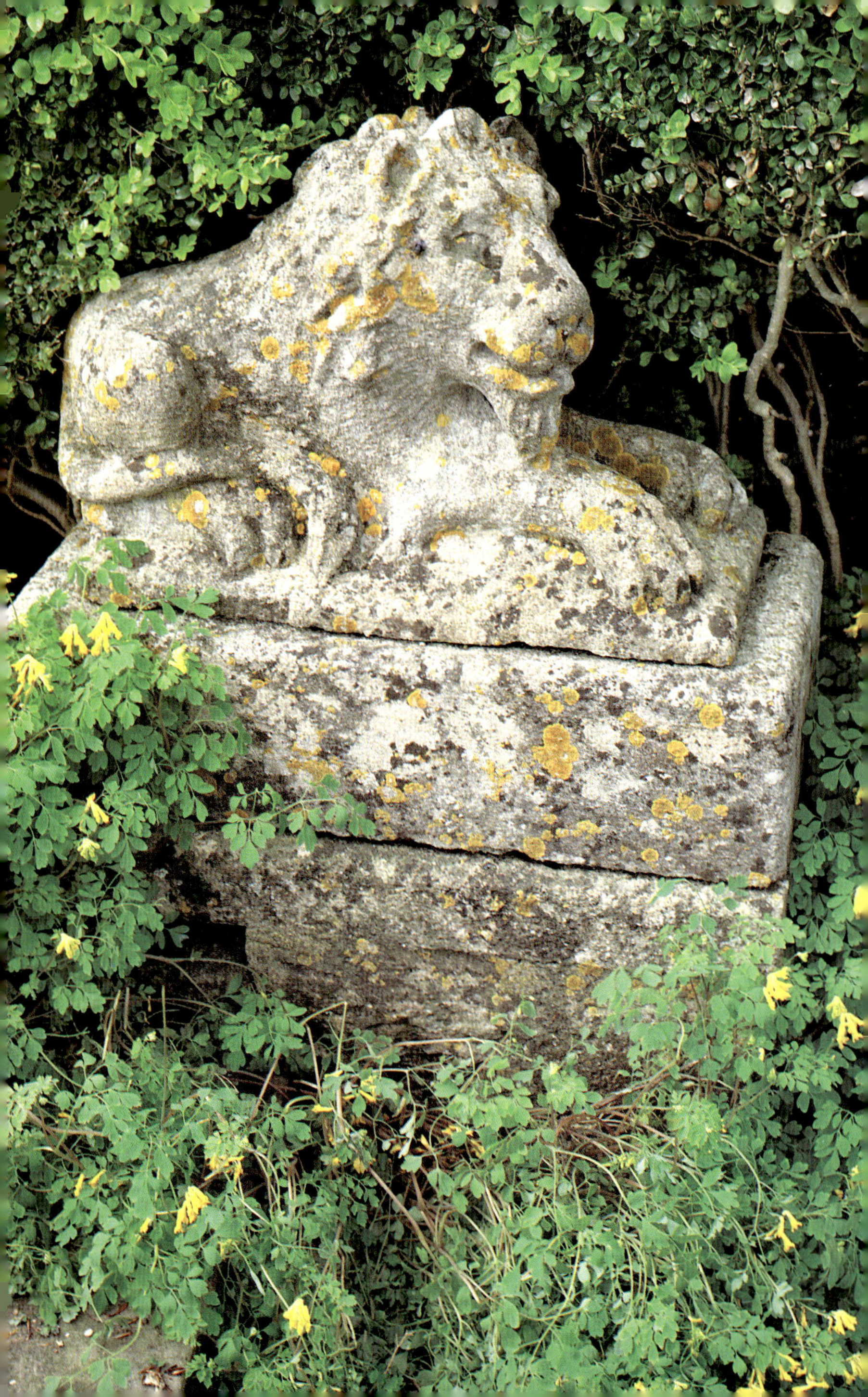

FOXGROVE PLANTS
Berkshire

Foxgrove Farm, Enborne, nr Newbury RG14 6RE
1m W of Newbury
Tel: 01635 40554/0831 176072

Open: Wed to Sun and Bank Hol Mon 10–5; closed throughout Aug

THIS LITTLE NURSERY has won several medals at RHS shows and elsewhere. Its speciality is smaller herbaceous plants and, although the stock is small, the plants are particularly well chosen. There are large selections of campanulas, geraniums, primulas (including some pretty auriculas), saxifrages, snowdrops (of which a special list is published) and violas. Louise Vockins has an eye for a good plant and the visitor is likely to find something unfamiliar and worth buying.

FURZEY GARDENS
Hampshire

Illustration opposite: The Courts

THIS GARDEN was started in 1922 on rough grazing land which benefited from some good old trees and a rich natural vegetation which in many parts of the garden has been preserved. The site is sloping, the soil is acid, and the garden is full of excellent

SOUTH-CENTRAL ENGLAND · 73

Minstead,
nr Lyndhurst SO4 37GL
9m W of Southampton by
A336
Tel: 01703 812464

Owner: Furzey Gardens
Charitable Trust

Open: Daily except 25 and
26 Dec 10–5 or earlier in
winter. 8 acres

plants, many of them unusual. The layout is
informal, with grassy walks descending the hill and
winding between groups of shrubs. Herbaceous
plantings fringe the paths. In spring an immense
number of bulbs – narcissi, dog's tooth violets and
fritillaries – is followed by azaleas and
rhododendrons, many of them rare and tender. The
garden is outstanding in autumn with brilliant foliage
colours from such shrubs as enkianthus and witch
hazels and large specimens of *Liquidambar styraciflua*
and the scarlet oak, *Quercus coccinea*.

GREATHAM MILL
Hampshire

Greatham, nr Liss
GU33 6HH
7m SE of Alton by B3006
Tel: 01420 538245

Owner:
Mrs E. Groves

Open: Apr to Oct, Sat, Sun
and Bank Hol Mon 2–6; by
appointment at other times

MRS PUMPHREY came to this mill house in 1949
and made a large and seductive garden on a
particularly attractive site – it is now run by her
granddaughter and grandson. Cottage-garden
profusion reigns at the front – an old plum tree
sprawls over richly planted beds of shrubs
underplanted with herbaceous plants. The plants have
been fastidiously chosen and there are substantial
groups of irises, geraniums and hostas. Mrs
Pumphrey also had an excellent eye for what goes
with what: a group of intense blue irises associating
with glaucous-leafed hostas, a wig-wam of golden
hop cooled down by a creamy flowered Scotch rose.
This gives the garden harmony rather than jumble.
Behind the house are old trees, a beautifully planted
bog garden, garlands of old roses and the occasional
well placed aristocratic shrub. Across a footbridge is
a nursery area with some good plants for sale.

GREEN FARM PLANTS
Hampshire

Illustration: Asphodelus ramosus *(syn.* A. aestivus*)*

Bentley, nr Farnham
GU10 5JX
In the village of Bentley 3m SW of Farnham by A31
Tel: 01420 23202
Fax: 01420 22382

Open: Mid Mar to mid Oct, Wed to Sat 10–6; other times by appointment

JOHN COKE AND MARINA CHRISTOPHER'S beautifully kept nursery is well worth seeking out because they have a connoisseur's eye for a good plant and there are many things here that you will not easily find elsewhere. Their specialities are smaller decorative shrubs and hardy herbaceous plants. Everything they choose has something distinguished about it, which gives their range the feeling of a house style. They do not have immense numbers of any particular genus but there are discerningly chosen groups of plants such as cimicifugas (a much underappreciated plant), cistus, penstemons, poppies and sages. There is no mail order but a catalogue is produced (three 1st-class stamps).

GREYS COURT
Oxfordshire

Rotherfield Greys,
Henley-on-Thames
RG9 4PG
3m W of Henley-on-Thames by A423
Tel: 01491 628529

Owner:
The National Trust

Open: Apr to Sept, daily except Thur and Sun (closed Good Fri) 2–6.
9 acres. House open

THE HOUSE, partly Tudor and partly Georgian, commands unforgettable views over the valley of beech woods and downland. Passing through a white garden and a garden of old roses underplanted with pinks, a path leads under a great canopy of *Wisteria sinensis*. In the former kitchen garden, paths are edged with *Rosa mundi* or espaliered fruit trees. Here a pergola veiled with vine and honeysuckle leads to the Archbishop's Maze. Turning back towards the house, by the Cromwellian Stables, is a brilliant little enclosed garden with knots of box hedges and topiary, London pride edging the paths, beds of herbaceous plants, with walls of pleached laburnum.

HARDY'S COTTAGE GARDEN PLANTS

Hampshire

The Walled Garden,
Laverstoke Park,
Laverstoke, Whitchurch
RG28 7NT
2m E of Whitchurch
signposted from the B3400
on the western edge of
Laverstoke village

Tel: 01256 896533
Fax: 01256 896572

Open: Mar to Oct, daily
9–5.30

THE STRENGTH of this nursery lies in the harmony of its range of plants rather than in great botanical curiosities. I once saw a consignment of Hardy's plants on their way to a show, and jumbled together before being loaded they resembled an excellent little herbaceous border. The stock is chiefly herbaceous and the emphasis is on good garden plants rather than dazzling rarities. Campanulas, euphorbias, geraniums, penstemons and phloxes are well represented. A few woody plants – such as an unusual range of lavateras – are also stocked. But the value of this place is Rosy Hardy's sure eye for a good plant. There is not a dud in the place. A catalogue is produced (three 1st-class stamps) but there is no mail order.

HEALE GARDEN AND PLANT CENTRE

Wiltshire

Illustration opposite: The apple tunnel at Heale Garden

ON LOW-LYING LAND on the banks of the Avon Heale House is an irresistibly decorative confection of rosy brick and stone dressings. The garden has a character all of its own and there are few places in England where a gardener is likely to

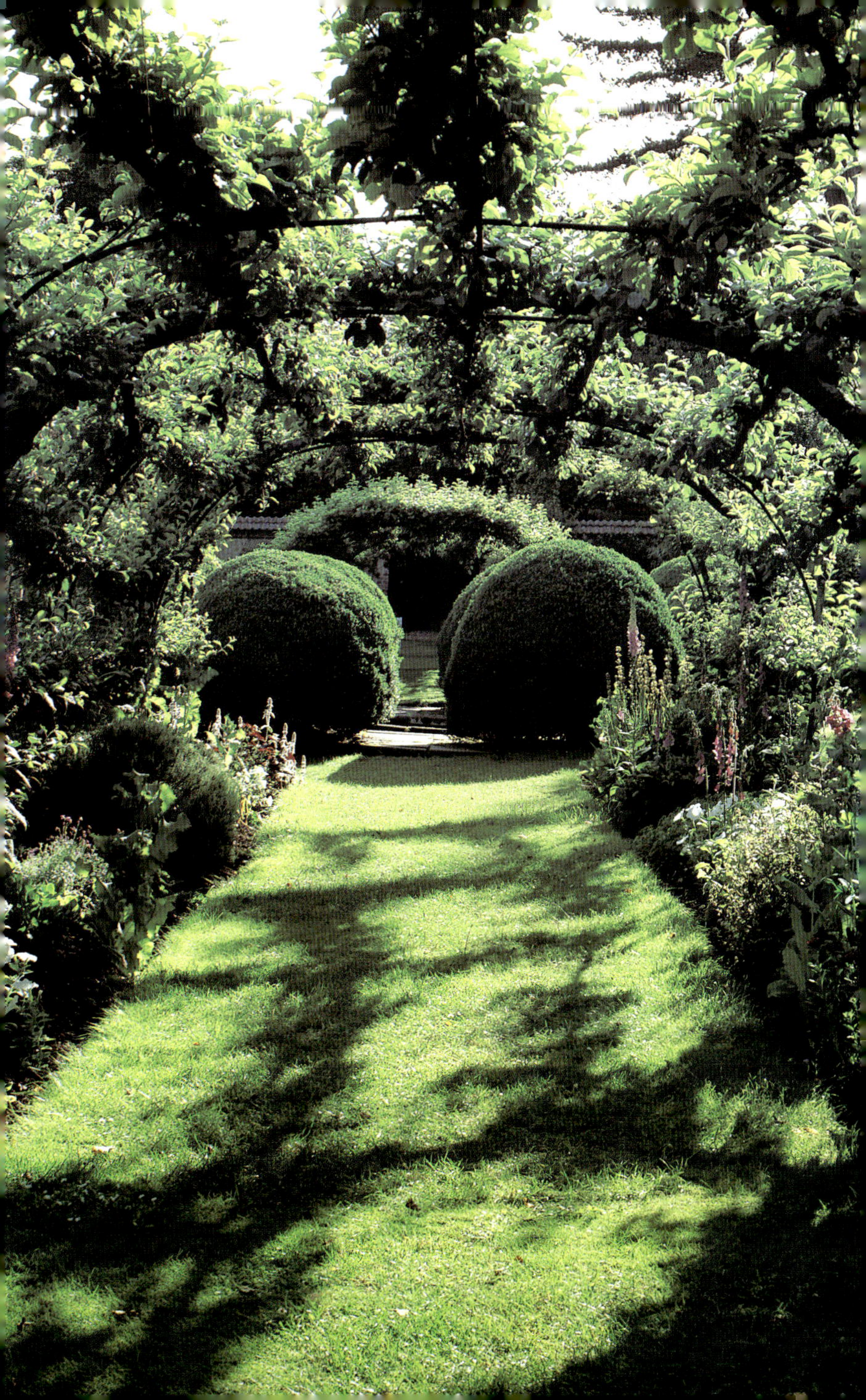

Middle Woodford,
nr Salisbury SP4 6NT
4m N of Salisbury in the
Woodford Valley by minor
roads
Tel: 01722 782504

Owner: Mr Guy Rasch

Open: Daily 10–5. 8 acres

have more fun. The 'landing stage' by the house and the scalloped fish ponds and rose terraces west of the house were designed by Harold Peto in 1910 for the Hon. Louis Greville who installed a Japanese garden with scarlet bridge and fragile tea-house after a tour of diplomatic duty in Japan before World War I. Nearby is a walled vegetable garden with broad tunnels of espaliered apples, clipped mounds of box surrounding a pool and a beguiling mixture of fruit, vegetables and masterly ornamental planting. Everywhere in the garden there are roses – particularly old shrub roses – an unforgettable sight in late June; but there is always something to admire at other times. An excellent plant centre, expanding all the time, sells exceptionally good plants including the beautiful 'Terrace' roses, apparently unique to Heale, which have so far resisted identification. A catalogue is produced but there is no mail order.

THE SIR HAROLD HILLIER GARDENS AND ARBORETUM
Hampshire

Jermyns Lane, Ampfield,
nr Romsey SO51 0QA
3m NE of Romsey by
A31
Tel: 01794 368787
Fax: 01794 368027

Owner: Hampshire County Council

Open: Apr to Oct, daily 10.30–6; Nov to Mar, daily 10.30–5. 160 acres

THIS IS ONE of the greatest collections of woody plants in the country, and had its origin as the private arboretum of Sir Harold Hillier. The arboretum holds the National Collection of oaks but its riches are so extensive and various that there is little point in beginning to list them. A visit at any time of the year will be splendidly rewarded and this is a marvellous place for even expert gardeners to learn more; for beginners it is an essential part of gardening education.

HILLIER'S NURSERIES LTD
Hampshire

THIS IS THE headquarters of the Hillier empire from which mail orders are serviced. This nursery has the largest single collection of woody plants commercially available in the country (and quite possibly in the world) and its catalogue is a standard reference book. Herbaceous plants are also sold but there is nothing like the same range and depth. There

Ampfield House, Ampfield, nr Romsey SO51 9PA
Tel: 01794 368733

Open: All branches: Mon to Sat 9–5.30, Sun 10–5.30; closed Christmas and New Year

are several garden centres in Hampshire, which include those at Jermyn's Lane, nr Romsey (01794 68407); in Romsey Road, west of Winchester (01962 842288); and at Botley Road, Romsey (01794 513459). These carry a good general stock – but it is only a pale reflection of the treasures available to order by mail or for collection from the headquarters.

HINTON AMPNER
Hampshire

Bramdean, nr Alresford SO24 0LA
1m W of Bramdean village by A272
Tel: 01962 771305

Owner:
The National Trust

Open: 30 Mar to Sept, Sat, Sun, Tue, Wed, Bank Hol Mon 1.30–5.30. 8 acres. House open

THIS IS AN exciting place to visit – an excellent old garden, redesigned in the 20th century and now being restored. The estate formerly belonged to Ralph Dutton, Lord Sherborne, who rebuilt the house, an 18th-century brick mansion, and laid out a new garden incorporating older features such as a superb lime avenue planted in 1720. It is a marvellous site and Dutton opened views into the exquisite surrounding parkland. Within the garden he laid out all sorts of decorative schemes – a cherry garden with formal hedges of box and yew, a yew walk backed with shrub roses, a leafy and mysterious dell, a sunken garden, yew topiary and much else. Everywhere there is a brilliant use of ornaments – statues and urns – which direct the gaze and emphasise a vista.

HOLLINGTON NURSERIES
Berkshire

Woolton Hill, Newbury RG20 9XT
5m SW of Newbury by A343
Tel: 01635 253908
Fax: 01635 254990

Open: Mid Mar to Sept, Mon to Sat 10–5.30, Sun and Bank Hol Mon 11–5; Oct to Mar, Mon to Fri 10–dusk

ALTHOUGH THIS marvellous place certainly sells herbs it is misleading to call it a herb garden because it is of much wider interest that that. Simon and Judith Hopkinson have laid out a series of borders, knots, parterres and raised beds to show their plants in action. All this – beautifully designed and executed – is bursting with ideas for gardeners. It is well worth visiting in iuts own right. In the nursery itself, apart from the very wide range of herbs there are also shrubs and trees with scented foliage, a small selection of conservatory plants and an interesting collection of ready-made topiary in cypress, box, yew and holly. A very good catalogue is produced (s.a.e.) and a separate list is available (s.a.e.) but there is no mail order.

IFORD MANOR
Wiltshire

Iford, nr Bradford-on-Avon
BA15 2BA
7m SE of Bath by A36
Tel: 01225 863146

Owner: Mrs Cartwright-Hignett

Open: Apr and Oct, Sun 2–5; May to Sept, daily except Mon and Fri 2–5. 2 1/2 acres

THE ARCHITECT and garden-designer Harold Peto came here in 1899 and on the steep wooded slopes of the Frome valley, above an 18th-century manor house, laid out a terraced garden embellished with classical statuary and architectural fragments. Steep flights of steps link the terraces with their pools, fountains, loggias, colonnades, urns and figures. Cypresses add to the Italian atmosphere and many trees and shrubs flower among the statues. The formal garden contrasts with its rural surrounds, and idyllic views open out over cattle grazing in meadows. In the woods above the garden a Japanese garden is being recreated by the present owners who have done a huge amount of restoration.

JENKYN PLACE
Hampshire

JENKYN PLACE is in the distinguished 20th-century tradition of gardens of compartments embellished with beautifully chosen, sometimes rare, plants. Laid out on a gentle slope, hedged in yew, beech or

Bentley, nr Farnham
GU10 5LU
In Bentley village, 4m
SW of Farnham on A31
Tel: 01420 23118

Owner: Mrs G.E. Coke

Open: Apr to Sept, Thur to
Sun and Bank Hol Mon
2–6. 6 acres

hawthorn, the garden has some very grand ingredients – a pair of large-scale true herbaceous borders, for example. But many of the most memorable features are of a simpler kind – waves of crinums planted under old apple trees, an avenue of pairs of different species of rowans, a single statue of a crouching lion at the end of a long, plain enclosure of beech hedging, and a long, refreshing grassy vista through old trees. The best quality of the garden is the unforced contrast of very different styles – an informal grassy walk among trees and shrubs, or the crisp formality of stone steps, statues and paths. Everywhere the visitor may see excellent plants used with real skill.

KELMSCOTT MANOR
Oxfordshire

Kelmscott GL7 3HJ
In the village of Kelmscott,
6 1/2m NW of Faringdon by
A417, B4449 and minor road
Tel: 01367 252486
Fax: 01367 253754

Owner: The Society of
Antiquaries

Open: Apr to Sept, Wed
11–1, 2–5. 1 1/2 acres

THE GABLED MANOR is 16th-century, handsomely set on the edge of the village by the wooded banks of the infant Thames. It is famous as the country house of William Morris and the garden preserves an atmosphere of simple rural charm. Recently, the custodians have been turning their attention to the garden. Their careful plantings, with well-chosen colours, now embellish this intensely atmospheric place which is still so redolent of Morris and his times. A historic survey has recently been carried out as a result of which new paths and beds have been made with the standard roses so popular in high Victorian times. The aim of this is to make the garden more closely resemble the picture of it shown in Morris's *News from Nowhere*.

LANGLEY BOXWOOD NURSERY

Hampshire

Rake, nr Liss GU33 7JL
6m NE of Petersfield by
B2070 (formerly A3) on the
W side of the road turning
off immediately after
garden centre and school
Tel: 01730 894467
Fax: 01730 894703

Open: By appointment

PERSONAL OBSESSIONS are often of no interest to other people unless you are a psychiatrist who studies compulsive behaviour. But Elizabeth Braimbridge's passionate devotion to box is inspiring. She has gathered together, deep in Hampshire woodland, the greatest range commercially available in this country. Here is the curious and wonderful sight of queues of topiary teddy-bears, pyramids, spheres, corkscrews, leaping horses and preening peacocks. In addition to topiary she also sells many cultivars of *Buxus sempervirens* and other species which, with their often strikingly ornamental foliage, make highly ornamental plants even without clipping. It is enough to make box fanatics of us all. An outstandingly informative catalogue is produced (four 1st-class stamps) and mail order is available.

THE LITTLE COTTAGE

Hampshire

FEW GARDENS cram in so many decorative devices as this 1/4-acre plot which bursts with Hidcotean ambitions. It is an awkward site on a busy main road which Lyn and Peter Prior have craftily divided into seven distinct compartments each with its own colour combinations. Every dinky vista has its eyecatcher

Southampton Road,
Lymington SO41 9GZ
On the A337 opposite Toll
House Inn on the northern
edge of Lymington
Tel: 01590 679395

Owner: Lyn and Peter
Prior

Open: Jun to Sept, Tues
10–1, 2–6 and at other
times by arrangement.
1/4 acre

and there is some resoundingly successful planting here. The entrance, with an avenue of lollipops of variegated euonymus and a colour-scheme of gold and blue, is enchanting – yellow daylilies, blue irises and geraniums, gold variegated ivy, periwinkles and hostas. To some gardeners' taste some of the colour schemes may be over the top. But the whole point about visiting gardens is to enjoy other people's ideas and the occasional jolt to the sensibilities never did anyone any harm – indeed for some gardeners it is an essential spiritual tonic.

LONGSTOCK WATER GARDENS
Hampshire

Longstock, Stockbridge,
Hampshire SO20 6EH
1 1/2m NE of Longstock
village
Tel: 01264 810894
Fax: 01264 810430

Owner: John Lewis
Partnership

Open: Apr to Sept, 1st and
3rd Sun in each month 2–5.
8 acres

THERE IS NOTHING in Britain quite like these mesmerising water gardens. A maze of little islands is linked by bridges and separated by streams and pools. Close-mown turf paths run along the waterside which is handsomely planted with bold drifts of herbaceous plants – geraniums, ornamental grasses, hostas, irises, ligularia and Asiatic primulas. Gold, grey and silver carp and orfe twist and sparkle in the water. Excellent trees such as swamp cypresses, Himalayan birches and *Liquidambar styraciflua* provide large-scale interest and in the background is fine woodland and ramparts of rhododendrons. Seats are placed here and there and the place, which is exquisitely maintained, exudes calm. Provided for the recreation of the staff ('partners') of The John Lewis Partnership, the public is occasionally admitted.

THE MANOR HOUSE
Hampshire

Upton Grey, nr Basingstoke
RG25 2RD
In the centre of Upton Grey village, 6m SE of Basingstoke by minor roads; Jnct 5 of M3
Tel: 01256 862827
Fax: 01256 861035

Owner: Mr and Mrs J. Wallinger

Open: May to Jul, by appointment

THE NAME OF Gertrude Jekyll seems to be on almost every gardener's lips these days but very few of her gardens survive and fewer still have been restored with such care and affection as this. The Wallingers came in 1984, long after the Jekyll garden had disappeared, and have now reinstated her original scheme with meticulous care. To one side of the entrance drive the wild garden has sinuous mown paths in long grass, rambling roses, thickets of bamboo and a flag-fringed pool. Behind the house the formal garden has a virtuoso Jekyll plat – two squares of triangular beds edged with grey stachys and brimming with swoony double pink peonies and the double pink rose 'Caroline Testout'. Terraces overlook it and the supporting dry-stone walls are rich with aquilegia, corydalis, hart's tongue ferns and valerian. Steps lead down to terraced bowling and tennis lawns hedged in yew. This is one of the very best Jekyll gardens from which to learn her essential ideas which may be put into practice in any garden.

THE MEAD NURSERY
Wiltshire

Illustration: Malva moschata *'Alba'*

Brokerswood, nr Westbury
BA13 4EG
3 m NW of Westbury between Woodland Park and Rudge
Tel: 01373 859990

Open: Feb to Oct, Wed to Sat and Bank Hol Mon 9–5, Sun 12–5

STEPHEN AND EMMA Lewis-Dale started their nursery only three years ago and already it is showing its paces. The heart of their stock is herbaceous perennials with several of the smaller shrubs like artemisias lavender, sages and thymes that make such valuable companion plants. An interesting range of hardy alpines is also stocked. You would have to possess the best-stocked garden in the world, or be impossible to please, to come away empty-handed. Some well-planned display areas show the plants performing. No mail order but a very good catalogue is issued (five 1st-class stamps).

MOTTISFONT ABBEY GARDEN
Hampshire

Mottisfont,
nr Romsey SO51 0LJ
4 1/2m NW of Romsey by A3057
Tel: 01794 341220/340757

Owner:
The National Trust

Open: 24 and 31 Mar, Apr to 30 Oct, Sat to Wed 12–6 or dusk if earlier (in Jun daily 12–8.30). 21 acres. House open

MOTTISFONT IS known for its Rose Garden in which an immense collection of shrub roses, with an emphasis on the older varieties, is arranged in the old walled kitchen garden. Here is housed the National Collection of pre-1900 shrub roses. Unlike many rose gardens, however, this is beautifully designed in box-edged beds divided by lawns and gravel paths, and the beds are enriched by all kinds of herbaceous plants which maintain interest when the roses are not performing. Visiting gardeners will not only meet many unfamiliar roses but they will discover an immense amount about their ornamental use in the garden. All this is a tribute to Graham

SOUTH-CENTRAL ENGLAND • 85

Stuart Thomas who rediscovered so many old roses and supervised the making of this garden. Nearer the house, partly medieval stone and partly Georgian brick, there are other things worth seeing: a pleached lime alley designed by Sir Geoffrey Jellicoe with carpets of chionodoxa in the spring; a dashing box parterre with summer bedding; and, down by the River Test which flows through the grounds, a stupendous London plane tree, one of the most memorable trees you will ever see.

THE OLD RECTORY
Berkshire

Burghfield, Reading
RG3 3TH
In Burghfield village 5m
SW of Reading

Owner:
Mr R.R. Merton

Open: Feb to Oct, second and last Wed in month 11–4 (parties by appointment in writing). 4 1/2 acres

THIS WONDERFUL GARDEN gets in only by the skin of its teeth because it is open so rarely, but it is so good that it would be worth planning a visit to these parts to coincide with its opening. Immediately behind the handsome brick house a marvellous cedar of Lebanon, the supreme garden ornament, is given full breathing space on a lawn. A pair of brilliant borders, separated by a crisp turf path and backed by yew hedges, leads towards a pool with a statue of Antinous, fringed with maples, bold foliage planting and flowering shrubs. All about the house are beautifully judged plantings (including some excellent troughs) and there is a splendid kitchen garden. On open days a plant *souk* appears in the yard and many good plants are sold. Esther Merton, who made this garden, died in 1995 but her garden continues. She was a great gardener whose name pops up repeatedly among those who love plants and gardens – usually in the form of 'Oh, yes, this was given to me by Mrs Merton, she found it on the Great Wall of China.'

OXFORD BOTANIC GARDEN
Oxfordshire

High Street,
Oxford OX1 4AX
In the centre of Oxford,
near Magdalen Bridge
Tel: 01865 276920

Owner: University of Oxford

Open: Daily except Good Fri and Christmas Day 9–5 (4.30 in winter); greenhouses 2–4. 4 1/2 acres

THIS WALLED GARDEN, with its lovely early 17th-century entrance gate, was founded in 1621, the first botanic garden in England. It still preserves its character of a 'repository of curious plants' but it is extremely attractively laid out and very well maintained. There are rectangular 'order' beds – with plants grouped according to botanical families – and there are also many ornamental trees and shrubs, some of them unusual (like the beautiful Himalayan birch, *Betula utilis jacquemontii*). Although much of the planting is severely botanical the ornamental aspects of horticulture are certainly not neglected: there are excellent borders and fine trees are well placed. Everything is impeccably labelled so it is an admirable place to learn about plants. To one side of the entrance, running along the High Street, is the 'Penicillin Garden', a parterre of roses and hedges of box and yew, designed by Dame Sylvia Crowe to celebrate Oxford's greatest medical discovery and to make the connection with the ancient physic garden.

OXFORD COLLEGE GARDENS
Oxfordshire

Illustration: The entrance to St John's College garden

ALL OXFORD COLLEGES have some sort of garden, presenting to outsiders enticing green views glimpsed through iron railings or gates. A few of these are well worth visiting – hidden gardens of sometimes surprising size. **Magdalen College** (High St; *Open:* 2–6) has a deer park which gives the adjacent early 18th-century New Building something of the air of a rural seat; in front of it is an immense and beautiful London plane. Behind it, Addison's Walk, a shady tree-lined path loved by the 18th-century philosopher, skirts Magdalen Meadow, a lovely pasture which in spring is alive with snake's head fritillaries. **New College** (Holywell Street; *Open:* 11–5) in its Garden Quad, screened by handsome iron gates and railings, has bold borders with a jolly gallimaufry of colours against the sombre stone, given structure by crafty repeated plantings. In other parts of the college there are further signs of imaginative and skilful gardening; for example, bold pairs of distinguished shrubs such as *Carpenteria californica* flanking the entrance to a quad; all this, no doubt, the doing of Robin Lane Fox, the excellent gardener-writer who is a New College don. **St John's College** (St Giles; *Open:* 1–5) has an especially attractive view of the garden through the gate from Canterbury Quad; here is a grand lawn, with substantial trees, fringed with borders. A path to one side leads to a rock garden. **Wadham College** (Parks Road; *Open:* 1.30–4.30) has a long, curving mixed border and an exceptional old purple beech.

POUND HILL HOUSE
Wiltshire

THIS IS THE KIND of garden that corresponds to many people's ideal. It fits the pretty 17th-century stone farmhouse perfectly, it is full of charm, it has much variety of both plants and of design and it is not so large and so lavish as to be beyond the realms of possibility to others. But there is much art in this unassuming artlessness and Barbara Stockitt is a skilful gardener. There are good mixed borders with lavish use of roses, an elegant

West Kington, Chippenham
SN14 7JG
8m NW of Chippenham by
A420 and B4039 and minor
roads
Tel: 01249 782822
Fax: 01249 782953

Owner: Mr and Mrs Philip Stockitt

Open: Tue to Sun 2–5, also Bank Hol Mons. Plant centre same days but 10–5. 2 acres

formal kitchen garden, a grassy walk of shrubs and roses and, behind the house, a splendid water garden. It lies at the head of a lawn, with deep mixed borders leading down towards the house. A stone-flagged courtyard has box topiary in pots and more good roses, including the curiously named but wonderfully blowsy pink climber 'Blairii Number Two'. An attractively laid out plant centre carries a good general stock of woody and herbaceous plants, well worth a visit in its own right.

ROCHE COURT SCULPTURE GARDEN
Wiltshire

THERE IS a renaissance of the use of ornaments in the garden and this is a splendid place to see them in action. The late Georgian house is in a wonderful position with wide views down a wooded valley, and the garden itself is rich in excellent old trees, yew hedges and old walls which make a very good setting in which to display ornaments. Roche

Winterslow,
nr Salisbury SP5 1BG
5m E of Salisbury by A30
Tel: 01980 862244

Owner:
The Earl and Countess of Bessborough

Open: May to Oct, Sat and Sun 11–5; also by appointment at other times

Court is partly a private garden and partly a gallery in which sculptures and pots are displayed for sale; some by well known artists such as Barbara Hepworth, others by the new and little known. The exhibits, which change constantly, benefit immensely from their open air display, and the ensemble of house, garden, views and works of art make it a memorable place to visit.

ROUSHAM HOUSE
Oxfordshire

Steeple Aston OX6 3QX
12m N of Oxford by
A4260 and B4030
Tel: 01869 347110

Owner: C. Cottrell-Dormer

Open: Daily 10–4.30.
30 acres. House open

THERE ARE FEW 18th-century landscape gardens surviving in England where it is still possible to see exactly what the designer intended. Rousham was designed between 1737 and 1741 by William Kent who devised a virtuoso arrangement of statues, buildings, water, a serpentine woodland rill and, above all, made a framework from which to admire the views over the River Cherwell towards the rural landscape beyond. Some of the individual garden buildings are exceptionally beautiful: Praeneste, a wonderful arcaded curve of golden stone, giving viewpoints of subtly changing aspect; Kent's little covered seat of trellis and boards; a solemn gothic temple half-shaded by the woods. The statues are of fine quality and almost all of them turn their backs on the garden and gaze out to the countryside. All this is done with the effortless ease of a conjuror pulling rabbits out of a hat. Nearer the house, in the old kitchen garden with its decorative dovecote, there is a charming arrangement of mixed borders and a box-edged rose parterre.

SPINNERS
Hampshire

Boldre, Lymington
SO41 5QE
1m NE of Lymington by A337
Tel: 01590 673347

Open: 14 Apr to 14 Sept, Wed to Sat 10–5 (also Suns in May); other times by appointment. 3 acres

ON ACID SOIL and surrounded by woodland, Spinners is both a garden and a nursery garden selling a diverse selection of woody and herbaceous plants, many rare. The paths that wind downhill are well planted with ornamental trees and shrubs, and nearer the house there are excellent borders. Most of the plants displayed in the garden may be bought at the nursery. There are, for example, many different magnolias, several maples and rhododendrons, many dogwoods, rare oaks and witch hazels – and that is only in the woody department. There are also choice herbaceous plants – 10 kinds of cyclamen, ferns, excellent grasses, dozens of geraniums and a host of hostas. No catalogue is produced and there is no mail order, so a visit is essential.

STOURHEAD
Wiltshire

Stourton, Warminster
BA12 6QH
In Stourton village, 3m NW of Mere by A303 and B3092
Tel: 01747 840348

Owner:
The National Trust

Open: Daily 9–7 or sunset if earlier (except 17 Jun and 22–25 Jul when garden closes at 5). 40 acres.
House open

ALTHOUGH THIS IS probably the most photographed and certainly the best-known landscape garden in England the experience of visiting it, in different seasons of the year, always provides some new pleasure. It was started in 1741 by the banker Henry Hoare who dammed the River Stour to make a sinuous lake about whose shores he disposed paths, temples, urns, a shivery grotto and, clothing the hillsides, a vast wealth of trees. Although there has been much subsequent planting, continuing in present times, the character of the original layout is unimpaired. Even at rhododendron time it is possible to escape the crush of visitors, ascend the precipitous paths that wind up away from the lake, and experience the authentic feeling of thrilling solitude such gardens inspired in the 18th century.

STOWE LANDSCAPE GARDENS
Buckinghamshire

Buckingham MK18 5EH
3m NW of Buckingham of A422
Tel: 01280 822850

Owner:
The National Trust

Open: 23 Mar to 14 Apr, daily 10–5; 15 Apr to 5 July, Mon, Wed, Fri, Sun 10–5; 7 Jul to 8 Sept, daily 10–5; 9 Sept to 3 Nov, Mon, Wed, Fri and Sun 10–5; 27 Dec to 5 Jan 1997, daily 10–5 or dusk if earlier. 250 acres. House open

STOWE MAKES all other gardens seem like light snacks – this is the full banquet. It is a giant 18th-century landscape garden in which the greatest garden designers of the day worked – Charles Bridgeman, William Kent and 'Capability' Brown, who was head gardener in 1741. In this vast landscape grass, trees, water, ornaments, buildings and huge vistas form a series of exquisite pictures. The monuments have all sorts of meanings and are often decorated with literary or political inscriptions. Even without unravelling their significance, visitors can revel in the marvellous shifting scenes – the contrast of immense views and corners of pastoral intimacy, of grazing cattle and classical temples. To walk about Stowe is one of the greatest of all garden experiences.

TUDOR HOUSE GARDEN
Hampshire

Tudor House, Bugle Street,
Southampton SO1 OA8
Centre of Southampton;
follow signs to old town
and docks
Tel: 01703 332513
Fax: 01703 339601

Owner: Southampton
County Council

Open: Tue to Fri 10–12,
1–5, Sat 10–12, 1–4, Sun 2–5

THIS IS a very attractive idea – a dashing recreation of a Tudor period garden, designed by Dr Sylvia Landsberg in 1982 as the annexe to an excellent museum in the old city of Southampton. A knot of box, plants of the period, characteristic columns painted in chevrons and surmounted by heraldic beasts, hives with honey bees, a rose arbour and a tunnel of vines give something of the true character of a garden of the period.

WADDESDON MANOR
Buckinghamshire

Waddesdon,
nr Aylesbury HP18 0JH
6m NW of Aylesbury by
A41
Tel: 01296 651211

Owner:
The National Trust

Open: 6 Jan to 25 Feb, Sat
and Sun 11–5; 28 Feb to 22
Dec, Wed to Sun, Bank
Hol Mon and Good Fri
11–6. 160 acres.

THIS IS a Rothschild garden and a splendid one. The house is a fantasy pastiche of a Loire château, finished in 1889 for Baron Ferdinand de Rothschild and built on a wonderful site – the top of a hill commanding views over the Vale of Aylesbury. The slopes of the hill are encircled with walks and clothed in splendid trees, and a marvellous collection of statues animates the scene. To the south of the house are terraced gardens which have recently been restored with elaborate bedding schemes to their original Edwardian splendour as shown in contemporary photographs. In 1995 40,000 bedding plants were used – with the Rothschild colours of blue and yellow in prominence. Further work is in progress in a 10-year programme to restore other parts of the gardens which were laid out by the French landscape architect Lainé who also worked on the estates of the French Rothschilds. To one side of the house a superb aviary of delicate wrought-iron tracery and rococo curlicues houses a splendid collection of exotic birds. The house, after a long period of restoration, looks more beautiful than ever.

GILBERT WHITE'S HOUSE
Hampshire

Selborne,
nr Alton GU34 3JH
In the village of Selborne,
5m SE of Alton by B3006
Tel: 01420 511275

Owner:
Oates Memorial Trust

Open: End Mar to end Oct daily 11–5; Nov to Dec, Sat and Sun 11–5 (closed 24 Dec)

GILBERT WHITE was as passionately observant about gardening as he was about natural history and his writings on the subject, contained in his *Garden Kalendar*, are still well worth reading. This place – his former house and garden – is sacred ground. Behind the house, which is in the village high street, the garden has wonderful views across to the wooded ridge known as the Hanger. A rose garden, yew hedges and topiary, a laburnum tunnel and herbaceous borders are well cared for. These are relatively modern features but there still remains much from White's time – the ha-ha he made in 1761, his fruit wall and a decorative sun-dial. Ambitious plans are now in place, with the help of his own writings, to restore the garden the garden to its state as he designed it. Already completed are a quincunx, wooden ha-ha, mount and beds of plants known to Gilbert White.

SOUTH-WEST ENGLAND

Cornwall
Devon
Dorset
Somerset

Map of Cornwall and Devon Gardens

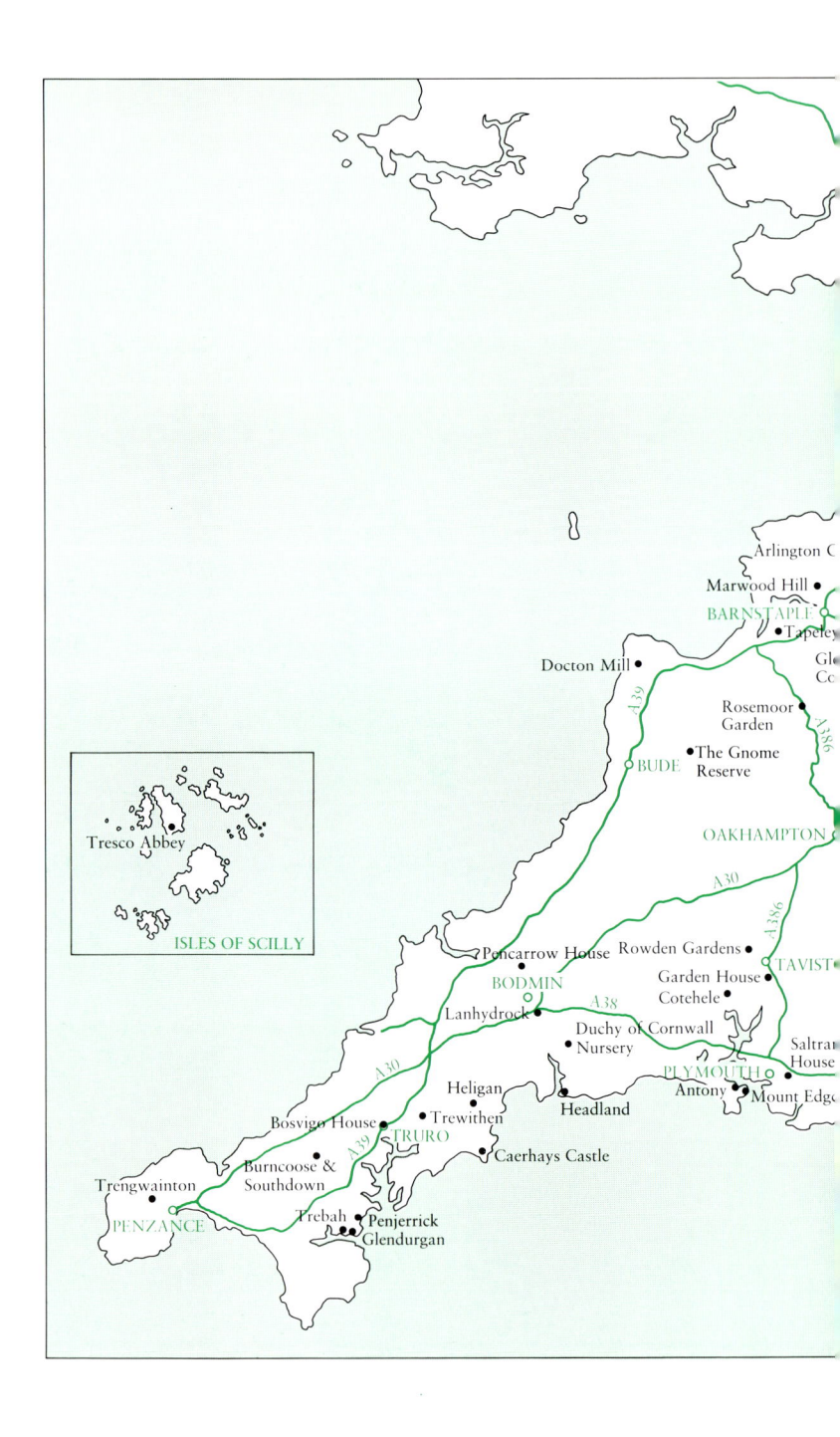

- Arlington C[ourt]
- Marwood Hill
- BARNSTAPLE
- Tapeley
- Docton Mill
- Gl[...] Co[...]
- Rosemoor Garden
- BUDE
- The Gnome Reserve
- OAKHAMPTON
- Tresco Abbey
- ISLES OF SCILLY
- Pencarrow House
- Rowden Gardens
- BODMIN
- Garden House
- Lanhydrock
- Cotehele
- TAVIST[OCK]
- Duchy of Cornwall Nursery
- Saltra[m] House
- Heligan
- PLYMOUTH
- Trewithen
- Headland
- Antony
- Mount Edg[cumbe]
- Bosvigo House
- TRURO
- Burncoose & Southdown
- Caerhays Castle
- Trengwainton
- PENZANCE
- Trebah
- Penjerrick
- Glendurgan

Map of South West England – Gardens and Nurseries

- The Monocot Nursery
- Manor House
- Blaise Castle
- BRISTOL
- BATH
- Bath Botanical Gardens
- Hannays of Bath
- Claverton Manor
- Blackmore & Langdon
- Prior Park Landscape Garden
- MINEHEAD
- Greencombe
- Dunster Castle
- Milton Lodge
- Hadspen House
- Hestercombe
- Kelways Nurseries
- Patricia Marrow
- Chiffchaffs
- TAUNTON
- Broadleigh Gardens
- Lyte's Cary Manor
- East Lambrook Manor
- Mallet Court Nursery
- Tintinhull House
- Avon Bulbs
- Montacute House
- Hare Lane Pottery
- Cotshayes Court
- Barrington Court
- Cranborne Manor
- Scott's Nurseries
- Lower Severalls
- Edmondsham House
- Killerton House
- YEOVIL
- EXETER
- Forde Abbey
- Sticky Wicket Garden
- Minterne
- Parnham House
- Mapperton House
- Athelhampton
- Compton Acres
- Castle Drogo
- Bicton College
- Bicton Park
- DORCHESTER
- POOLE
- Abbotsbury
- Kingston Maurward Gardens
- Arlington Hall
- Coleton Fishacre
- Overbecks

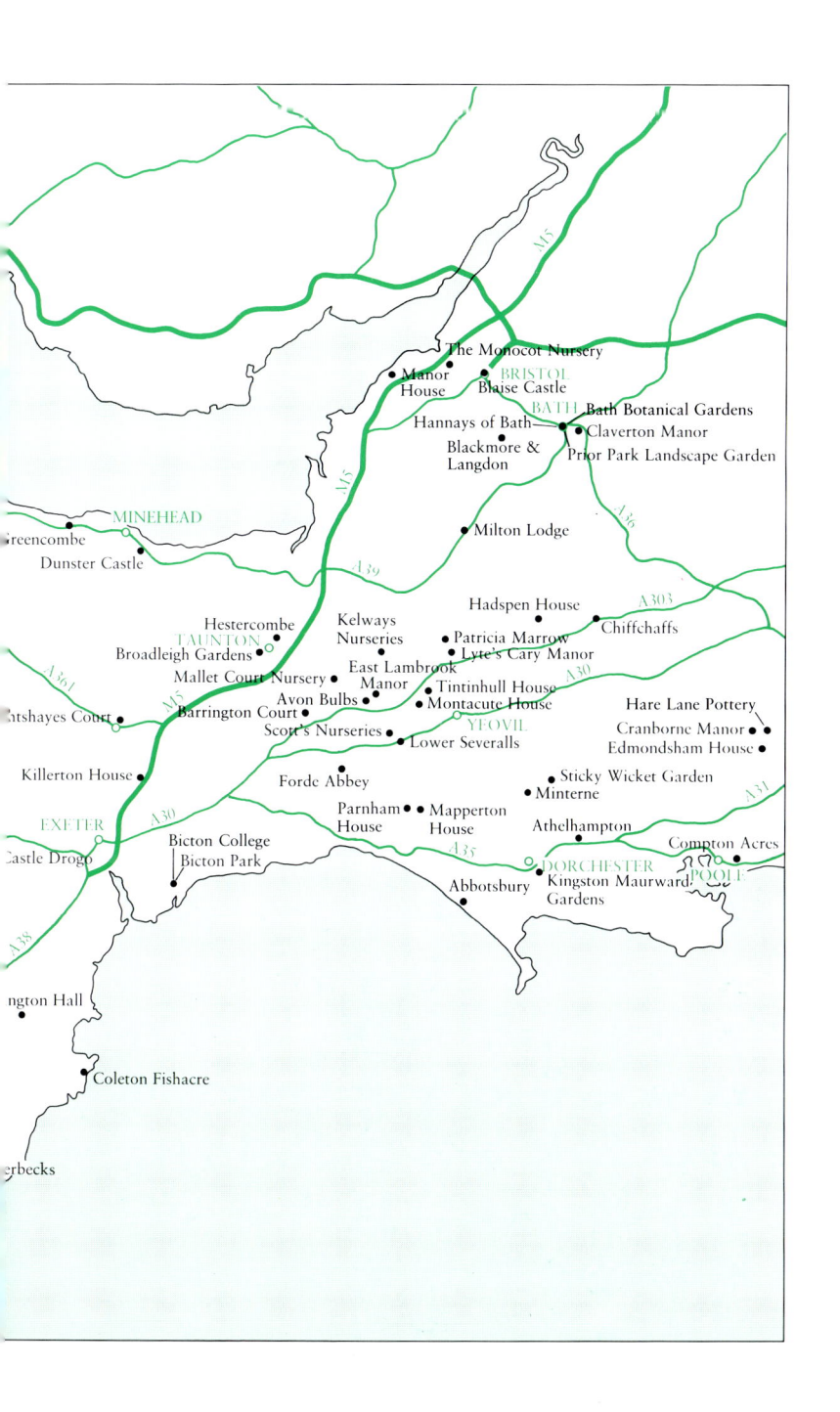

ABBOTSBURY SUB-TROPICAL GARDENS
Dorset

Abbotsbury,
nr Weymouth DT3 4LA
1/2m W of Abbotsbury
village, 9m NW of
Weymouth by B3157
Tel: 01305 871412/871344
Fax: 01305 871092

Owner: Ilchester Estates

Open: Daily 10–5 (dusk in winter); closed 25 Dec. 20 acres

BENEFITING FROM a remarkably mild microclimate, Abbotsbury Gardens have an immense range of plants. The garden was started in the 1760s but the 4th Earl of Ilchester introduced many new plants in the 19th century. From the original walled garden with its beautiful wingnut (*Pterocarya fraxinifolia*), paths lead to the valley garden, a gentle combe with camellias, magnolias and rhododendrons in old woodland. Asiatic primulas enliven the banks of the stream in spring, followed by gunnera, petasites, rodgersias and rheums. It is a garden worth visiting at any time of the year; in winter, for example, it is full of interest. Everywhere there is something to catch the eye in the jungle-like luxuriance. A plant centre has some good plants for sale.

ANTONY HOUSE
Cornwall

Torpoint PL11 2QA
5m W of Plymouth by
Torpoint car ferry and A374
Tel: 01752 812191

Owner:
The National Trust

Open: Apr to Oct, Tue, Wed, Thur and Bank Hol Mon 1.30–5.30; Jun to Aug, also Sun 1.30–5.30. 25 acres. House open

WHEN A HOUSE is as beautiful as Antony there is always a danger that any garden will be outfaced. As it is, helped by the genius of Humphry Repton, the two go together in perfect harmony. The house – an early 18th-century dream of silver Pentewan stone – presents its north façade to land which slopes gently towards the distant Tamar estuary. The view from the house, over shallow rose-planted terraces, is towards an immense lawn broken in the middle ground only by a superb old black walnut (*Juglans nigra*). Far beyond this, Repton pierced an opening through a deep belt of woodland to give glimpses of the shimmering water in the distance. In the woods there are marvellous trees, including some ancient holm oaks which Repton admired and was careful to preserve. A flower garden, and a recently made knot of box and germander, are enclosed in yew, and in the old vegetable garden there is an immense collection of daylilies of which Antony holds a National Collection. South of all this is a giant cork oak (*Quercus suber*), a wonder to see.

ANTONY WOODLAND GARDEN AND WOODS
Cornwall

Torpoint PL11 2QA
5m W of Plymouth by Torpoint car ferry and A374

Owner: Carew Pole Garden Trust

Open: 15 Mar to 31 Oct, Mon to Sat 11–5.30; Sun 2–5.30. 100 acres

ADJOINING THE HOUSE and garden at Antony, and still owned by the family that built it, is an atmospheric woodland garden. Sir John Carew Pole started to plant it before World War II but was interrupted by active service. Since then he has added an immense number of magnolias and rhododendrons which flourish in the naturalistic setting of a wooded combe protected to the west by windbreaks. The woods fringe the estuary of the River Lynher and an idyllic walk gives glimpses of the mainland and the castellated silhouette of Ince Castle.

ARLINGTON COURT
Devon

Arlington, nr Barnstaple
EX31 4LP
7m NE of Barnstaple by A39
Tel: 01271 850629

Owner:
The National Trust

Open: Apr to Oct, daily except Sat (open Sat Bank Hol weekends) 11–5.30. 25 acres. House open

THE PLEASURES of Arlington are not dramatic but they are distinctive. The best thing here is a little Victorian garden with, as its central ornament, a handsome gabled glasshouse crowned with a decorative metal heron, the crest of the Chichester family who owned the estate for many centuries. The garden is backed by a high wall and the ground descends in bold turfed terraces to the entrance steps which are flanked by a pair of cast-iron herons holding wriggling worms in their beaks. On either side of a central pool and fountain, arbours are festooned with roses in summer. The Victorian garden is some distance from the house which is set in lawns with fine specimen trees, including the recent addition of a collection of species of ash. The lake was made at about the same time as the Victorian garden and a classical urn on a plinth to its north-east is in memory of Miss Rosalie Chichester who gave the estate to the National Trust.

ATHELHAMPTON HOUSE
Dorset

Athelhampton, Dorchester
DT2 7LG
5 1/2m NE of Dorchester
by A35(T)
Tel: 01305 848363

Owner: Patrick Cooke

Open: Easter to end Oct, Tue, Wed, Thur and Sun 12–5; Jul and Aug, also Mon and Fri.
15 acres. House open

THE GREAT THING about the garden at Athelhampton is the beauty of its design. This is a late medieval manor house of rare character and the garden, which was designed in the 1890s by F. Inigo Thomas, fits it to perfection. A balustraded terrace ornamented with two elegant summer houses overlooks a narrow canal and beyond, disposed on a sunken lawn with a pool, are twelve giant pyramids of clipped yew. On the far side a gate leads through to a series of enclosed gardens – cunningly connected to the house by penetrating vistas – which are richly ornamented with statues, fountains, obelisks, beautifully detailed walls and gate piers in golden Ham stone. The whole place is a virtuoso performance, a garden that is harmoniously related to house and site.

AVON BULBS

Somerset

Illustration: Albuca nelsonii

Burnt House Farm, Mid Lambrook, South Petherton TA13 5HE
10m W of Yeovil by A3088 and A303 to South Petherton
Tel and Fax: 01460 242177

Open: Mid Feb to mid Apr; end Sept to mid Nov, Thur to Sat 9–4.30 (check by telephone; also by appointment)

AVON BULBS WINS Gold Medals at Chelsea regularly and its list is stuffed with good things. There is an emphasis on species or natural forms and many genera are represented in quantity (e.g. 15 species and forms of fritillary and over 20 snowdrops). There is an excellent range of cyclamen, camassias, erythroniums, irises, narcissi and tulips. Keep an eye open for all sorts of rare, tender bulbous plants which make superb pot plants, such as albuca, eucomis and tulbaghia. The nursery's business is chiefly bulbs but it strays into other desirable areas such as hellebores, of which a choice selection is offered, and, increasingly, beautiful species peonies. There are several excellent woodland plants such as asarum, corydalis, dicentra and smilacina. The list (four 2nd-class stamps) is exceptionally good, beautifully illustrated in colour and full of advice on cultivation. A mail order service is provided.

BARRINGTON COURT
Somerset

nr Ilminster TA19 0NQ
5m NE of Ilminster off A303
Tel: 01985 847777

Owner:
The National Trust

Open: Apr to Sept, daily except Fri 11–5.30.
9 acres. House open

THE BEAUTIFUL gabled manor house, of golden Ham stone, was built in 1514. The gardens have a pronounced Arts and Crafts atmosphere with marvellous basket-weave brick paths and fine masonry in walls and outhouses. Much of this is the work of the architects Forbes and Tate in the 1920s and for whose intricately planned enclosures Gertrude Jekyll designed the planting, one of her very last commissions. The lily garden to one side of the stable block, shows her touch, with central pool and raised beds of azaleas and bold clumps of crinums. East of it there is a charming new white garden, designed by Christine Middleton, the present head gardener, in segmental beds radiating from the centre. A gate leads through to the iris garden of Jekyllesque flavour, with a colour scheme of pink and lavender. A beautifully kept walled kitchen garden provides fruit and vegetables which are sold in season.

BATH BOTANICAL GARDENS
Somerset

Royal Victoria Park, Upper Bristol Road, Bath BA1 2NQ
W of city centre by Upper Bristol Road

Owner: City of Bath

Open: Daily 9–sunset

AS BOTANIC GARDENS go this is on a modest scale but it is very attractively laid out on a fine sloping site and is rich in good plants. Here, it is the trees and larger shrubs that are of special distinction. There are excellent specimens, many mature, of the golden *Catalpa bignonioïdes*, Japanese cherries, an exceptional dogwood, *Cornus kousa chinensis*, superb magnolias and Japanese maples. An atmospheric dell, across the road to the north of the gardens, has a monument to Shakespeare and lovely drifts of anemones and bluebells in season. The whole is excellently cared for by the city parks department.

BICTON COLLEGE OF AGRICULTURE
Devon

Illustration: Agapanthus praecox *sbsp.* minimus

East Budleigh, Budleigh Salterton EX9 7DP
6m NE of Exmouth by A376
Tel: 01395 568353

Owner: Bicton College

Open: Daily 10.30–5.
19 acres

PART OF THE SAME ESTATE as Bicton Park, Bicton College now opens its doors to members of the public, who will find much to interest them. An avenue of monkey-puzzles leads towards the house, beyond which are several collections of trees and shrubs – among them camellias, cherries, eucalyptus, magnolias maples. The college holds the National Collections of agapanthus and pittosporum; the former is a real eye-opener (especially the lovely, and rarely seen, species). In a 2-acre walled garden a nursery has many excellent plants for sale, including several tender rarities.

BICTON PARK GARDENS
Devon

THINGS ARE CHANGING at Bicton Park, which is being restored to its true character as a pleasure garden. At the heart of it is a formal arrangement, the Italian Garden, which in essence dates from the early 18th century but now has a jolly Victorian character with bedded-out parterres, fountains, urns

East Budleigh, Budleigh
Salterton EX9 7DP
6m NE of Exmouth by
B3178
Tel: 01395 568465
Fax: 01395 568889

Owner: Bicton Park Trust

Open: Mar to Oct, daily
10–6 (4 in Mar and Oct).
50 acres

and palm trees. To the north is a range of glasshouses with collections of fuchsias and pelargoniums and, to the west, a stunning curvaceous palm house, like a ship's prow seen from below. Recently restored, this very early building dates from 1820, and has been planted with a splendid range of conservatory plants. To one side of the Italian Garden there is an ornamental shell-house set in a ferny rock garden and, another relic of the early 19th century, an American garden in which plants from North America were grown. A woodland railway through the grounds gives views of a fine arboretum and the brick mansion. There is much to see and admire here, not least the high standards of maintenance.

BLACKMORE & LANGDON
Somerset

Stanton Nurseries,
Pensford, Bristol BS18 4JL
6 1/2m S of Bristol by A37
Tel: 01275 332300

Open: Daily 9–5 (Sun 10–4)

OLD-ESTABLISHED FAMILY firms such as this are becoming very rare. Blackmore & Langdon was founded in 1901, and has won over 60 Gold Medals at the Chelsea Flower Show and countless others elsewhere. It is best known for delphiniums, border phlox and begonias, and many varieties of these are available only from Blackmore & Langdon whose catalogue every year advertises interesting new cultivars. It also sells gloxinias and polyanthus. The catalogue (s.a.e.) is particularly informative, and excellent specialist pamphlets on growing some of these plants are issued. A mail order service is provided and various sundries, including special wire supports for begonias, are available. A visit at delphinium time is a wonderful treat.

BLAISE CASTLE
Bristol

THE BLAISE CASTLE ESTATE, all but engulfed in pretty horrible suburbia, is an enchanting relic of English landscape taste. The Great House at Henbury, a Tudor manor, was acquired in 1762 by Thomas Farr who in 1766 commissioned a splendid Sham Castle from the architect Robert Mylne. It remains on a lofty eminence rising above trees – 'The

Henbury, Bristol BS10 7QS
5m NW of Bristol by A4108
Tel: 0117 9506789

Owners: Bristol City Council; National Trust

Open: Daily dawn to dusk

finest place in England; worth going fifty miles at any time to see' as Jane Austen's Isabella Thorpe said in *Northanger Abbey*. Later in the century Humphry Repton came to landscape the park and his 'Red Book' is on view at Blaise Castle House. Repton's colleague John Nash was called in in the early 19th century to design Blaise Hamlet, a group of wildly picturesque staff cottages. This, owned by the National Trust, is impeccably kept and of devastating charm. It lies on the other side of the main road from the park – but is an essential part of a visit.

BOSVIGO HOUSE
Cornwall

Bosvigo Lane, Truro
TR1 3NH
In the western suburbs of Truro by A390; at Highertown turn down Dobbs Lane (near Sainsbury roundabout). Bosvigo House is 500 yards on the left
Tel: 01872 75774

Owner: Michael and Wendy Perry

Open: Mar to Sept, Wed to Sat 11–6. 3 acres

BOSVIGO HOUSE is a surprising and very attractive place to find on the suburban edge of Truro. In the garden, however, all that seems far away. The Perrys are perfectionists, and have made one of the most attractive of recent gardens. To one side of the handsome 18th-century house is a woodland garden, whose 'hot' borders explode into life in late summer with blazing crocosmias, dahlias, roses, nasturtiums and alstroemerias. About the house are several beautifully planted enclosures showing exciting and fastidious colour harmonies. It is rare in Cornwall for a garden to keep up the interest well into September as Bosvigo certainly does. The Perrys also sell excellent plants, some rare. There is a good catalogue (four 2nd-class stamps) but no mail order.

BROADLEIGH GARDENS
Somerset

Illustration: Tulipa bakeri *'Lilac Wonder'*

Bishops Hull,
Taunton TA4 1AE
3m SW of Taunton by A38
Tel: 01823 286231
Fax: 01823 323646

Open: Mon to Fri 9–4 to view only. Mail order and pre-booked sales only

THIS IS AN outstanding nursery specialising in bulbs but also with many herbaceous plants. Although the business is mail order only, you may visit the garden and view the plants on the spot. Spring is, of course, a good time but Lady Skelmersdale has all sorts of bulbous treats up her sleeve throughout the year – a rare selection of colchicums and autumn-flowering crocuses, for example. This is not a place for instant gardeners but you can go round, notebook in hand, making a list to order from the excellent catalogues (two 1st-class stamps) which are issued in January and June.

BURNCOOSE & SOUTH DOWN NURSERIES
Cornwall

Gwennap, Redruth
TR16 6BJ
3m SE of Redruth on A393
Tel: 01209 861112
Fax: 01209 860011

Open: Mon to Sat 8.30–5, Sun 11–5. *Garden:* 30 acres

THE NURSERY is in the ownership of the Williams family, famous plant collectors who also own Caerhays Castle. It carries a varied stock, of over 2,000 kinds, but there are specialities for which it is outstanding, some of which would be considered hopelessly tender anywhere outside the privileged south-west (for example, *Metrosideros*). The emphasis is on woody plants with some major groups, such as camellias, magnolias and rhododendrons, of which it has especially good selections. Several rarities are stocked (for example *Pittosporum tenuifolium* 'Silver Magic') which are scarcely to be found anywhere else. A very good catalogue (£1.00) is published, from which mail orders may be placed. Alongside the nursery is a fine old woodland garden in which camellias, magnolias and, above all, magnificent rhododendrons are attractively displayed among handsome trees.

CAERHAYS CASTLE
Cornwall

nr Gorran FA1 7DE
In the village of Caerhays
10m S of St Austell by minor roads
Tel: 01872 501310
Fax: 0872 501870

Owner: F.J. Williams

Open: 18 Mar to 3 May, Mon to Fri 11–4.30; also Easter Sun 7 Apr, Sun 21 Apr and Bank Hol Mon 6 May 11–4.30. 100 acres

THIS IS a special place for the three greatest groups of ornamental Asiatic shrubs: camellias, magnolias and rhododendrons. The Williams family, who own it, sponsored some of the great plant hunters – such as George Forrest and E.H. Wilson – and their discoveries found a marvellous home in this wild coastal setting. North of the early 19th-century castle designed by John Nash, woodland sweeps up the hill. It is a place for the observant visitor because the garden's chief glories may lie hidden in the jungle and the excitement of discovery is one of the exceptional pleasures here. Apart from the great trio of flowering shrubs there are many others, some of them exceptionally rare and first planted here – such as the exotically scented *Michelia doltsopa* with its flowers of creamy yellow. The lavish feast of spring blossom, in this wildly romantic place, is a marvellous sight.

CASTLE DROGO
Devon

Drewsteignton EX6 6PB
21m W of Exeter by A30
Tel: 01647 433306

Owner:
The National Trust

Open: Apr to Oct, daily 10.30–5.30. 12 acres.
Castle open

CASTLE DROGO, the last castle to be built in Britain, was designed by Edwin Lutyens and started before World War I. It has a dramatic position on a rocky bluff near Dartmoor, commanding wide views with the River Teign in the distance. The garden, to the north of the drive, is concealed behind ramparts of yew strongly echoing the bold forms of the castle. Granite steps and a path lead to a rectangular sunken garden of subtly varying levels. Here, in each corner, is a shady arbour of *Parrotia persica* trained over a framework, and around two central lawns are lavishly planted mixed borders, among which scalloped paths of Mughal influence thread their way. In late spring an immense old wisteria snakes along the terrace walls, its flowers dripping to the beds below. Granite steps rise to a path lined with flowering shrubs, leading to a huge croquet lawn (which visitors may use) hedged in yew, devoid of ornament but with powerful atmosphere.

CHIFFCHAFFS
Dorset

Chaffeymoor, Bourton, Gillingham SP8 5BY
At W end of Bourton village, 3m E of Wincanton by A303; leave A303 (Bourton bypass) at sign to Bourton
Tel: 01747 840841

Owner:
Mr and Mrs K.R. Potts

Open: Garden: 31 Mar to 29 Sept, Sun, Wed and Thur (closed 2nd Sun in month and 1st and 2nd Sun in Jul and Aug) and Bank Hol weekend 2–5.30; Nursery: Tue to Sat 10–1, 2–5, and whenever garden is open. At other times by appointment. 11 acres

THIS GARDEN, in a surprisingly secluded valley just off the A303, was started from nothing fourteen years ago, and the owners recently incorporated within it their nursery garden, Abbey Plants. The sloping site has been skilfully terraced and linked with stone paths and steps. The soil is acid and a very wide range of plants is grown in beds separated by curving lawns. The different levels, and secluded nooks and crannies, provide a variety of sites in an attractively informal setting. Across a field is a woodland garden threaded with streams where moisture-loving plants such as primulas, gunnera and rheums thrive in the shade of rhododendrons and many ornamental trees. All this is an exceptional example of what can be achieved by skilled gardeners in a remarkably short time. The nursery has an excellent general range of plants at modest prices and a visit is essential as no mail order service is provided.

CLAVERTON MANOR
Somerset

Claverton, nr Bath
BA2 7BD
4m SE of Bath by A36
Tel: 01225 460503
Fax: 01225 480726

Owner: The American Museum in Britain

Open: end Mar to beginning Nov, daily except Mon 1–6 (Sat and Sun 12–6; Bank Hol Sun and Mon 11–6). 10 acres. House open

CLAVERTON MANOR, with its wonderful views across the Avon valley, is an elegant Bath stone mansion designed by Sir Jeffry Wyatville. The position of the garden, on south-facing slopes, is beautiful, with excellent old trees – evergreen oaks, limes and beeches – providing a backdrop for the gardens made here since the American Museum came in 1961. A transatlantic flavour is given by a collection of herbs used in colonial times, disposed in box-edged beds with a bee-skep at the centre. The George Washington garden to the west of the house is inspired by the great man's Virginian estate of Mount Vernon. Here are sweeping beds edged in brick or box, gravel paths and an elegant octagonal pepper-pot gazebo. Farther down the slopes an arboretum planted with American trees and shrubs vividly reminds the visitor of the debt owed by British gardens to American flora. All this is impeccably maintained.

COLETON FISHACRE GARDEN
Devon

THIS IS a remote corner of south Devon and to find a garden here at all seems pretty unlikely; to find one of such special charm as this is amazing good fortune. The house, built by Oswald Milne, a follower of Edwin Lutyens, for the D'Oyly Carte

Coleton, Kingswear,
Dartmouth TQ6 0EQ
4m S of Brixham off B3205
Tel: 01803 425466

Owner:
The National Trust

Open: Mar, Sun 2–5; Apr to Oct, Wed to Sun (except Sat), also Bank Hol Mon 10.30–5.30 or dusk if earlier. 20 acres

family, looks down a narrow valley that descends to the sea. The garden has a very warm microclimate and the sea adds to the humidity. Plants flourish here and many tender things, tricky if not impossible to grow elsewhere in Britain, seem luxuriantly at home. A stream runs the whole length of the garden, occasionally breaking out into little pools whose banks are finely planted with moisture-loving herbaceous perennials. The sides of the valley, threaded with winding paths, are densely planted with trees and shrubs. There are many camellias and rhododendrons but also far more exciting things – tender exotics such as the crape myrtle (*Lagerstroemia indica*), *Mandevilla suaveolens* and great thickets of mimosa (*Acacia dealbata*).

COMPTON ACRES
Dorset

IN SPITE of Compton Acres' popularity, garden snobs should not turn their backs on it for it has an immense amount to offer. The precipitous site, with old pine woods close to the sea, reveals occasional splendid views to the Isle of Purbeck. The garden is arranged in a series of thematic episodes,

Canford Cliffs Road, Poole
BH13 7ES
1 1/2m W of Bournemouth
by A35 and B3065
Tel: 01202 700778
Fax: 01202 707537

Owner:
Pamlion Properties Ltd

Open: Mar to Oct, daily
10.30–6.30. 10 acres

each of which is beautifully arranged to give surprise: an Italian garden with a long pool, splashing fountains, clipped hedges and statues; a palm court with a Moorish flavour; an elaborate water garden with conifers and paths winding over rocks; and an immense Japanese garden of great character, shady, richly ornamented and dramatic. There are many excellent plants – in particular rhododendrons in a valley garden and many conifers and heathers in the heather dell. All this is done with panache and maintained to exemplary standards.

COTEHELE
Cornwall

St Dominick, nr Saltash
PL12 6TA
8m SW of Tavistock off
A390
Tel: 01579 350434

Owner:
The National Trust

Open: Apr to Oct, daily
11–5.30 or dusk if earlier.
10 acres. House open

THE GABLED and towered courtyard house, built in late Tudor times of moody grey granite by the Edgcumbe family, is at the centre of a garden that has many different faces. The house itself and its splendid outhouses and courtyards provide sheltered corners for all sorts of tender things such as the yellow-flowered *Jasminum mesnyi*. North-west of the house is a meadow which in spring is bright with daffodils. From here a gate leads through to a garden of more formal atmosphere, with a pool at the centre and a good border running along the northern wall. East of the house a series of terraces is planted with wallflowers in spring, followed in summer by roses, and there are some superb magnolias on the lower lawn. From the bottom terrace a secret passage leads through to a complete change of atmosphere. Here is a woodland garden in a steep valley, with a pool and ancient dovecote shaped like a giant beehive. In the woods paths amble among many camellias, magnolias and rhododendrons richly underplanted with ferns and moisture-loving plants; hostas, primulas and the bold foliage of *Gunnera manicata* relish the banks of a rushing stream.

CRANBORNE MANOR GARDENS
Dorset

Cranborne, nr Wimborne
BH21 5PP
In the village of Cranborne
16 1/2m SW of Salisbury
by A354 and B3081
Tel: 01725 517248
Fax: 01725 517248

Owner: Viscount and Viscountess Cranborne

Open: Garden: Mar to Sept, Wed 9–5; Garden Centre: All the year, Tue to Sat, 9–5 (Sun 10–5). 10 acres

THE MANOR house, once a medieval hunting lodge, has been in the Cecil family since the 17th century. There are excellent borders, an enclosed herb garden, walks of espaliered apple trees, a 17th-century mount and the exceptional charm of an ancient place embosomed in even more ancient woods. The garden centre next door to the manor is in fact a nursery garden and a particularly good one. It carries a wide general stock but with especially good collections of old and shrub roses and clematises. It also sells ornaments, furniture, trellis-work and some very good pots. A mail order service is provided for roses only, a speciality, and a catalogue (£1.00) of them is issued.

DARTINGTON HALL
Devon

Dartington, nr Totnes
TQ9 6EL
2m NW of Totnes by A384
Tel: 01803 862271

Owner: Dartington Hall Trust

Open: Daily, dawn–dusk. 30 acres

THE HOUSE is one of the most spectacular medieval mansions in Devon and the garden which lies chiefly to the south-west of it is designed on a heroic scale. The natural combe has been sculpted into great grassy terraces looking down onto an expanse of turf – according to legend, a medieval jousting lawn. The formal arrangement to the north of the terraces was designed by the American garden designer Beatrix Farrand, her only work in England. On the highest terrace, in the shade of immense old sweet chestnuts, a splendid stone carving by Henry Moore of a reclining woman turns her back on the terraces below. Nearby, a vertiginous flight of steps sweeps down the hill and giant magnolias ornament each side. At the far end of the terraces more steps lead up to an ornamental pond with a fountain of carved swans in the shade of a very large *Elaeagnus umbellata* 'Parvifolia', and farther to the west glades open out in old woodland.

DOCTON MILL
Devon

Spekes Valley,
nr Hartland EX39 6EA
3m S of Hartland follow signs to Elmscott and Lymebridge Cross; the garden is between Lymebridge Cross and Milford
Tel: 01237 441369

Owner:
Mr and Mrs M.G. Bourcier

Open: Mar to Oct, daily 10–5. 8 acres

THIS GARDEN has been made since 1980 and is a model of sensitive planting and design in an exceptionally beautiful site. In a secluded valley near the sea it possesses a favourable microclimate. In spring the garden explodes into life with an immense collection of daffodils and the upper slopes of the valley sparkle with the young foliage of many shrubs and ornamental trees. An excellent bog garden and the banks of streams are planted with moisture-loving plants – lysichitons, ligularias, candelabra primulas and hostas, with bold contrasts of foliage shape and colour. The intricate planting near the house contrasts well with a woodland garden that merges with the surrounding landscape.

DUCHY OF CORNWALL NURSERY
Cornwall

Penlyne, Cott Road,
Lostwithiel PL22 0BW
2m NE of Lostwithiel off
the A390

Tel: 01208 872668

Open: Daily except Bank
Hols 9-5 (Sun 10-5)

THIS IS THE KIND of nursery which, in an ideal world, every gardener would have just down the road. Its exceptional qualities are its range of plants – almost 3,000 both woody and herbaceous – and their very high quality. Being in Cornwall it stocks many tender things that flourish in those balmy parts – corokias, drimys, feijoa, several myrtles and prostantheras. In every department there is a wide range and something worth having. It is impeccably run and prices are more than fair. There is an excellent catalogue (£1.00) but no mail order.

DUNSTER CASTLE
Somerset

Dunster, nr Minehead
TA24 6SL
3m SE of Minehead by
A396
Tel: 01643 821314

Owner:
The National Trust

Open: Jan to Mar, Oct to
Dec, daily 11–4 (closed 25
Dec); Apr to Sept, daily
10–5 (including Good Fri).
17 acres. Castle open

THE CASTLE OCCUPIES a marvellous position on its great wooded tor. It is partly 13th-century but much added to, especially in the 19th century by Anthony Salvin. The microclimate here is very privileged and the spectacular rocky crag on which the castle is built provides shelter to tender plants. The garden, which is informally arranged to spiral up the wooded slopes to a secluded plateau at the summit, has many plants from Australasia – such as pittosporums, mimosas, olearias and the lovely white banksian rose. A large lemon tree on a sunny terrace, over 100 years old, with winter protection fruits handsomely. Camellias and magnolias are brilliant in early spring. The National Trust has been restoring and adding to this garden in recent years – planting an unusual grove of strawberry trees, for example.

EAST LAMBROOK MANOR
Somerset

*Illustration opposite: East
Lambrook Manor*

THE GARDEN was made by Margery Fish from 1938 and, publicised by her excellent books, became one of the best known gardens in England. Mrs Fish invented a style of inspired cottage gardening, often using carefully chosen forms of wild

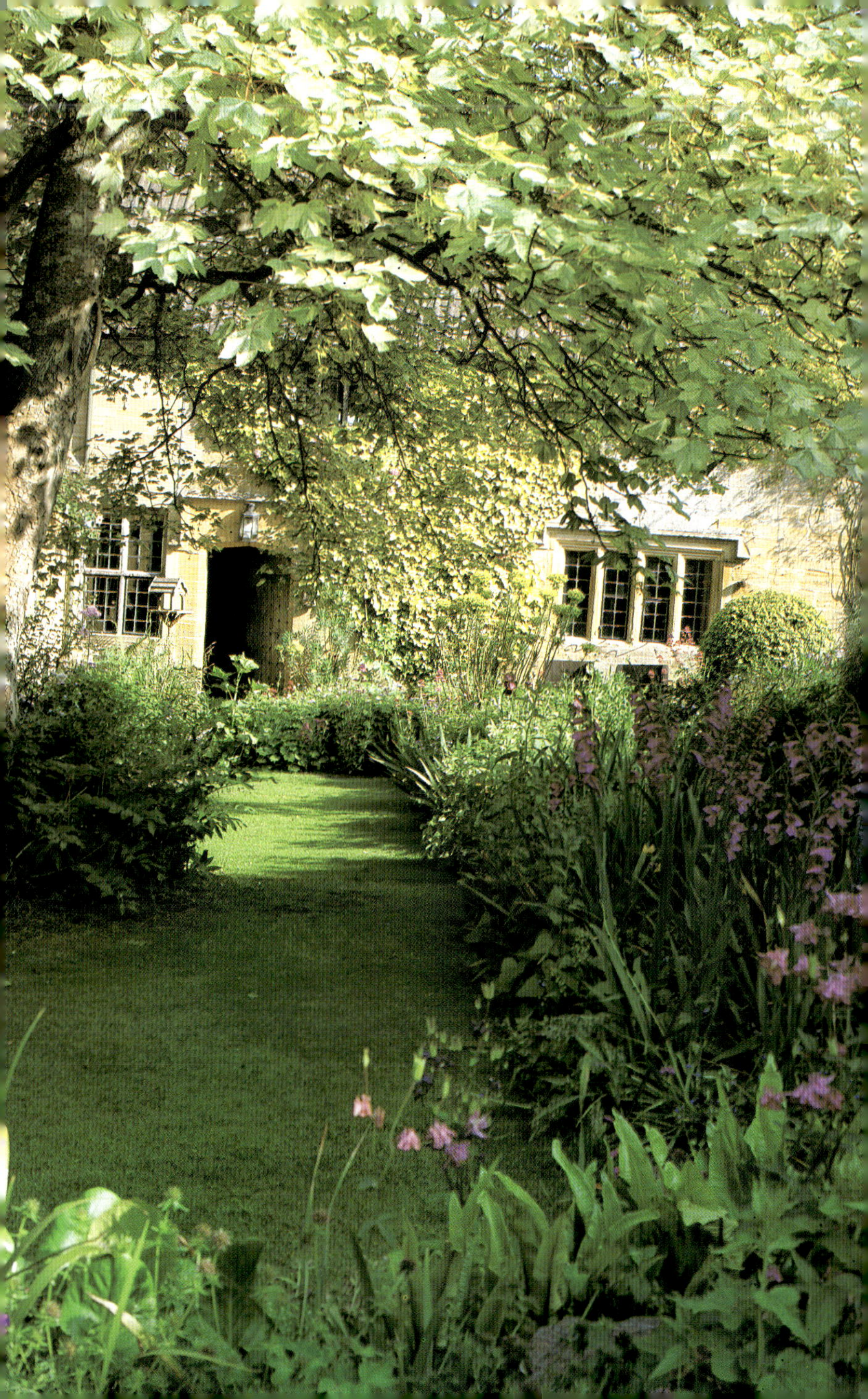

East Lambrook, South
Petherton TA13 5HL
3m N of the A 303 to
South Petherton
Tel: 01460 240328
Fax: 01460 242344

Owner: Mr and Mrs
Andrew Norton

Open: Garden: Mar to Oct,
daily except Sun (open
May Bank Hol weekend)
10–5; *Nursery:* daily except
Sun 10–5. 1 1/2 acres

plants. The design is informal and, although it is given structure by clipped evergreens and pollarded willows, there is scarcely a straight line in the place. Her garden, restored since 1985 by new owners, is full of excellent plants very well grown and many rare. It is also full of lessons for all gardeners about the importance of siting plants and choosing those that perform in every season. It is especially strong on herbaceous plants and contains the best collection of species and primary hybrids of hardy geraniums (a National Collection) in the country. An excellent nursery sells a very good range of the kind of plants grown in the garden, chiefly herbaceous and many of them unusual, at excellent prices; some of them, including new cultivars of geraniums, have been introduced by the nursery. A catalogue (50p) is produced and there is a mail order service; but it is much better to visit, admire, and buy, on the spot.

EDMONDSHAM HOUSE
Dorset

Edmondsham, nr
Wimborne BH21 5RE
17m SW of Salisbury
by A354 and B3081
Tel: 01725 517207

Owner: Mrs J. Smith

Open: Apr to Oct,
Wed and Sun, Bank
Hol Mons 2–5. 6 acres

THE HOUSE at Edmondsham is marvellous, and splendidly two-faced – ornately Tudor and Jacobean on one side, suavely Georgian on the other, and framed by excellent old trees. The chief garden interest here is an old 1-acre kitchen garden, walled in brick and cob, cultivated entirely organically. Fruit and vegetables are bursting with vigour, and broad double herbaceous borders flank a path. With its impeccable potting shed, its old well and pump and its beautifully restored pit house, this is a fascinating example of the kitchen gardens of the past upon which households were absolutely dependent.

FORDE ABBEY
Dorset

Chard TA20 4LU
7m W of Crewkerne by B3165
Tel: 01460 220231
Fax: 01460 20296

Owner: M. Roper

Open: Daily 10–4.30. 20 acres. House open

THE LATE medieval monastic buildings are spectacular, and near the house old yew hedges with wambly tops and a procession of sentinel clipped yews provide bold ornament. At some distance, across undulating turf with many fine specimen trees, a lake is overlooked by a curious summer house of pleached beech; beyond, is a fine bog garden. In the old kitchen garden The Abbey Nursery sells a wide range of excellent plants, emphasising the tender and unusual.

GARDEN HOUSE
Devon

Buckland Monachorum, Yelverton PL20 7LQ
5m S of Tavistock by A386

Tel: 01822 854769

Owner: The Fortescue Garden Trust

Open: Mar to Oct, daily 10.30–5. 8 acres

ON THE VERY edge of Dartmoor the Garden House is hidden in a wooded valley. Here, around some romantically decaying 16th-century ruins, Lionel Fortescue from 1945 onwards made a suitably romantic garden, surrounded by old walls and built on precipitous terraces from which there are lovely views over garden and country. Clematis and roses scale the stone walls and there are wonderful riches of plants, especially herbaceous, artfully disposed. Here are no cold and calculating vistas – everything depends on the quality of the planting and meticulous upkeep. Fortescue's successor, Keith Wiley, has now expanded the garden beyond the walls with ambition and skill. An impeccable nursery sells marvellous plants, none commonplace and all good value.

GLEBE COTTAGE PLANTS
Devon

Illustration: Geranium pratense *'Mrs Kendall Clark'*

Pixie Lane, Warkleigh,
Umberleigh EX37 9DH
6m W of South Molton by
B3226
Tel and Fax: 01769 540554

Open: Apr to Oct, Wed to
Sat 10–5; also by
appointment

CAROL KLEIN specialises in herbaceous plants with a few woody herbs. She sells exactly the kind of plants that many people want to grow in their gardens and she has excellent collections of particular groups – campanulas, pinks, a long and distinguished list of hardy geraniums, many penstemons and a marvellous range of primulas. Most of these may be seen growing in her garden next to the nursery. An elegantly hand-lettered list (£1.00) is produced, plants may be supplied by mail.

GLENDURGAN GARDEN
Cornwall

Helford River, Mawnan
Smith, nr Falmouth
TR11 5JZ
4m SW of Falmouth on
road to Helford Passage
Tel: 01208 74281/01326
250906

Owner:
The National Trust

Open: Mar to Oct, Tue to
Sat and Bank Hol Mon
(closed Good Fri)
10.30–5.30. 25 acres

THE FOXES are a great Cornish family and their garden exploits contributed immensely to the horticultural life of the county. Glendurgan was bought by Alfred Fox in 1821 and his family have been here ever since. The glen is a deep ravine which tumbles down to the sparkling water of the Helford estuary. On either side of the steep banks paths follow the contours but the bottom of the valley is not so densely planted as to obscure the marvellous views across to trees and shrubs on the other side of the ravine. Deftly infiltrated into the informal planting is a wandering maze of cherry laurel, planted in 1833 by Alfred Fox, and making a lively evergreen garden ornament. Like other Cornish gardens Glendurgan is abundantly rich in camellias, magnolias and rhododendrons but it also has exceptional trees such as an unforgettable tulip tree with wide spreading branches, one of the largest in the country. It would be wrong to think of Glendurgan as merely a spring garden – the pleasures continue throughout the gardening season. In any season, the view from the terrace of the house, at the head of the glen, perfectly composed, is one the visitor will not quickly forget.

THE GNOME RESERVE
Devon

West Putford, nr
Bradworthy EX22 7XE
7 1/2m N of Holsworthy
by A388 and minor roads
(follow rose sign)
Tel: 01409 241435

Open: Daily, 21 Mar to
Oct, 10–6. 4 acres

IF THERE IS a larger collection of gnomes than this, I do not know it. Here in rural north Devon at least 1,000 of them live in comfort, doing their gnomely thing cushioned in moss or ivy under the shade of splendid beeches. Gravel paths snake through the woods and the visitor soon succumbs to the enchanted atmosphere; pointed felt hats are issued to make humans appear more congenial to the natives. A gnome museum traces their history, new gnomes are produced (if that is the word) on the premises and may be seen being dressed (i.e. painted). To one side the 2-acre Pixies' Wildflower Garden has a fine display of over 250 wildflowers, ferns, herbs and grasses arranged in appropriate habitats.

GREENCOMBE
Somerset

Porlock TA24 8NU
1/2m W of Porlock by road
to Porlock Weir
Tel: 01643 862363

Owner: Greencombe
Garden Trust

Open: Apr to Jul, Sat to
Tue, 2–6. 3 1/2 acres

MUCH OF THE character of this remarkable garden is determined by its site – on slopes overlooking Porlock Weir and the Bristol Channel, with a very benign microclimate. The garden was started after World War II by Horace Stroud but it is under Miss Joan Loraine, who made the present garden and formed the Trust that now owns it, that it has come to full and unforgettable life. Near the house there are beds and flowing lawns with strong contrasts of shapely plants – mounds of Japanese maple and soaring spires of cypress. Above them, roses pour down slopes and walls; to the west, paths lead into ancient woodland in which immense hollies, oaks and old coppiced sweet chestnuts provide the background to wonderful magnolias, rhododendrons and maples underplanted with all kinds of shade-loving plants. There is nothing fiddly or fussy; the whole place has an air of marvellous inevitability. The National Collection of eythroniums is kept here – it is worth making a visit especially to see them.

HADSPEN GARDENS
Somerset

nr Castle Cary BA7 7NG
2m SE of Castle Cary by
A371
Tel: 01749 813707

Owner: N. and S. Pope

Open: Mar to Oct, Thur to
Sun and Bank Hol 9–6.
5 acres

*Illustration opposite: The
red and purple border at
Hadspen*

THE VERY PRETTY late 18th-century house in its park-like setting is sheltered by wooded slopes rising to the north behind it. The garden beyond the house has 18th-century origins but most of its present distinction is more recent. Penelope Hobhouse restored and replanned it after 1968 and in 1987 a further impetus came from lively new gardeners from Canada, Nori and Sandra Pope. In the old walled kitchen garden a dazzling but subtle double border of yellow and white followed by hostas shaded with beech hedges descends the slope, and brilliant colour borders round the walls are alive with the Popes' new plantings of subtle harmonies. Nearby, above a huge rectangular pool, a high brick wall affords protection to many tender plants. A nursery sells excellent plants, some bearing the 'Hadspen' name, and new introductions are constantly being made. There is a catalogue (three 1st-class stamps) but no mail order.

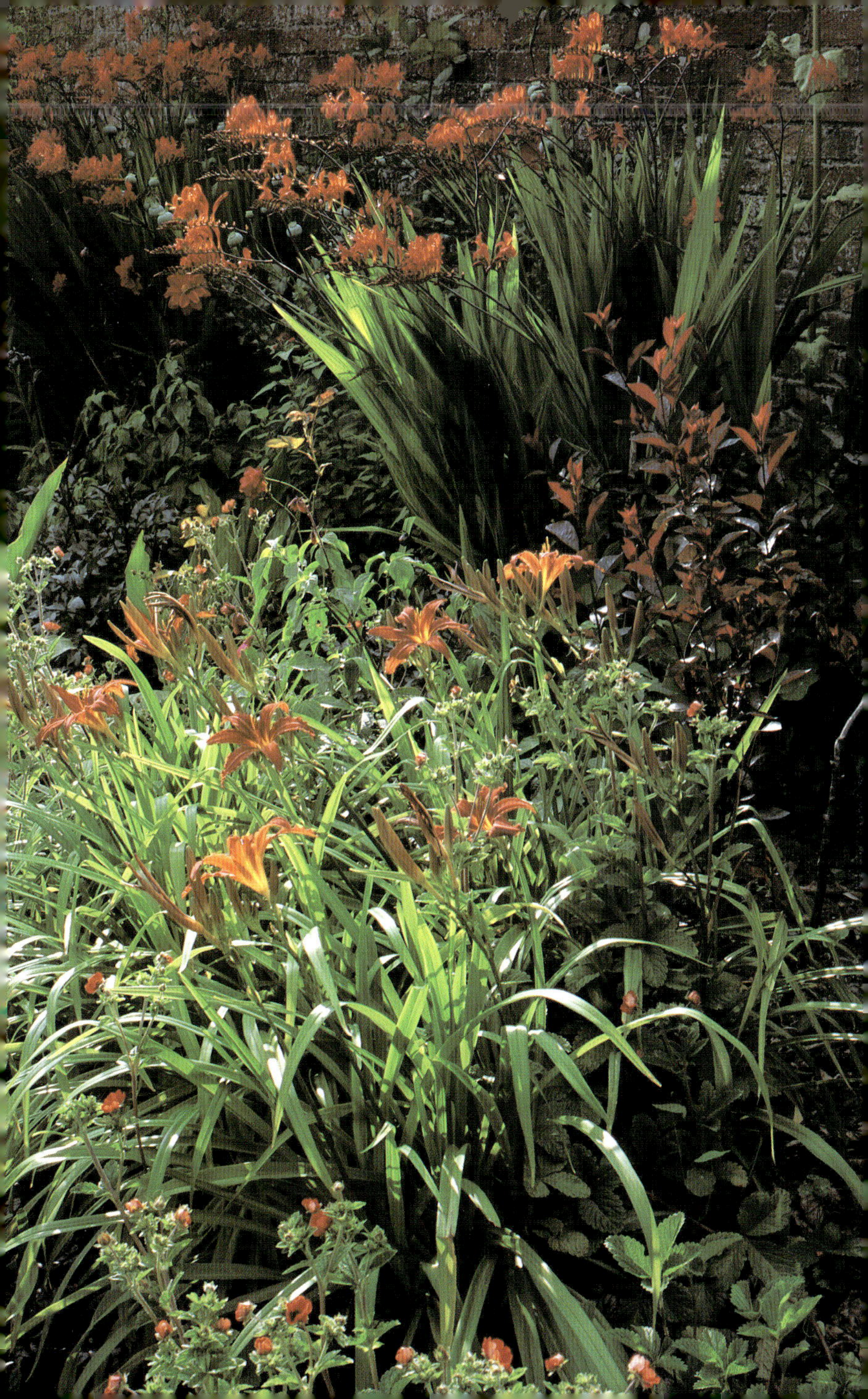

THE HANNAYS OF BATH
Somerset

Sydney Wharf Nursery,
Bathwick, Bath BA2 4ES
In Bath at bottom of
Bathwick Hill via Sydney
Mews
Tel: 01225 462230/317577

Open: Mar to Oct, daily
except Tue 10–5

THE HANNAYS are mad about plants and a visit to their nursery is always rewarding because you will certainly find excellent and unfamiliar ones. Some may come from the Hannays' own collecting expeditions. They are especially good on herbaceous plants and on their wild forms; adenophoras, cimicifugas, dieramas, euphorbias and geraniums are well represented. Among woody plants cistus, phlomis and sages are outstanding. A very good catalogue (£1.40) is produced, with much valuable information, but there is no mail order.

HARE LANE POTTERY
Dorset

nr Wimborne BH21 5QT
2m E of Cranborne on
Alderholt road
Tel: 01725 517700

Open: Sat and Sun 9–5 and
mostly during the week;
please phone to check

HANDMADE GARDEN POTS, made from local clay and fired in a wood-burning kiln were once common; today they are extremely rare. Jonathan Garratt makes a wide range of beautifully fashioned pots, alpine pans and various kinds of planter. They vary in colour, some having an attractive darker tinge, but all are finely made and are available only at the pottery. All the pots are guaranteed against frost damage; pots planted with bulbs having withstood −12°C at the pottery.

HEADLAND
Cornwall

3 Battery Lane,
Polruan-by-Fowey
PL23 1PW.
In the centre of Polruan.
Park in main car park and
walk down St Saviour's
Hill, turning left at Coast
Guard Office.
Tel: 01726 870 243

Owner: Jean and John Hill

Open: 20 May to 30 Sept,
Thurs 2–8. 1 3/4 acres

JEAN AND JOHN HILL came to Headland in 1976 after several years of experience of gardening in the south. Nowhere else, however, had quite the same problems and possibilities as this. On a splendid rocky promontory jutting out into the mouth of the Fowey estuary, the Hills have made a garden of vital interest to all gardeners who battle against wind and salt-laden air. Paths wind along the contours of precipitous slopes with marvellous outcrops of natural rock. Hedges of escallonia, euonymus and privet have proved their worth as shelters. A few handsome mature trees, in particular

Monterey pine (*Pinus radiata*) and *Cupressus macrocarpa*, although relishing the seaside climate, suffered grievously from storm damage. Many other woody plants – arbutus, cistus, cotoneaster, hebes – provide wind- and salt-proof ornament. Frosts are rarely severe and such herbaceous plants as aeonium, lampranthus and osteospermum flourish. This is a garden that will also be enjoyed by gardeners not seeking practical guidance about coastal gardening; the winding paths, well-kept plantings, and exquisite views across the estuary give rare pleasure.

HELIGAN
Cornwall

nr Mevagissey, St Austell PL26 6EN 4m S of St Austell by B3273; turn to right after village of Pentewan.
Tel: 01726 844157
Fax: 01726 843023

Owner: The Heligan Manor Garden Project Ltd

Open: Daily 10.30–5. 57 acres

THE PRESIDING GENIUS of this extraordinary place, Tim Smit, is a man of such astounding energy that he could probably make a memorable event out of the restoration of a bus shelter. Here at Heligan, however, he has found a subject truly worthy of his skills. The lost garden of the Tremaynes, famous in its day, became neglected and forgotten. Tim Smit rediscovered it and with his partner John Nelson formed a trust to restore it. Work started in the spring of 1991 – paths were laid bare and resurfaced, immense brambles uprooted, glades cleared, and gradually a garden of fabulous enchantment was revealed. It is rich in rhododendrons (including several Hooker introductions of the 1840s), many rare and grown to exceptional size, and trees of exceptional beauty. It also possesses a unique range of garden buildings – a peach house, an ingenious pineapple pit, melon frames, bee boles and beautiful frames with fish-tail glazing. All these, and tool- and potting-sheds, are now restored. A magnificent walled flower garden and vast early glasshouses are now being tackled. Already the garden gives pleasure of the most varied kind. There is much to excite the most demanding of plant lovers, but the special quality of Heligan is that its wild and romantic atmosphere has been triumphantly preserved.

HESTERCOMBE

Somerset

Cheddon Fitzpaine, nr Taunton TA2 8LQ
4m NE of Taunton off A361
Tel: 01823 337222

Owner: Somerset County Council

Open: Mon to Fri 9–5 (also May to Sept, Sat and Sun 2–5). 8 acres

THE GARDEN at Hestercombe was designed by Gertrude Jekyll and Edwin Lutyens just before World War I and is one of their great masterpieces. Since 1973 it has been rescued from the brink of irretrievable collapse by Somerset County Council who have restored it with authenticity. Here is a marvellous distillation of the essence of the Lutyens/Jekyll garden wizardry – an enclosed area of shifting levels with lively stonework, a symmetrical parterre-like 'Great Plat', iris-fringed rills fed by water-spouting masks, and Miss Jekyll's boldly unfussy planting of massed grey-leafed plants, glossy bergenias, ramparts of rosemary and a pergola of roses and clematis. In addition to all this, there is a round pool in a round walled garden filled with wintersweet and roses, a Dutch garden of lamb's ears, lavender and roses, and the most beautiful orangery of the 20th century. All gardeners can draw practical inspiration from this exquisite garden.

KELWAYS NURSERIES
Somerset

Langport TA10 9EZ
In Langport, 10m E of
Taunton by A358 and
A378
Tel: 01458 250521
Fax: 01458 253351

Open: Mon to Fri 9–5, Sat
and Sun 10–5

THIS IS ONE of the best of all nurseries for daylilies, irises and peonies, and the many cultivars bearing the 'Langport' or 'Kelway' name are evidence of the work of this famous place in the raising of garden-worthy plants. After a fallow period it is looking up again. Excellent catalogues are issued twice a year, from which orders are fulfilled by post.

KILLERTON
Devon

Broadclyst, Exeter
EX5 3LE
5m NE of Exeter by B3181
and B3185; or by Jnct 28
on M5
Tel: 01392 881345

Owner:
The National Trust

Open: Daily 10.30–dusk.
22 acres. House open

THE CHARMS of Killerton reveal themselves gradually, and because of that tend to stick in the mind. Near the house a gravel path leads between a pair of fortissimo mixed borders – originally planted with the advice of William Robinson – ornamented with elegant Coade stone urns. Beyond, the lawn unrolls, interrupted by countless trees and shrubs of an acid-loving type – magnolias, rhododendrons, stewartias, styrax and maples. A half-hidden rustic summer house, with a touch of Grimm's fairy tales, has a wonderful interior of rattan and wickerwork, and a ceiling with patterns of pine cones. Behind it is a masterly rock garden, of a naturalistic kind, built in an old quarry; hellebores, hostas, geraniums and many other herbaceous plants flourish among mossy rocks under a canopy of old camellias, maples and daphnes. In late spring the air is scented with sheets of *Cyclamen repandum*.

KINGSTON MAURWARD GARDENS
Dorset

THE HOUSE at Kingston Maurward is a grand early 18th-century stone mansion built for the Pitt family. The estate was eventually acquired by the Hanbury family, a great horticultural dynasty, owners of the famous subtropical garden at La Mortola in Italy, and donors of land to Wisley gardens. It is now a college of agriculture and

Dorchester DT2 8PY
On the E edge of
Dorchester by A35 bypass
Tel: 01305 264738
Fax: 01305 250059

Owner: Kingston
Maurward College

Open: Mid-Apr to
mid-Oct, daily 10–5.
20 acres

horticulture which has pulled off the remarkable feat of restoring the gardens on a lavish scale, opening to the public in 1995. It still looks a bit raw but it has tremendous promise. Here are burgeoning borders, fine Edwardian terraced gardens, a Japanese garden, a penstemon terrace (the National Collection is held here) and a rose garden. For many gardeners the most interesting thing is the use of tender bedding plants which hit their stride in late summer. Cannas, bananas with leaves as big as elephant's ears, castor-oil plants, sages and other exotic things vividly show the dramatic possibilities of this neglected style of gardening.

KNIGHTSHAYES COURT
Devon

Bolham, Tiverton
EX16 7RQ
2m N of Tiverton by A396
Tel: 01884 254665

Owner:
The National Trust

Open: 16 Mar to Oct, daily
11–5.30. 40 acres.
House open

THE GARDENS at Knightshayes have two faces, both of them very handsome. Near the house are generously planted borders and a formal garden with yew hedges, standard wisterias, lead figures and a cool pool overhung by a weeping pear. Looking away from the house are marvellous rural views. East of this is one of the best small woodland gardens in the country, in which exceptional shrubs and ornamental trees are disposed to brilliant effect. At first sight it seems just a very attractive piece of woodland but the more you look the more you will see rare plants used with rare skill. In spring the display of bulbs is a fabulous sight, with *Erythronium* 'Knightshayes Pink' spreading like a lovely weed. A small selection of very good plants is for sale.

LANHYDROCK

Cornwall

Bodmin PL30 5AD
2 1/2m SE of Bodmin by
A38 or B3268
Tel: 01208 73320

Owner:
The National Trust

Open: Apr to Oct, daily
11–5.30 (5 in Oct). 25
acres. House open

THE HOUSE, a romantic mixture of the 17th and 19th centuries, is set in exquisite parkland, and an avenue of sycamores and beeches marches to the castellated entrance lodge. Beyond it a formal courtyard garden has rows of vast clipped Irish yews, beds of modern roses and ornate bronze urns. Behind the house and church is a yew-hedged circular garden with herbaceous beds containing the National Collection of crocosmias which make the garden particularly worth visiting in late summer. Beyond this a woodland garden is rich in flowering shrubs and trees, especially rhododendrons and exceptional magnolias, of which there are 120 different kinds.

LOWER SEVERALLS HERB NURSERY

Somerset

Lower Severalls, nr
Crewkerne TA18 7NX
1 1/2 NE of Crewkerne off
A30 on Haselbury–Merriott
road
Tel: 01460 73234
Fax: 01460 76105

Open: Daily except Thur
10–5 (Sun 2–5)

MARY COOPER'S nursery is arranged in the garden of a very attractive Ham stone farmhouse. As well as medicinal and culinary herbs, she is particularly interested in those with especially good scents – of lemon, pineapple and so on. She also has a selection of tender and half-hardy plants for containers and bedding. There is a well chosen range of herbaceous perennials – including over 50 cranesbills and some very good sages (around 25 varieties). Apart from the excellent plants, the garden is extremely attractive. Orders are fulfilled by mail and a catalogue (four 1st-class stamps) is produced.

LYTE'S CARY MANOR
Somerset

Charlton Mackrell,
Somerton TA11 7HU
4m SE of Somerton by
B3151
Tel: 01985 847777

Owner:
The National Trust

Open: Apr to 30 Oct, Mon, Wed and Sat 2–6 or dusk if earlier. 3 acres. House open

THE ENTRANCE to the late medieval manor house is through a forecourt with a central path flanked by yew topiary clipped into cottage-loaf shapes. This mixture of formality and simplicity characterises the garden. A door leads through to a lavish mixed border of herbaceous plants under old roses, while, on the other side of the path, a yew hedge is clipped into buttresses with decorative finials. Beyond a formal orchard, open lawns and statues lead to a shady tunnel of hornbeam and a secret garden. Lytes Cary is no horticultural masterpiece but it provides the perfect garden setting for a rare house.

MALLET COURT NURSERY
Somerset

Curry Mallet, nr Taunton
TA3 6SY
In village of Curry Mallet
5m SE of Taunton by A358 and A378
Tel: 01823 480748
Fax: 01823 481009

Open: Mon to Fri 9–1, 2–5

JAMES HARRIS is known among tree-lovers as 'Acer' Harris, and sells one of the finest selections of maples commercially available – almost certainly the largest in the country. His nursery is primarily devoted to trees and shrubs, with a particular emphasis on those grown from seed collected in the wild. He sells, for example, a vast range of oaks (160 kinds), many birches, rowans and magnolias, and shrubs, from China, Korea and Japan. There is a catalogue (£1 plus 29p s.a.e.) and mail order service but a visit is always worthwhile to discover treasures that have not yet found their way onto the list.

THE MANOR HOUSE
Somerset

Walton-in-Gordano, nr
Clevedon BS21 7AN
2m NE of Clevedon by
B3124
Tel: 01275 872067

Owner: Simon and Philippa Wills

Open: Mid Apr to mid Sept, Wed and Thur 10–4; also by appointment. 4 acres

PROTECTED BY WOODED hills to the north, this garden has a balmy microclimate which allows the owners to grow a very wide range of plants. In a very attractive setting, there is much to see and admire, with an exceptional range of both herbaceous and woody plants, some quite rare, and a lively sense of horticultural endeavour everywhere apparent. A few plants propagated in the nursery, some unusual, are for sale at modest prices.

MAPPERTON GARDENS
Dorset

Beaminster DT8 3NR
2m SE of Beaminster by
B3163
Tel: 01308 862645

Owner: The Montagu family

Open: Mar to Oct, daily 2–6. 12 acres. House open by appointment to groups only

TO THE EAST of the fine 17th-century house, the garden, hidden in a long combe, comes as a surprise – a splendid formal arrangement of descending terraces and cross vistas. At the head of the valley an orangery looks down flagged paths past a rose-festooned pergola and along the central vista, guarded by stone eagles, which ends with two long rectangular pools. All this is copiously ornamented with topiary of yew and box, handsome urns and statues, and plenty of places to sit and admire the garden and the gabled house rising above it. This lively pastiche of a 17th-century garden, with all the trimmings, was laid out as recently as the 1920s. It is beautifully executed and makes an entirely unexpected and wonderful contrast to idyllic views of cattle grazing in the park-like countryside beyond.

PATRICIA MARROW
Somerset

Kingsdon, nr Somerton
TA11 7LE
In the middle of Kingsdon, 2m SE of Somerton off B3151
Tel: 01935 840232

Open: Daily, dawn–dusk but check by phone

AS SO MANY of the old-established nursery gardens cut back on their stock, much smaller, specialist nurseries have become one of the best sources of more unusual plants. Mrs Marrow is a gardening institution in the West Country – a demon propagator who chooses her plants with great care. There is nothing commonplace here and much that you will not find easily elsewhere. She stocks a very large number of hardy plants, woody and herbaceous, some of which may not be quite so hardy in the frozen north. She issues no catalogue and provides no mail order service, but part of the essential charm of the place lies in meeting her. She does not bully customers but she talks about her plants so seductively that you will certainly bear away more than you bargained for.

MARWOOD HILL GARDENS
Devon

Barnstaple EX31 4EB
4m NW of Barnstaple,
signed from A361
Barnstaple–Braunton road
Tel: 01271 42528

Owner: Dr J.A. Smart

Open: Garden: daily,
dawn–dusk; *Nursery:* daily
11–5. 20 acres

THERE ARE many reasons for visiting Marwood Hill but the chief interest of the garden lies in the very large number of plants grown in appropriate habitats in the attractive valley setting. It was started in 1949 by Dr Jimmy Smart who took over a neglected old garden. Flowering shrubs and ornamental trees clothe the slopes of the upper garden and at the bottom of the valley small lakes are linked together by streams. A bog garden between two of the lakes burgeons with ligularias, candelabra primulas and irises. In high summer the banks are covered by the plumes of an immense number of astilbes – 135 different species and cultivars, a National Collection. In addition, National Collections of *Iris ensata* and tulbaghias are held here. There is also a excellent general nursery. A catalogue (70p) is produced but there is no mail order, so a visit is essential.

MILTON LODGE
Somerset

nr Wells BA5 3AQ
1/2m N of Wells off A39
Tel: 01749 672168

Owner: D.C. Tudway Quilter

Open: Good Fri to Oct, daily except Sat 2–6. 12 acres

Here is a garden that takes full advantage of its exquisite position – with the city of Wells and its great cathedral below it to the south, and Glastonbury Tor in the distance beyond the vale of Avalon. From the 18th-century house a terrace overlooks the steeply sloping site with mixed borders, yew hedges and vertiginous descents giving way to parkland with ornamental trees. At some distance from the house, on the other side of the Old Bristol Road, is a real rarity – the Combe, an 18th-century gentleman's arboretum now in splendid maturity. This walled and bosky valley, full of fine trees to which the present owner adds, has immense charm.

MINTERNE
Dorset

Minterne Magna, Dorchester DT2 7AU
9m N of Dorchester by A352 in the village of Minterne Magna
Tel: 01300 341370

Owner: Lord and Lady Digby

Open: Apr to Oct, daily 10–7. 21 acres

At MINTERNE THE rare quality of the garden lies in the gradual revealing of exotic flowering trees and shrubs in a beautiful setting. From the house there are views down a shallow valley to a sinuous lake set in parkland ornamented with superlative old trees. The woodland below is rich in exceptional examples of *Davidia involucrata*, magnolias, maples and rhododendrons. In the valley the banks of a stream are richly planted – vast drifts of primulas as well as exotic shrubs and trees, many of spectacular size. The visitor either follows the lower walk, nose-to-nose with the plants, or takes the upper, with views across the valley. The path arrives at a more open setting, a bridge arches over the stream, and on the bank sheep graze among superb oaks and limes.

THE MONOCOT NURSERY
Somerset

The daringly botanical name of this little nursery is a good clue to what it is. Mike Salmon sells bulbs, specialising in species and natural forms. If you are looking for overweight daffs and beefy multi-coloured tulips this is *not* the place for you.

Illustration: Narcissus *'Eystettensis'*

Jacklands, Jacklands Bridge, Tickenham, Clevedon BS21 6SG
Near the village of Tickenham, on the B3130; 8m W of Bristol by B3128
Tel: None

Open: Daily 10–6

Instead, here are exquisite narcissi (every species you have ever heard of and some you haven't), rare tulbaghias, thirty species of crocus (not counting forms), a long list of colchicums and all sorts of treasures many of which are not to be found elsewhere. The nursery is a charming mess but Mr Salmon knows his alliums and he is one of the finest sources in the country for rare bulbs. There is a mail order service (for seeds as well as bulbs) and fascinating lists are produced (s. a. e.).

MONTACUTE HOUSE
Somerset

Montacute TA15 6XP
In the village of Montacute, 4m W of Yeovil by A3088
Tel: 01935 823289

Owner:
The National Trust

Open: 30 Mar to 3 Nov, daily except Tue 11.30–5.30 or dusk if earlier; 6 Nov to 28 Mar 1997, Wed to Sun 11.30–4. 12 acres. House open

THE LATE Tudor house, built of lovely golden Ham stone, is well situated in a garden to match. To the east of the house a walled forecourt has good herbaceous borders with lively colour schemes. The Tudor walls are ornamented with stone finials and, in each corner, an airy Elizabethan gazebo gives views to the deer park beyond. North of the house a raised walk overlooks a deep border planted with shrub roses underplanted with peonies, and a stately lawn surrounded by clipped Irish yews with a circular poool at its centre. All about are venerable yew hedges, some handsomely blowsy with age, and the view is constantly drawn to the great house. Do not miss the splendid view of the house from the western wrought iron gate with the drive lined with an avenue of clipped Irish yews backed by limes, oaks and cedars of Lebanon.

MOUNT EDGCUMBE
Cornwall

Cremyll,
Torpoint PL10 1HZ
2 1/2m SE of Torpoint
Tel: 01752 822236
Fax: 01752 822199

Owner: City of Plymouth
and Cornwall County
Council

*Open: Park and formal
garden:* daily dawn–dusk;
*Earl's Garden (entrance via
house):* Apr to Oct, Wed to
Sun and Bank Hol Mon
11–5. 865 acres. House open

IT IS HARD to pin down the rare character of this place – but there is certainly nowhere like it. The site, on a sloping headland overlooking Plymouth Sound, is beautiful, and the castellated mansion turns its face to this, down an immense triple avenue of limes. The Edgcumbe family, also of Cotehele, came here in the mid 16th century and their estate became so famous that Admiral Medina Sidonia vowed that he would live there after his Armada had beaten the English. At the foot of the hill there are formal gardens – a French garden, an English garden, a conservatory and an Italianate garden with double staircase ornamented with flamboyant statuary, a pool, bedding schemes and orange trees in Versailles boxes. All this has recently been undergoing restoration. The parkland, laced with marvellous walks, runs to the very edge of the cliffs – interrupted with picturesque ruins and a columned temple from which there are lovely views of the sea.

OVERBECKS GARDEN
Devon

Sharpitor,
Salcombe TQ8 8LW
1 1/2m SW of Salcombe by
minor roads
Tel: 01548 842893/843238

Owner: The National Trust

Open: Daily 10–8 or sunset
if earlier. 6 acres

OVERBECKS IS a very unusual place, lost on the precipitous heights above Salcombe estuary. It was the creation of Otto Overbecks who left it to the National Trust in 1937. It enjoys a remarkably mild microclimate and, with views through trees of shimmering water, it is fairly easy to imagine yourself on the *corniche* on the Côte d'Azur. Even the steps leading down into the garden, with their sinuous handrail, have a Mediterranean feel to them. The garden is terraced and its very sharp drainage and abundant sunshine permits many tender plants to flourish as they do in few other places on mainland Britain – callistemons, Chusan palms, mimosa, olearias, olives and tender pittosporums. On the lower slopes, an old *Magnolia campbellii*, planted in 1901, is a famous sight in spring, covered with its hot pink flowers. The earlier part of the year is a wonderful time to visit, when the garden is extraordinarily floriferous and the air laden with sweet scents. In high summer it takes on the character of an exotic jungle.

PARNHAM HOUSE
Dorset

Beaminster DT8 3NA
1m S of Beaminster by A3066
Tel: 01308 862204

Owner: John Makepeace

Open: Apr to Oct, Wed, Sun and Bank Hol weekends 10–5. 14 acres. House open

SWARMING WITH decoration – gables, castellations and bristling chimneys – Parnham House is a Tudor mansion comprehensively done over by John Nash in the early 19th century. The estate was acquired in 1976 by the famous furniture maker, John Makepeace, who has restored it with energy and imagination. To the south, a deep terrace with stone gazebos at each end overlooks an immense lawn with rows of giant yew cones and water runnels. Beyond, superb woodland is framed by great cedars of Lebanon. On the east side of the house the entrance forecourt has decorative walls crowned with finials, and borders planted with roses. Beyond the house, behind old yew hedges and brick walls, Jennie Makepeace has been breathing new life into herbaceous borders.

PENCARROW HOUSE
Cornwall

Washaway, Bodmin
PL30 3AG
3 1/2m NW of Bodmin by A389
Tel: 01208 841369

Owner: The Molesworth-St Aubyn Family

Open: Easter to mid Oct, daily dawn–dusk. 50 acres. House open

PENCARROW IS ONE of those rare places in which the character of the whole amounts to much more than the sum of the parts. It is set in a broad valley with the very pretty 18th-century house facing south along it. The Italian Gardens, an arrangement of turfed terraces, urns and a fountain, lie immediately south of the house. Beyond this, a vast meadow opens out, edged on either side by ramparts of magnificent trees and shrubs. From a Victorian rock garden on one side a path leads through the woodland garden, a lake and an American Garden. The visitor should return by the path on the other side, with lovely views of the house framed in great trees and old rhododendrons with, in spring, an exquisite bluebell grove splashed with wild garlic. The whole is a marvellous English scene – fine house, formal gardens, enticing woodland and distant views of cattle grazing on rich Cornish pasture.

PENJERRICK
Cornwall

Budock, nr Falmouth
TR11 5ED
3m SW of Falmouth by minor roads
Tel: 01326 250074/01872 870105

Owner: Mrs R. Morin

Open: Mar to Sept, Wed, Fri and Sun 1.30–4.30. 15 acres

FEW GARDENS HAVE the wonderful atmosphere of Penjerrick – another creation of the Fox family, the great Cornish master gardeners. Penjerrick has a valley site sloping towards the sea. But here there is a character of wildness which provides exactly the right contrast to some of the more swaggering rhododendrons which are such a striking feature of the garden. Superlative old beeches, copper and ordinary, date from the early 1800s and provide a stately background to more exotic planting. Here are exceptional tree ferns, many examples of the tender large-leafed rhododendrons, an exceptional *Davidia involucrata* and the most magnificent *Podocarpus salignus* in the country.In early spring many outstanding magnolias flaunt their flowers in the lovely jungle that surrounds them. The garden continues beyond a road, spanned by a bridge, and here in a jungle-like setting thickets of bamboos edge a lake and alluring fern-fringed paths wind up the side of the valley.

PRIOR PARK LANDSCAPE GARDEN
Somerset

1m S of the centre of Bath in the village of Combe Down
Tel: 01985 843600

Owner: The National Trust

Open: Times were not fixed when we went to press. Phone number above for details

THE PALLADIAN MANSION of Prior Park (now a school) was built in the 1730s for Ralph Allen, probably to the designs of John Wood. In the combe to the north a miniature landscape park was laid out, at first with advice from Allen's friend Alexander Pope. In 1750 an enchanting Palladian Bridge was added, making an architectural focal point for the scene and spanning the neck of a miniature lake. Some buildings (such as a Gothic temple) no longer survive but a handsome classical Sham Bridge does. The essence of the place, as a visitor wrote in 1746, consist of 'The natural beauties of wood, water and prospect, hill and dale, wilderness and cultivation.' The National Trust has recently taken over the garden and has done much to restore and preserve the precious Elysian atmosphere of this miniature landscape park so close to the heart of Bath.

ROSEMOOR GARDEN
Devon

Great Torrington
EX38 8PH
1m SE of Great Torrington by B3220
Tel: 01805 624067
Fax: 01805 624717

Owner: The Royal Horticultural Society

Open: Mar and Oct, daily 10–5; Apr to Sept, daily 10–6; Nov to Feb, daily 10–4. 40 acres

THERE ARE two gardens at Rosemoor: one was made in the early 1960s by Lady Anne Palmer – an intimate woodland garden with less informal planting nearer the house; the other is a more razzmatazz affair complete with Visitors' Centre, ambitious formal rose gardens, giant borders and ornamental vegetable garden, all of which have been made by the Royal Horticultural Society since it became the owner in 1988. The two gardens are separated by the B3220 under which visitors may pass by a subterranean passage. A lake and stream garden will make an attractive prelude to the tunnel. Lady Anne's garden has an excellent collection of trees and shrubs of the kind which relish the acid soil – dogwoods (a National Collection), eucryphias, maples, pieris, rhododendrons and vacciniums. By the house there are lawns, borders and a tennis court that has been transformed into a Mediterranean garden. At the Visitors' Centre a shop sells a wide range of well grown plants and marvellous pots.

ROWDEN GARDENS
Devon

Illustration: Ranunculus ficaria *'Brazen Hussy'*

Brentor, nr Tavistock
PL19 0NG
NW of village of Brentor, on road to Liddaton and Chillaton
Tel: 01822 810275

Open: Apr to Sept, Sat, Sun and Bank Hol Mon 10–5; other times by appointment.

SOMETHING NEW always seems to be happening at Rowden Gardens nursery which has in the past specialised in aquatic plants but now has a wider range – in all, over 3,000 species and varieties with a strong emphasis on herbaceous perennials. There are particularly good collections of crocosmias, primulas and rheums. Some of the plants are very rare, including those bred at the nursery and bearing the 'Rowden' name. Behind the nursery there are rows of canal-like pools, displaying the plants in very decorative fashion. There is an informative (£1.50) list and a mail order service. Many plants that are not listed are to be seen at the nursery, and John Carter will probably seduce you into buying them. This is the home of probably the largest collection of polygonums in the country, of which Rowden holds the National Collection. A new acquisition is the National Collection of celandines (*Ranunculus ficaria*), known in south Devon as 'gooley cups'.

SALTRAM
Devon

ALTHOUGH WITHIN sight of the urban sprawl of Plymouth, Saltram still preserves its character of a gentlemanly house set in parkland. The early 18th-century house was enriched by spectacular new rooms by Robert Adam for the Parker family. The

Plympton, Plymouth PL7 3UH
3m E of Plymouth by A38
Tel: 01752 336546

Owner:
The National Trust

Open: Mar, Sat and Sun
11–4; Apr to Oct, daily
except Fri (but open Good
Fri) and Sat 10.30–5.30. 21
acres. House open

parkland – in the 18th-century grazed by deer to the very walls of the house – is now embellished with ornamental trees, superb sweet chestnuts and the Spanish plane (*Platanus* × *hispanica*) among them. From the stately pedimented orangery, built in 1775, paths lead to a gothic pavilion. An avenue of limes, with pale narcissi in spring, forms a boundary. All this is understated and, of its kind, perfect.

SCOTTS NURSERIES LTD
Somerset

Merriott TA16 5PL
2m N of Crewkerne by the
A356
Tel: 01460 72306
Fax: 01460 77433

Open: Mon to Sat 9–5, Sun
10–5

THIS OLD-ESTABLISHED nursery is one of the best in the West Country. It sells a wide range of plants, with good collections of shrub roses and of fruit, and many old cultivars of apples, pears, plums and soft fruit. Good trees and flowering shrubs are stocked, as well as herbaceous plants and alpines. A marvellous catalogue (£1.50) is issued, which many gardeners treat it as a bible. A mail order service is available.

STICKY WICKET GARDEN
Dorset

STICKY WICKET is a glorious name for a garden and Peter and Pam Lewis have fashioned a rare place. They came in 1986 and found the going sticky, with no drainage to alleviate the heavy clay. The garden they made is quite distinctive. They are interested in

Buckland Newton DT2 7BY
10m N of Dorchester by
B3143. In the village
between the church, the
school and the Gaggle of
Geese pub
Tel: 01300 345476

Owners: Peter and Pam
Lewis

Open: Mid-June to
mid-Sept, Thurs 10.30–8.
3 3/4 acres

colour and they want to garden in collaboration with nature rather than against it. There are marvellous plants here, including a profusion of roses, and they are disposed with a sharp eye for colour. In the Round Garden plants are arranged in segments following the spectral wheel but elsewhere the associations have a basis of pure beauty. The ecological side of the garden extends to providing water for frogs, berries for birds, a dovecote and a haven for ducks and poultry. As a gardener you may have no interest in such things but they will not intrude on the pleasure of a beautifully kept garden brimming with good plants admirably used.

TAPELEY PARK
Devon

Instow EX39 4NT
2m N of Bideford by A39
Tel: 01271 860528

Owner: N.D.C.I. Ltd

Open: Easter to Oct, daily
except Sat 10–5. 10 acres

TAPELEY PARK deserves to be much better known. The mid 18th-century tycoon's mansion of pink brick, occupies an unforgettable position in parkland, with wonderful views down to the River Torrington. South of the house is a dazzling Italian garden designed by the neo-classical architect John Belcher in the early 20th century. Terraces gently descend the hill, with a sundial at the centre, and a row of sentinel Irish yews guards the lowest terrace to the west. Handsome statues decorate the walls, and others, on the far side of the lawn, gaze out towards the countryside. Borders have recently been replanted to the lively designs of Mary Keen and Carol Klein. In the woods on one side are a Gothic pavilion and an ice-house with a walled kitchen-garden beyond.

TINTINHULL HOUSE
Somerset

Tintinhull,
nr Yeovil BA22 8PZ
In village of Tintinhull, off
A303 5m SW of Yeovil
Tel: 01935 822545

Owner:
The National Trust

Open: 31 Mar to 29 Sept,
daily except Mon and Tue
(open Bank Hol Mon)
12–6. 3/4 acre

THE DESIGN of this small garden, created by Phyllis Reiss between the wars, is so clever that it provides an inexhaustible model for gardeners. Divided into separate 'rooms' by walls or hedges, each area has a distinctive atmosphere. The Eagle Court west of the house has a central flagged path edged with clipped mounds of box and richly planted borders. The path leads to a little white garden, hedged in yew, in which white anemones, roses and lilies glow under miniature silvery willows. An opening leads through to a decorative kitchen garden. The pool garden above it, with its canal planted with irises, and summer house at one end, has a pair of masterly borders – one with hot colours of red and yellow, and the other with cool silvers and mauves.

TREBAH
Cornwall

Mawnan Smith,
nr Falmouth TR11 5JZ
4m SW of Falmouth,
tourism signs from A394
and A39 approaches to
Falmouth
Tel: 01326 250448
Fax: 0326 250781

Owner: Trebah Garden
Trust

Open: Daily 10.30–5.
25 acres

TREBAH IS the creation of Charles Fox who came here in 1831. By 1981 when Major and Mrs Hibbert started to restore it, the place had suffered years of neglect. Set in a long, slender ravine, the garden sweeps down south to the Helford river with paths running along each side of the valley, giving vertiginous views over great rhododendrons, magnolias, groves of the great tree-fern *Dicksonia antarctica*, and palms. A stream runs along the bottom of the ravine, with a waterfall and pools, and thickets of hydrangeas and *Gunnera manicata*. The contrast of exotic foliage, seen from above and below, is the most memorable thing at Trebah.

TRENGWAINTON GARDEN
Cornwall

SIR EDWARD BOLITHO was the chief creator of this garden in the 1920s, when he added to it some of the spectacular new discoveries of the plant-hunters, especially those of Frank Kingdon-Ward. From the entrance lodge a very long

Madron,
nr Penzance TR20 8RZ
2m NW of Penzance by
B3312
Tel: 01736 63021

Owner: The National Trust

Open: Mar to Oct, Wed to
Sat, Bank Hol Mon and
Good Fri 10.30–5.30 (5 in
Mar and Oct). 15 acres

drive provides the main axis of the garden. On one side an extraordinary walled kitchen garden now protects especially tender exotics. These flourish among rare magnolias and other ornamental trees and shrubs such as eucryphias, michelias, stewartias and *Styrax japonica*. Beyond the drive an excellent stream garden is beautifully planted with candelabra primulas, meconopsis, ligularias and skunk cabbage. In the woodland behind are immense rhododendrons – with spectacular examples of some of the large-leafed species such as *R. sino-grande*, *R. macabeanum* and *R. falconeri*. At the end of the drive the house looks out across a lawn to far views of St Michael's Mount, a splendid eye-catcher.

TRESCO ABBEY
Cornwall

Tresco,
Isles of Scilly TR24 0QQ
Access by helicopter or
ferry from Penzance
Tel: 01720 422849
Fax: 01720 422807

Owner: R. Dorrien Smith

Open: Daily 10–4. 16 acres

THERE IS certainly no other garden like this in the world. Tresco, one of the Scilly Isles, has an extraordinarily benign microclimate with moderate rainfall but high humidity from the sea. The garden was started by Augustus Smith in 1834, who, after planting windbreaks, gradually built up terraces on which to cultivate a staggering range of plants, especially those of the Southern Hemisphere. This, greatly added to by his descendants, is the garden that visitors may see today. It is primarily a collection of plants, but it is craftily designed with gravel paths leading along terraces, and cross vistas giving thrilling views through the sub-tropical luxuriance. The garden contains countless plants which you will see in no other British garden. There are, however, emphatic repeated plantings – of different kinds of palms, of the splendidly architectural *Echium pininiana* with its soaring spires of flowers, and of the giant purple-flowered *Geranium maderense* – giving structure to the abundance. It gives unique and exhilarating pleasure.

TREWITHEN
Cornwall

Grampound Road,
nr Truro TR2 4DD
7m W of St Austell by A390
Tel: 01726 882763/883647
Fax: 01726 882301

Owner: A.M.J. Galsworthy

Open: Mar to Sept, Mon to Sat 10–4.30. 25 acres. House open

TREWITHEN IS another Cornish garden with an outstanding collection of camellias, magnolias and rhododendrons – but it is strikingly unlike any of the others. Behind the elegant 1723 house there is an immense lawn, 200 yards long, with trees and shrubs crowding in on either side. From the far end of the lawn, this is seen to provide a marvellous setting for the house, like an immensely deep stage framed in wonderful plants. The garden was made by George Johnstone who came here in 1903 and cleared existing woodland, enriching the planting with many of the Asiatic plants newly introduced in the 1920s. Paths wind through this woodland and at every turn there is something wonderful to see. It is at its most spectacular in early to late spring but it has many pleasures to offer later in the year. Nor is it only a woodland garden. The formal walled garden should not be overlooked: with its wisteria-draped pergola, Irish yews and beautifully planted borders it is an admirable piece of work. An excellent plant shop sells many of the plants particularly associated with the garden (e.g. the beautiful *Ceanothus arboreus* 'Trewithen Blue').

WALES AND WEST-CENTRAL ENGLAND

Cheshire
Gloucestershire
Hereford and Worcester
Shropshire

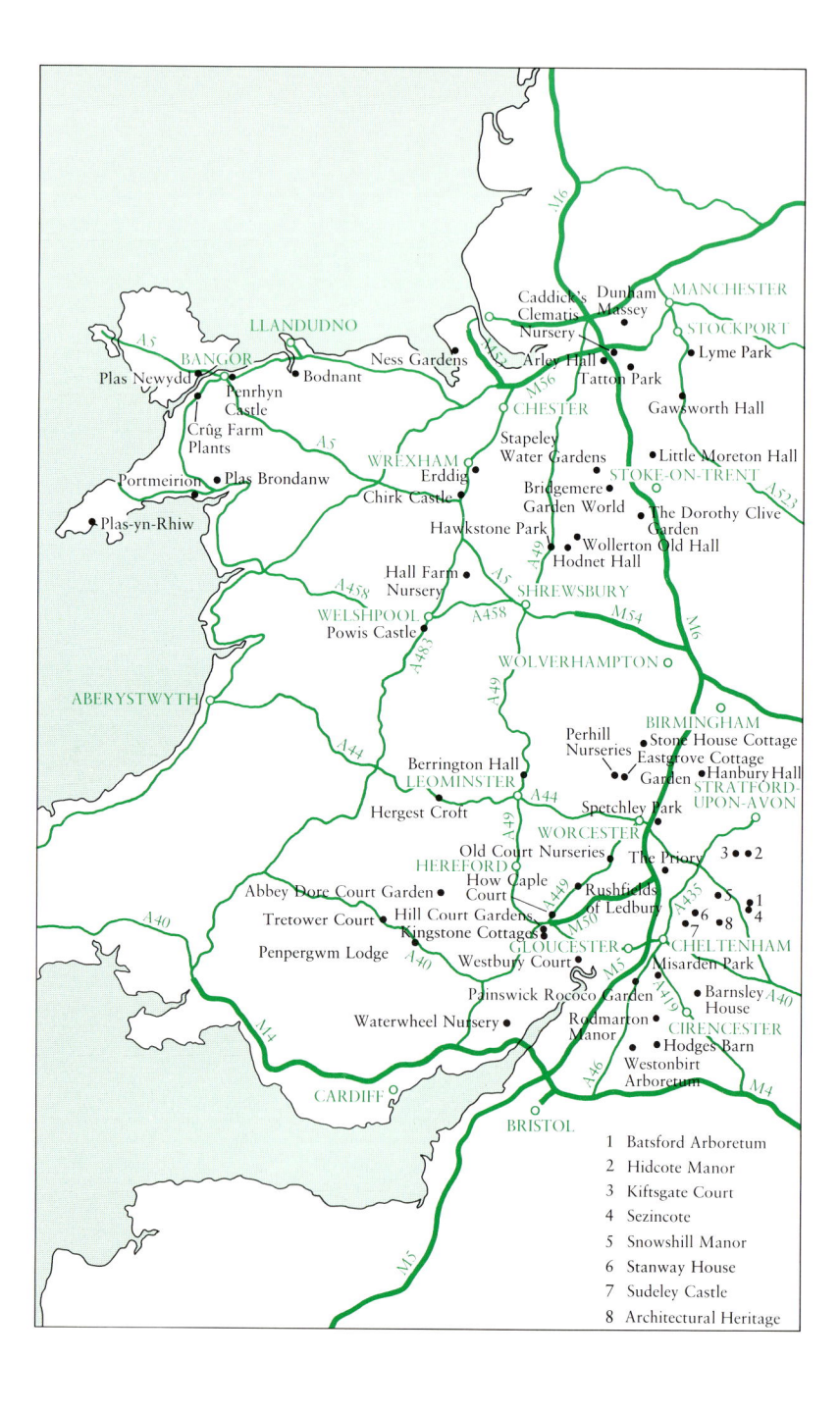

1. Batsford Arboretum
2. Hidcote Manor
3. Kiftsgate Court
4. Sezincote
5. Snowshill Manor
6. Stanway House
7. Sudeley Castle
8. Architectural Heritage

ABBEY DORE COURT GARDEN
Hereford and Worcester

Abbey Dore,
nr Hereford HR2 0AD
11m SW of Hereford by
A465 and B4347
Tel: 01981 240419
Fax: 01981 240279

Owner: Mrs C.L. Ward

Open: Mar to 3rd Sun in
Oct, daily except Wed 11–6
(also open before Mar for
hellebores; telephone for
dates). 5 acres

ABBEY DORE COURT on the banks of the River Dore has both an attractive garden and a nursery with a good range of the woody and herbaceous plants that may be seen growing in the garden. There is no catalogue and no mail order service, so a visit is essential. Abbey Dore keeps a National Collection of euphorbias, those fashionable and valuable greenery-yallery plants (40 species and cultivars). Throughout the garden the planting is of a very high standard; especially beautiful is a pair of mixed borders planted predominantly in yellow- and white-flowered plants, with gold and variegated foliage and the occasional sombre note of rich purple.

ARCHITECTURAL HERITAGE
Gloucestershire

Taddington Manor,
nr Cutsdean, Cheltenham
GL54 5RY
14m NE of Cheltenham by
B4632, B4077 and minor
roads; 15m E of Jnct 9 of
M5
Tel: 01386 584414
Fax: 01386 584236

Open: Mon to Fri
9.30–5.30 (but closed Bank
Hols); Sat 10.30–4.30

IN AND AROUND the handsome outhouses of a Cotswold manor house Architectural Heritage displays an alluring collection of garden urns, seats, fountains and statues – from frolicking dolphins to coy maidens. You will need a long purse to take away any of these lovely treasures but you may then possess a potently decorative garden antique of high quality. The stock changes all the time and, although they will find things for you, it is worth visiting to see what they have.

WALES AND WEST-CENTRAL ENGLAND · 145

ARLEY HALL

Cheshire

Arley, nr Northwich
CW9 6NA
5m W of Knutsford by
minor roads; Jncts 19 and
20 of M6; Jnct 10 of M56
Tel: 01565 777353

Owner:
The Hon. M.L.W. Flower

Open: Apr to Oct, Tue to
Sun and Bank Hol Mon
12–5. 12 acres

A PAIR OF herbaceous borders was laid out at Arley in 1846, a great novelty, and they survive to this day, beautifully maintained: pairs of topiary yew 'dumb waiters' form entrances at each end, and a broad grass path separates the borders which have yew buttresses on each side, breaking up an otherwise uncomfortably long stretch of planting. From June to the end of the gardening season they are one of the great garden sights of England. A path leads from the borders to a procession of giant columns of clipped holm oak and views over fields. There are also borders of shrub roses, old walled gardens with good mixed borders, a simple terraced walk above a ha-ha, and much else to see. Still in private ownership, Arley Hall preserves the atmosphere of a garden kept for its own delight.

BARNSLEY HOUSE GARDEN

Gloucestershire

THIS IS a famous garden, made by David and Rosemary Verey since 1951. Influenced by her knowledge of garden history Mrs Verey contrived a heady mixture of ingredients – a pleached lime walk, knot gardens, an ornamental *potager*, temples and statuary. The real distinction, however, lies in the planting, especially in the use of herbaceous plants and subtle associations of form and colour. Barnsley

Barnsley, nr Cirencester
GL7 5EE
In Barnsley village 4m NE of Cirencester by A433/B4425
Tel: 01285 740281
Fax: 01285 740628

Owner: Charles Verey

Open: Mon, Wed, Thur and Sat 10–6 or dusk if earlier. 4 acres

House is well known through Mrs Verey's own excellent books – but there is no substitute for a visit to the garden itself, which is in a constant state of gentle but stimulating change as new discoveries are made. It is one of those rare gardens that opens throughout the year and a winter visit, with the structural bones laid bare, is especially rewarding. A nursery sells an excellent stock of choice and often rare plants of the sort grown in the garden.

BATSFORD ARBORETUM
Gloucestershire

Moreton-in-Marsh GL56 9QF
1m NW of Moreton-in-Marsh by A44
Tel: 01608 650722
Fax: 01608 650290

Owner: The Batsford Foundation

Open: Mar to 5 Nov, daily 10–5. 50 acres

THIS ARBORETUM, started in the 1880s, has recently been revitalised with an enormous amount of new planting. It is now well worth visiting at any time of the year and even demon dendrologists will find marvellous things – over 90 kinds of oak, for example, and many wonderful individual specimens. But for less rarified tastes the place is full of interest, with all trees well labelled and the landscape enlivened by statues (including a fine bronze Buddha) and ornamental buildings. It is a marvellous place in which to walk and learn about trees. There is also a large nursery which carries a good general stock.

Illustration opposite: Statue at Bodnant

BERRINGTON HALL
Hereford and Worcester

nr Leominster HR6 0DW
3m N of Leominster by A49
Tel: 01568 615721

Owner:
The National Trust

Open: Apr, Fri, Sat and Sun (open Bank Hol Mon but closed Good Fri) 1.30–5.30; May to Jun and Sept, Wed to Sun and Bank Hol Mon 1.30–5.30; Jul and Aug, daily 1.30–5.30; Oct, Fri, Sat and Sun 1.30–5.30. 10 acres.
House open

THE BROWN STONE mansion was designed by Henry Holland and completed in 1781, and the unspoilt landscape park was laid out by his partner and father-in-law 'Capability' Brown. There was no house or garden here before so this is an unusual period piece. From the vast Arch of Triumph at the entrance, an avenue of clipped mounds of golden yew leads towards the front door of the house. On one side a magnificent brick-walled 18th-century kitchen garden has a recently planted collection of historic varieties of apple and, leading up to the wrought-iron entrance gate, a pair of good mixed borders. The walls provide protection for some unusual tender plants including the grandest of all buddlejas, *B colvillei*, with huge panicles of red flowers.

BODNANT
Gwynedd

Tal-y-Cafn, Colwyn Bay, Clwyd LL28 5RE
8m S of Llandudno by A470
Tel: 01492 650460

Owner:
The National Trust

Open: 16 Mar to 31 Oct, daily 10–5. 80 acres

BODNANT WAS started in the late 19th century at the height of the rhododendron craze. The steep slopes of the Conwy valley provided a wonderfully romantic site for their cultivation, and with the rushing waters of the River Hraethlyn at his feet, the visitor today may convincingly imagine himself in a dream-like valley of the Himalayas. Rhododendrons and camellias flourish under a high canopy of conifers. Nearer the house there is a completely

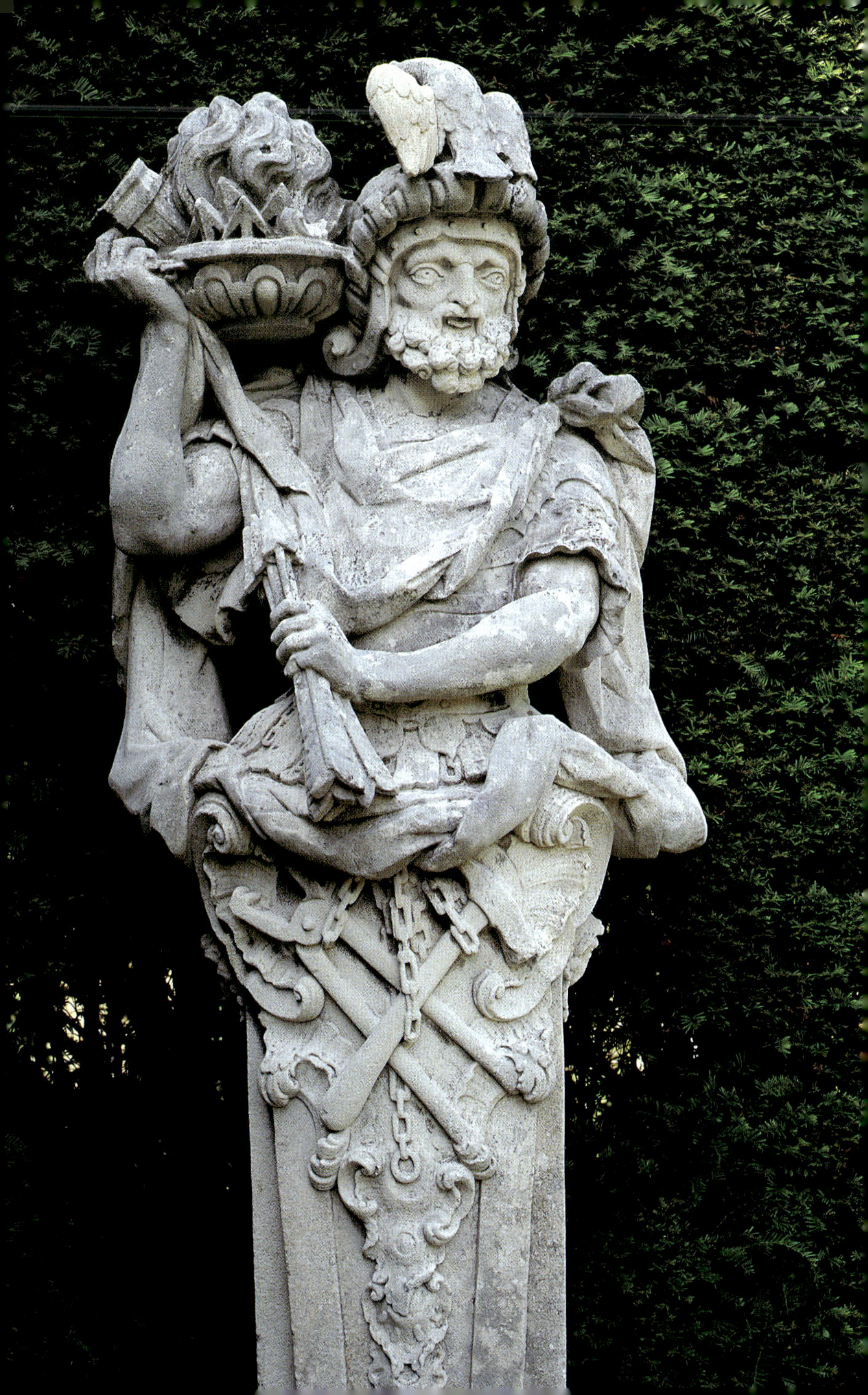

different garden – formal terraces descend in stately progression to a vast lily pool and the crispest yew hedges you will ever see. At the upper level is one of the most photographed garden sights in Britain – a curved tunnel of laburnum which in May and June drips gold and still has the power to take your breath away. This is an old-fashioned garden, almost a period piece, if only in terms of the superlative maintenance – even the yew hedges are still clipped by hand. The Head Gardener has been a Puddle for three generations and what they don't know about running a garden is probably not worth knowing. A large nursery, especially good for acid-loving shrubs, also sells plants by mail order.

BRIDGEMERE GARDEN WORLD
Cheshire

Bridgemere, nr Nantwich
CW5 7QB
6m SE of Nantwich on A51
Tel: 01270 520381
Fax: 01270 520215

Open: Mon to Sat 9–8, Sun 10–8; closes 5 in winter

NO OTHER garden centre has the sense of horticultural excitement that you will find here. It is a huge place – 25 acres in all – and there are enormous numbers of plants of every kind; it probably carries the greatest commercially available range in the country. They are grouped in a way that is useful to the gardener – both under type of plants (herbaceous, roses, etc) or by use (ground-cover, shade-loving, etc). A separate 6-acre display garden, 'The Garden Kingdom', shows the plants in action. There is no mail order, but all gardeners will enjoy a visit to see excellent and unfamiliar plants.

CADDICK'S CLEMATIS NURSERIES
Cheshire

Lymm Road, Thelwall,
Warrington WA13 0UF
At Thelwall village, just off
A56. 10 mins from Jnct 20
of M6 and Jnct 9 of M56
Tel: 01925 757196

Open: Daily except Mon
(but closed 15 Dec to 31
Jan) 10–5

CADDICK'S WAS STARTED only in 1984, by Harry Caddick, a Lockmaster on the Manchester Ship Canal. He now sells a a wonderful collection of clematis, that essential garden plant, beautifully displayed in new premises. Caddick's sells nothing but these essential garden plants, and its catalogue (£1.00) of over 300 varieties is one of the best. A mail order service is provided.

CHIRK CASTLE
Clwyd

Chirk LL14 5AF
1/2m W of Chirk village by A5
Tel: 01691 777701

Owner:
The National Trust

Open: 2 Apr to 27 Sept daily except Mon and Sat (open Bank Hol Mon) 11–6; Jul and Aug also open Sat; 5 to 29 Oct, Sat and Sun 11–6. 5 acres. Castle open

CHIRK IS a 13th-century border castle, and its massive defensive towers are echoed in the billowing old topiary cones of yew that march down its east side. An opening cut into a yew hedge guarded by a pair of bronze nymphs leads through to the upper lawn and a deep mixed border punctuated by groups of flowering cherries. On this windy site woodland provides protection for magnolias, rhododendrons and more unusual plants such as the Chilean firebush (*Embothrium coccineum*) with its scarlet flowers, and *Eucryphia glutinosa*.

THE DOROTHY CLIVE GARDEN
Shropshire

Willoughbridge, nr Market Drayton TF9 4EU
9m SE of Nantwich by A51
Tel: 01630 647237

Owner: Willoughbridge Garden Trust

Open: Apr to Oct, daily 10–5.30. 8 acres

FEW GARDENS have such diversity of interest as this. The garden was started in 1940 by Col. Harry Clive who realised the attractions of the site: a former gravel pit with acid soil on a fine south-facing, well watered slope, which provides habitats for a very wide range of plants. At the very top of the hill, in the old quarry, Col. Clive's original woodland garden is now fully mature; it is rich with azaleas, maples, rhododendrons and other ornamental trees and shrubs. A rushing multi-tiered waterfall is a brilliant sight in high summer, fringed with the coloured plumes of astilbes and ligularias. On the slopes below the old quarry a garden of a completely different character, planned by the garden designer John Codrington, was developed after Col. Clive's death. In the upper reaches, broad grassy paths running along the contours of the hill divide mixed borders lavishly planted with woody and herbaceous plants. Paths then run downhill at a brisker pace, between informal and scree beds, with a lily pond at the bottom.

CRÛG FARM PLANTS
Gwynedd

Griffith's Crossing, nr Caernarfon LL55 1TU
2m NE of Caernarfon off A487
Tel: 01248 670232
Fax: 01248 670232

Open: 24 Feb to 21 Sept, Thurs to Sun and Bank Hols 10–6

BLEDDYN WYNN-JONES was bitten by the love of plants and gave up farming to start this dazzling nursery five years ago with his wife Sue. The climate here on the edge of Snowdonia is balmy and wet, providing good conditions for the cultivation of the woodland plants that they love. Here are many anemones, asarums, daphnes, dicentras, hellebores, hostas, pulmonarias and trilliums. An exceptional list of hardy geraniums includes some new introductions of the Wynn-Joneses. They have formed the habit of going on plant-collecting jaunts to the great Asiatic hunting grounds whence new plants flow to the

Illustration: Trillium cuneatum

nursery. In all departments there are very unusual plants, many of which may be seen displayed in the owners' garden alongside. There is no mail order service but a useful catalogue is produced (s.a.e. and one 2nd-class stamp).

DUNHAM MASSEY
Cheshire

Altrincham WA14 4SJ
3m W of Altrincham by A56
Tel: 01619411025

Owner:
The National Trust

Open: 30 Mar to 27 Oct, daily 11–5.30. 250 acres. House open

ONE OF THE great successes of many National Trust gardens is their willingness to give full emphasis within a single garden to garden styles of different periods. At Dunham Massey, with its grand early 18th-century house, there are remains of a pattern of formal avenues of the same period, charging towards the horizon. Much replanting of beeches, limes and oaks has given this new life. From the house a double staircase leads to a sprightly Edwardian parterre, bedded in summer with zonal pelargoniums mixed with verbena and edged with rich blue lobelia. Clipped mounds of holm oak and hedges of golden yew give permanent ornament. To one side of the house informal lawns spread out, overlooked by an 18th-century orangery with, half-concealed in the woods behind, a well house disguised as a rustic retreat. Grassy walks lead along a moat whose banks are densely planted with astilbes, ferns, hostas, irises and rodgersias. The walk continues to a simple lawn, from which views are suddenly revealed of the house reflected in the tranquil waters of the moat.

EASTGROVE COTTAGE GARDEN

Hereford and Worcester

Sankyns Green, Little Witley WR6 6LQ
8m NW of Worcester, on the road between Shrawley (on B4196) and Great Witley (on A443)
Tel: 01299 896389

Owner: Malcolm and Carol Skinner

Open: Apr to Jul, Thur to Mon 2–5; Sept to 19 Oct, Thur to Sat 2–5 (closed throughout Aug). 1 acre

IF YOU DID NOT know what a cottage garden should look like this would be a good place to learn. The cottage itself, tiled and ancient, is set in lovely countryside and the garden, flawlessly kept, is full of lively planting and cunning design. There are formal ingredients – a splendid zigzagging hedge of the neatest possible *Lonicera nitida*, carefully placed benches in enclosures, and a great rose arbour; the garden itself is chiefly composed of curving borders and sweeps of lawn. A very wide range of plants, some extremely unusual, is grown. Malcolm and Carol Skinner, who made the garden, also run an outstanding nursery which concentrates on herbaceous perennials, hardy and half-hardy, and in which even the keenest gardeners will make discoveries. A very good list is produced (five 2nd-class stamps) but there is no mail order service.

ERDDIG

Clwyd

nr Wrexham LL13 0YT
2m S of Wrexham by A525
Tel: 01978 313333

Owner:
The National Trust

Open: Apr to Sept, daily except Thur and Fri (open Good Fri) 11–6 (Jul and Aug 10–6); 2 Oct to 3 Nov, daily except Thur and Fri 11–5. 13 acres. House open

THE FORMAL GARDEN to the east of the long, low early 18th-century house is one of the very few in Britain to survive the craze for landscape gardens in the second part of the 18th century. It has now been sensitively restored by the National Trust and is full of delights. It is enclosed in brick walls on which are espaliered old varieties of fruit trees. These are underplanted with many varieties of daffodil, and the central area has formal orchards of apple trees. A gravel path leads from the Edwardian parterre under the east windows of the house, by tubs of Portugal laurel clipped into mushroom shapes, towards a slender canal flanked with old limes. At its end, exquisite wrought-iron gates give views of the country beyond. A flowery Victorian parterre has variegated maples, agapanthus, clematis and cheerful bedding and nearby, on the north wall, is the National Collection of ivy. A path continues to a pair of stone urns and a memorably gloomy moss walk in the woods of shady holly and laurel.

GAWSWORTH HALL
Cheshire

Gawsworth, nr
Macclesfield SK11 9RN
3m S of Macclesfield by
A536
Tel: 01260 223456
Fax: 01260 223469

Owner: Mr and Mrs
Timothy Richards

Open: Apr to Oct, daily
2–5. 20 acres. House open

GAWSWORTH HALL is a lovely late Elizabethan half-timbered house of the characteristic Cheshire type. In front, lawns with specimen trees run down to a pool, and from the forecourt a paved path leads to a formal garden of rose beds, hedges of holly and yew and an ornamental bronze fountain. Beyond the house lie the ghostly remains of a princely 16th-century garden. Magnificent Tudor brick walls survive, enclosing a great space, where a pattern of terraces, and the site of a wilderness garden and of a formal canal, are visible. This has been the subject of an archaeological dig, very well described in a booklet on sale at the house. No plants survive from this early garden but it still has great atmosphere.

HALL FARM NURSERY
Shropshire

Illustration: Salvia sclarea
var. turkestanica

Kinnerley, nr Oswestry
SY10 8DH
In the village of Kinnerley
2m W of the A5 midway
between Shrewsbury and
Oswestry
Tel: 01691 682135

Open: Mar to Oct, Tue to
Sat 10–5, Sun 11–5

Christine Ffoulkes-Jones has been building up the reputation of her nursery with a fine crop of medals at RHS shows and a burgeoning catalogue of herbaceous perennials. She is interested in garden-worthy plants rather than botanical curiosities although there are certainly some rarities in her list. She has fine collections of campanulas, epimediums, geraniums (over 80 kinds listed), penstemons, primulas, pulmonarias and violas. In addition there are distinguished ornamental grasses and a specialist list of alpines. There is no mail order but a good catalogue is produced (four 1st-class stamps).

HANBURY HALL
Hereford and Worcester

Hanbury, Droitwich
WR9 7EA
4 1/2m E of Droitwich by
B4090 and minor road;
Jnct 5 of M5
Tel: 01527 821214

Owner: The National Trust

Open: 31 Mar to 30 Oct,
Sun to Wed 2–6. 15 acres.
House open

HANBURY HALL, built of brick and stone in 1701, is one of the prettiest houses in England and the view of it as you approach it across fields will take the breath away. The Vernon family who built it also commissioned a great garden from George London, the leading designer of the day, which was destroyed in the 1780s at the height of the landscaping craze. The National Trust have now reinstated London's formal gardens to the west of the house to dazzling effect. A four-square giant sunken parterre edged in box is planted with bold blocks of plants with a topiary figure at the centre of each bed. Beyond it is a formal 'wilderness' and to one side a formal orchard. It all suits the house to perfection.

HAWKSTONE PARK
Shropshire

Weston-under-Redcastle,
Shrewsbury SY4 5UY
14m NE of Shrewsbury by
A49 or A53 and minor
roads
Tel: 01939 200300

Owner: Hawkstone Estate

Open: Apr to Oct, daily
9–5. 100 acres

THIS WILD AND WOOLLY landscape garden has recently been brought spectacularly back to life and now offers the most complete experience of a high-style 'picturesque' garden. It was created by the Hill family from the 1740s onwards. Their trump card was the splendid lie of the land, with marvellous red sandstone crags erupting from wooded slopes. They made tunnels through the rock, and a labyrinthine grotto, and embellished the heights with splendid ornaments and buildings. A 100ft-tall column is crowned by a giant figure of a 16th-century Hill. Inside, a vertiginous spiral staircase takes the intrepid visitor to a gusty viewing platform from which the views are remarkable. Dr Johnson visited in 1774 and was thrilled by 'striking scenes and terrifick grandeur' – and you will be, too.

HERGEST CROFT
Hereford and Worcester

Illustration opposite:
Hanbury Hall

THIS IS ONE of the best private collections of woody plants in Britain, and has an exceptionally attractive atmosphere. The house was built in 1896 by William Hartland Banks who also started the

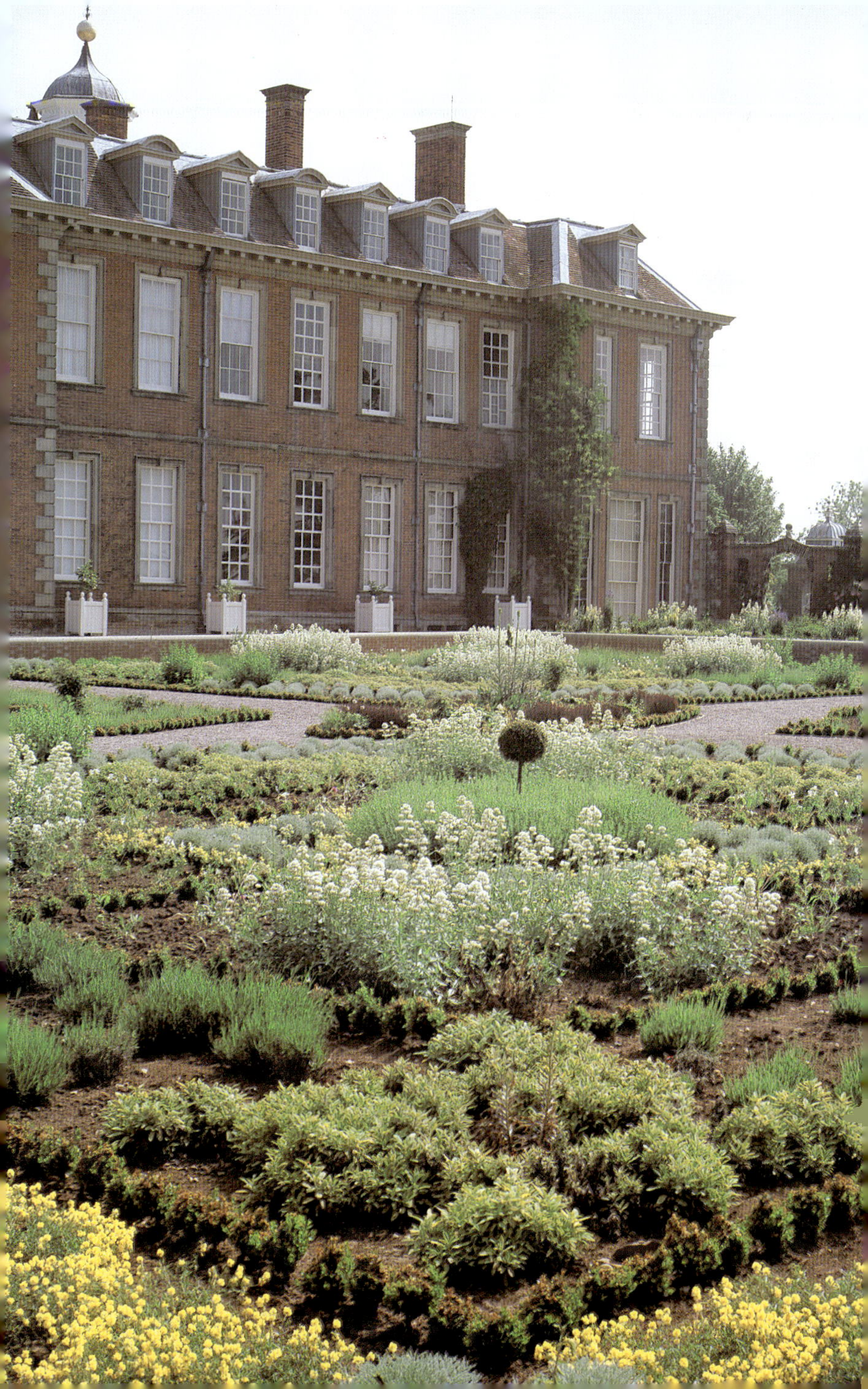

Kington HR5 3EG
1/2m W of Kington
signposted off A44
Tel: 01544 230160

Owner: W.L. Banks and R.A. Banks

Open: Easter to Oct, daily 1.30–6.30. 50 acres

collection of plants, many of which were raised from seed gathered in the wild. The garden falls into two chief parts – that near the house and Park Wood which lies across fields with exotic trees and contains a fine collection of rhododendrons. It is useless to attempt to list the great riches of this place. There are marvellous plants everywhere, and of particular interest are the National Collections of maples (excluding *Acer japonicum* and *A. palmatum* cultivars) and of birches. An exceptionally pretty kitchen garden has good borders.

HIDCOTE MANOR GARDEN
Gloucestershire

Hidcote Bartrim, nr
Chipping Campden
GL55 6LR
4m NE of Chipping
Campden by B4632
Tel: 01386 438333

Owner:
The National Trust

Open: Apr to Oct, daily except Tue and Fri 11–7 (closes at 6 in Oct). 10 acres

ALTHOUGH AMONG the best-known gardens in Britain, Hidcote still has the power to startle. It was begun before World War I by an American, Major Lawrence Johnston, who devised a type of garden that many think of as quintessentially English. First, it is a garden built up of separate 'rooms', each connected to the next but often with dramatic contrasts. For example, a pair of blazing red borders leads through to a cool green alley of pleached hornbeams. Second, the firm layout provides a disciplined setting for an immense range of plants of which Johnston was a pioneer rediscoverer – especially of old roses – and which he used in a swashbuckling manner in contrast with the crisp authority of his layout. Everywhere something enticing is glimpsed through an opening, across a pool, down steps or framed by a distant gate.

HODGES BARN
Gloucestershire

Shipton Moyne, Tetbury GL8 8PR
E of the village of Shipton Moyne, 2 1/2m S of Tetbury by A433 and minor road
Tel: 01666 880202
Fax: 01367 718096

Owner: Mr and Mrs Charles Hornby

Open: Apr to mid Aug, Mon, Tue and Fri 2–5. 8 acres

HODGES BARN IS an exceptionally pretty house, a pair of lovely ancient domed dovecotes converted into an elegant house in the 20th century. The garden was started after 1946 by the present owner's grandmother who planted many trees and laid out an excellent, bold design which has been enriched by the present owners. Enclosed areas about the house, hedged or walled, are skilfully planted and make the most of lovely views of the house or of the rural countryside beyond. Everywhere there are excellent roses - climbers and shrubs near the house and the species and wilder types among trees. A naturalistic woodland garden is marvellous in spring and in a more formal woodland glade the former stew pond is edged with moisture-loving plants. Deft touches of formality – a procession of Irish yews, well placed ornaments or lively topiary – give crisp contrast to the lavish planting. All is impeccably kept and sparkles with the excitement of gardening.

HODNET HALL
Shropshire

Hodnet, nr Market Drayton TF9 3NN
5 1/2m SW of Market Drayton by A53; 12m NE of Shrewsbury by A53
Tel: 01630 685202
Fax: 01630 685853

Owner: Mr and the Hon. Mrs A.E.H. Heber-Percy

Open: Apr to Sept, Mon to Sat 2–5, Sun and Bank Hol Mon 12–5.30. 70 acres

HEBERS HAVE been at Hodnet for an immense time but the garden can never have been in a better state than it is today. The main house is a neo-Elizabethan extravaganza built in 1870 by Anthony Salvin on an eminence with views south over a lake; a decorative Tudor dovecote forms an eye-catcher in the distance. Immediately below the south terrace of the house there are good mixed borders, and steps lead down towards the lake which is part of a chain of pools whose banks have been brilliantly planted with with moisture-loving plants –

astilbes, ferns, *Gunnera manicata*, hostas, rodgersias, and primulas. By the east end of the lake, partly concealed by woodland, is a circular bed with a figure of Father Time surrounded by concentric beds of hydrangeas, peonies and roses.

HOW CAPLE COURT GARDENS
Hereford and Worcester

nr Ross-on-Wye HR1 4SX
4m N of Ross-on-Wye by A449 and B4224
Tel: 01989 740626
Fax: 01989 740611

Owner: Mr and Mrs Peter Lee

Open: Apr to Oct, Mon to Sat 9–5.30, Sun 10–5. 11 acres

THIS MARVELLOUS PLACE is undergoing restoration but already so much has been done that it is well worth visiting. The house is an ancient one with medieval origins, rebuilt in the early 17th century and once again at the turn of the century. The present owner's grandfather was mad about gardens and laid out an ambitious and exciting scheme thoroughly appropriate to the spectacular site. On one side of the house he made a series of dramatic terraces linked by steps with views across the Wye valley towards the Brecon Beacons to the south. The bottom terrace has a pool, Italianate statues, sentinel Irish yews and cascades of old roses. In the wooded valley alongside the house there is a dell garden, a vast circular pool, a Florentine garden with a pattern of canals, the remains of a huge pergola and a loggia – all of which are undergoing restoration. A small nursery in the stable yard sells some good plants, particularly shrub roses.

KIFTSGATE COURT
Gloucestershire

Chipping Campden
GL55 6LW
3m NE of Chipping
Campden by B4632
Tel: 01386 438777

Owner: Mr and Mrs A.H. Chambers

Open: Apr to Sept, Wed, Thur and Sun 2–6; Jun to Jul, also Sat and Bank Hol Mon 2–6. 6 acres

THE NAME KIFTSGATE means to many gardeners that beautiful and embarrassingly vigorous rambling rose *R. filipes* 'Kiftsgate', but although the garden, started in the 1920s by Heather Muir, is certainly full of roses there is much else to admire. The house has a splendid setting, teetering on the edge of a precipitous valley across which, through the woods, are views of the Vale of Evesham. About the house is a series of enclosed gardens in which formality is blurred by generous planting. Four Squares has peonies, penstemons and rodgersias among berberis, indigofera and kolkwitzia. The rose borders have a central path hedged in *Rosa versicolor* behind which rise ramparts of shrub roses, and the 'Kiftsgate' rose zips 50 feet into the branches of a copper beech. Below all this, paths wind steeply down the valley side where, under the canopy of trees, cistus, hebes, phlomis and senecio relish the dry conditions. A choice selection of plants is for sale.

KINGSTONE COTTAGES
Hereford and Worcester

Weston-under-Penyard,
Ross-on-Wye HR9 7NX
2 m E of Ross-on-Wye by
A40 and minor roads
Tel: 01989 565267

Owner:
Mr and Mrs M. Hughes

Open: May to 20 Jun, Mon
to Fri 9–4 or by
appointment

SOPHIE HUGHES is an expert on pinks and at Kingstone Cottages she holds the National Collection of old garden varieties – over 140 species and cultivars. Some are displayed in a little parterre, like a bed in a physic garden, but many more are used to great effect in the excellent mixed plantings of her charming cottage garden. There are good plants for sale, pinks, of course, but others too.

LITTLE MORETON HALL
Cheshire

Congleton CW12 4SD
4m SW of Congleton by
A34
Tel: 01260 272018

Owner:
The National Trust

Open: 23 Mar to 27 Oct,
Wed to Sun (closed Good
Fri) 12–5.30; Bank Hol
Mon 11–5.30; 2 Nov to 22
Dec, Sat and Sun 12–4 or
dusk if earlier. 1 acre.
House open

THE HALF-TIMBERED famously wambly 15th-century house is surrounded by a moat. Little is known about what sort of garden the house had in its heyday but there are the remains of an artificial mound of the sort that might have been used for viewing a formal knot or parterre. With this in mind Graham Stuart Thomas laid out a charming little knot garden of box hedges, gravel and topiary yew obelisks based on a 17th-century pattern. At each side a pattern of square beds hedged in box contains a standard gooseberry bush underplanted with blocks of a single herbaceous plant – germander, strawberries, London pride or woodruff. All this is perfectly appropriate to the setting and a model of what may be done in a small space.

LYME PARK
Cheshire

Disley, Stockport
SK12 2NX
6 1/2m SE of Stockport by A6
Tel: 01663 762023

Owner:
The National Trust

Open: Apr to Oct 11–5; 2 Nov to 30 Mar, Sat and Sun 12–4. 15 acres. House open

AT LYME PARK the best parts of the garden have an exciting Victorian flavour that contrasts strikingly with the grand Frenchified house of the early 18th century. To one side of the house a well planted orangery of 1862 overlooks a parterre with Irish yews and urns, whose beds are planted in spring and summer with bright bedding schemes. On a terrace above, a rose garden with flagged paths and a central pool is enclosed in yew hedges and partly shaded by a pair of beautiful old limes. To one side a path sweeps uphill between deep herbaceous borders whose colour scheme modulates from oranges and yellows to blues and violets as it recedes from the house. North-west of the house, suddenly revealed below a high terrace, is an eye-stopping sight: the so-called Dutch garden, a dazzling arrangment of a fountain, statues of the four seasons, and a geometric pattern of beds edged in tightly clipped ivy and planted with single blocks of begonias, yellow or orange marigolds, santolina or purple verbena. For those who scoff at bedding this comes as a revelation.

MISARDEN PARK
Gloucestershire

Miserden, Stroud GL6 7JA
7m SE of Gloucester
Tel: 01285 821303

Owner:
Major M.T.N.H. Wills

Open: Apr to Sept, Tue to Thur 9.30–4.30. 12 1/2 acres

THE HOUSE is of the early 17th century with additions in 1920 by Sir Edwin Lutyens who also influenced the style of the terrace garden and forecourt alongside the house. The site is marvellous, on the edge of a valley with long views over wooded country. South and east of the house are excellent ornamental trees, and pleasure gardens are disposed on the slopes above. At their heart is a long walk of yew hedges whose tops are decorated by a series of undulating topiary humps. On one side a pair of great mixed borders is separated by a broad grass walk, and on the other a formal rose garden is backed with elegant trellis fencing. The garden is extremely well kept and is full of interest. A nursery sells the kinds of plants seen in the garden.

NESS GARDENS
Cheshire

Ness, Neston L64 4AY
11m NW of Chester by A540
Tel: 01513 362135/367769
Fax: 01513 531004

Owner: The University of Liverpool

Open: Mar to Oct, daily 9.30–sunset; Nov to Feb, daily (except 25 Dec) 9.30–4. 63 acres

NESS GARDENS WERE founded by A.K. Bulley, who sponsored the first expeditions of two of the greatest plant hunters of the 20th century – George Forrest to western China in 1904 and Frank Kingdon-Ward to Yunnan in 1911. Other expeditions followed and the plants that these men introduced are among the best specimens to be seen in the gardens to day. The site of the garden was good – with undulating land, acid soil and natural outcrops of stone. Bulley planted windbreaks of holly, evergreen oak, pines and poplars, and built up a very wide range of plants. Some parts of the collection – such as azaleas, rhododendrons and sorbus – are particularly good. From the gardener's point of view, however, there are other valuable features: a heather garden, herbaceous borders, a large rock garden, many roses, immense numbers of flowering trees and shrubs, and a woodland garden.

OLD COURT NURSERIES LTD
Hereford and Worcester

Illustration: Astrantia
'George Chiswell'

Colwall, nr Malvern
WR13 6QE
3m SW of Malvern by
A449 and B4218
Tel: 01684 540416

Open: Apr to Oct, Wed to Sun 10–1, 2.15–5.30

THE GREAT GLORY of Old Court Nurseries is the collection of Michaelmas daisies, one of the National Collections and a wonderful sight in September and October. But the nursery also sells an excellent collection of herbaceous perennials and rock garden plants. These are handsomely displayed in the adjoining Picton Garden which is open at the same times as the nursery. Nursery and garden together make an extremely attractive place to visit. Paul Picton has an excellent eye for a good plant and any gardener will find something desirable. Michaelmas daisies only are sold by mail order and a list of them is issued for that purpose.

PAINSWICK ROCOCO GARDEN
Gloucestershire

THIS IS ONE of the most ambitious restorations of a private historic garden ever undertaken. The garden had all but disappeared but has now been almost entirely restored, using a painting of it by Thomas Robins of 1748. In a secret combe behind

Painswick,
nr Stroud GL6 6TH
1/2m N of Painswick by B4073
Tel: 01452 813204

Owner: Painswick Rococo Garden Trust

Open: 2nd Wed in Jan to 30 Nov, Wed to Sun and Bank Hol Mon, 11–5. 10 acres

the house are wonderful garden buildings, woodland walks, pools, and a snowdrop grove to take your breath away. A mysteriously two-faced gothic gazebo looks down a yew alley towards a distant pond. Paths snake up and down the wooded slopes of the combe, giving glimpses of alcoves, temples and pools. Work continues – the Eagle House, filigree Gothic Exedra and vegetable garden have been reconstructed with great success. More recently the Red House is red once again and a fine laburnum tunnel has been built. If you think you know it well, it's worth another visit.

PENPERGWM LODGE

Gwent

Abergavenny NP7 9AS
3m E of Abergavenny by B4598; turn N opposite King of Prussia
Tel: 01873 840208

Owner: Mr and Mrs Simon Boyle

Open: Mid Apr to mid Oct, Thur to Sat 2–5. 3 acres

CATRIONA BOYLE INHERITED some good bones when she took over the garden at Penpergwm Lodge, to which she has added much finely judged ornamental planting. Lawns by the house have excellent trees and a south-facing paved terrace burgeons with *Carpenteria californica*, cistus, diascias, indigofera, myrtle and penstemons. This is a surprisingly mild part of the country and the garden enjoys excellent frost drainage. On the far side of the house a stately procession of 'rooms' is hedged in yew: the former vegetable garden has arches of roses and vines with ebullient herbaceous planting below; a shady apple tunnel; a pair of rose borders backed with purple beech; and a new vine walk. There are some good specialist plants for sale, chiefly herbaceous. This is the home, too, of Catriona Boyle's Garden School which gives lively one-day courses with talks and demonstrations from very distinguished gardeners.

PENRHYN CASTLE

Gwynedd

Illustration opposite: The Eagle House at Painswick

THE GIANT CASTLE – commissioned from Thomas Hopper in 1827 by a local millionaire quarry owner – is in neo-Norman style, built on a bluff with marvellous views north to Beaumaris Bay and south towards Snowdon. Parkland surrounds the castle but the chief horticultural interest lies in the old kitchen

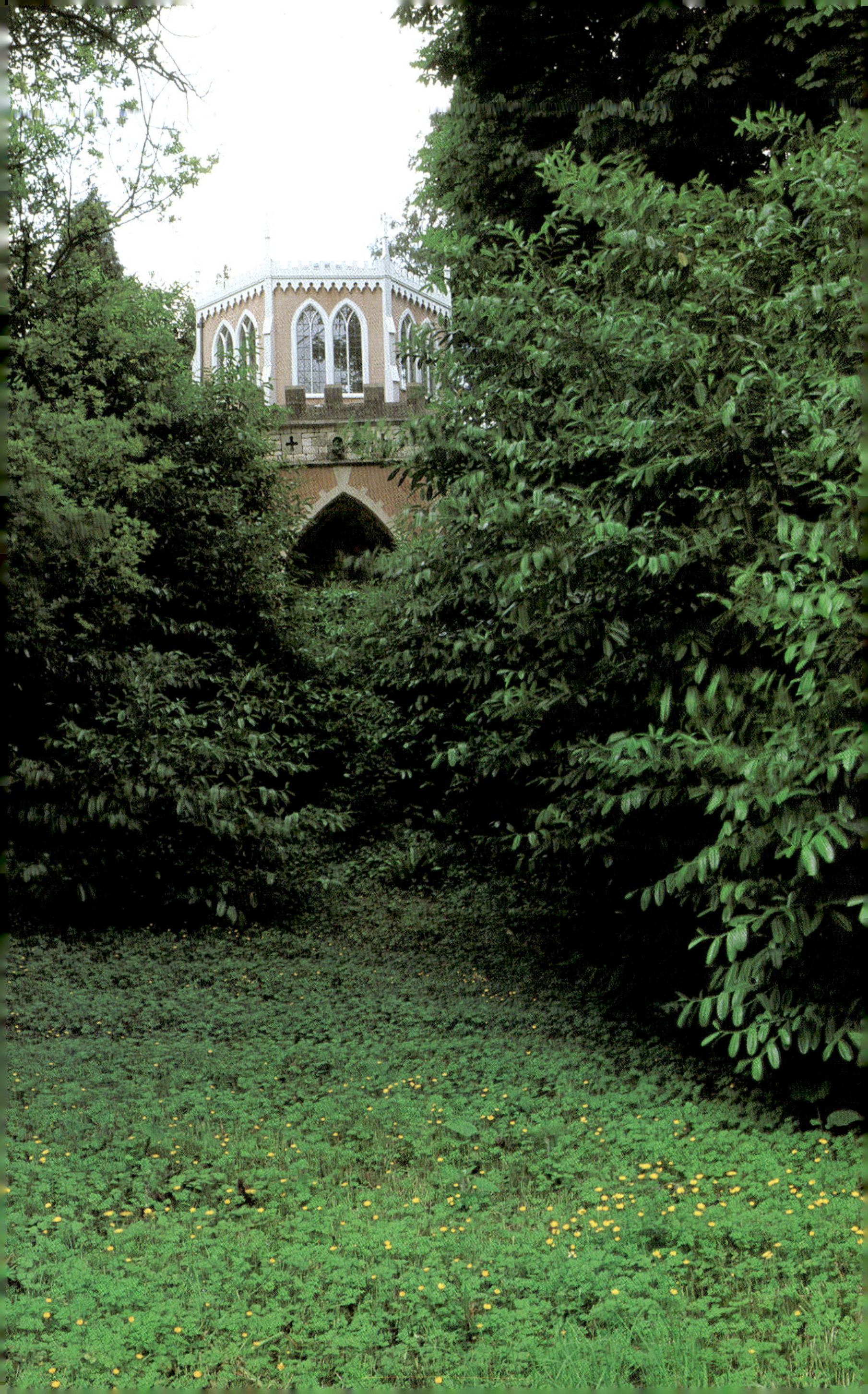

Bangor LL57 4HN
1m E of Bangor by A5122
Tel: 01248 353084

Owner:
The National Trust

Open: 27 Mar to 3 Nov,
daily except Tue 11–6 (Jul
and Aug 10–6). 47 acres.
House open

garden to the south. This is built on a steep slope with a formal terrace, parterres of roses and penstemons, and a rose arbour at the top; at a lower level are ornamental trees and shrubs – eucryphias, magnolias, sophoras and styrax; at the lowest level are trained fuchsias on a long pergola with clematis intertwining and views to the stream garden below, with the huge leaves of *Gunnera manicata* splendidly placed against groves of elegant purple-leafed maples.

PERHILL NURSERIES
Hereford and Worcester

Illustration: Phygelius
'Winchester Fanfare'

Worcester Road, Great
Witley WR6 6JT
On A443 1/4m SE of
village
Tel: 01299 896329
Fax: 0299 896990

Open: Mon to Sat 9–6, Sun
9–5. No mail order

ALPINES AND HERBACEOUS perennials are the speciality of this nursery, which carries a stock of over 2,200 different species and varieties. There are particularly good collections of campanulas, penstemons, phlox, pinks, salvias, silenes and sisyrinchiums. There are always too many plants to be listed so a rummage around will always reveal something desirable. There is no mail order but a plant list is produced (six 2nd-class stamps).

PLAS BRONDANW GARDENS
Gwynedd

TO MANY GARDEN VISITORS places that are completely unlike any other have an irresistible allure. Plas Brondanw belonged to the architect of Portmeirion, Sir Clough Williams-Ellis, who worked on the garden, on and off, from 1902 into the 1960s.

Llanfrothen,
Penrhyndeudraeth LL48
6SW
3m N of Penrhyndeudraeth
by A4085
Tel: 01766 770484

Owner: Trustees of the
Second Portmeirion
Foundation

Open: Daily 9–5. 4 acres

On wooded slopes on the very fringe of Snowdonia, Plas Brondanw has one of the most magnificent natural settings of any garden in Britain. Williams-Ellis laid out an inventive formal garden enlivened by the cheerful panache that makes him such an attractive figure (who else could make such a delightful pavilion out of *corrugated iron*, exquisitely shaped and painted, as that which lurks in the woodland here?). Yew hedges connect the house to the garden, and 'borrowed landscapes' are given full emphasis, including a breathtaking view of Snowdon and a neatly framed picture of Cnicht through a *claire voie*. The place swarms with architectural trimmings – an orangery, terraces, balustrades, urns, statues and *jeux d'esprit*. Under no circumstances miss the walk through the woods behind the house to the spectacular rocky ravine with its watchtower.

PLAS NEWYDD

Gwynedd

THE HOUSE of Plas Newydd is a famously decorative piece of gothic fantasy built in 1793 by James Wyatt overlooking the waters of the Menai Strait. This is a mild but windy place and one of the

Llanfairpwll, Anglesey
LL61 6EQ
1m S of Llanfairpwll by A5
Tel: 01248 714795

Owner:
The National Trust

Open: 29 Mar to 30 Sept,
daily except Sat 11–5; Oct
to 3 Nov, Fri and Sun
11–5. 31 acres. House open

striking things about the garden is the decorative use of unfamiliar hedging plants – fuchsia, griselinia and potentilla. There is a pretty little formal terraced garden between the house and the strait but the real garden excitement comes with the parkland to the west, known as 'West Indies', in the design of which Humphry Repton had a hand. Here countless good ornamental trees and shrubs – camellias, magnolias, maples and the Chilean firebush – flourish among older cedars, an exceptional sycamore and Monterey cypresses. A rhododendron garden, three-quarters of a mile to the north of the house, has recently been restored and is open only during flowering time from the beginning of April to the end of May.

PLAS-YN-RHIW
Gwynedd

Rhiw, Pwllheli LL53 8AB
12m from Pwllheli on S
coast road to Aberdaron
Tel: 01758 780219

Owner:
The National Trust

Open: Apr to Sept, daily
except Sat 12–5.
1 acre. House open

THE LLEYN PENINSULA is the most westerly part of Wales, and this enchanting little garden is one of the most remote on the mainland of Britain. The elegant stone house is built on precipitous wooded slopes giving beautiful views over Hell's Mouth Bay. Cobbled paths and box hedges divide the densely planted garden, and old plants of sweet bay, a fig, myrtles and artemisias give a Mediterranean air. The microclimate is very benign here so plants like *Euphorbia mellifera* grow to great size, and the tender climber *Lapageria rosea* flourishes. Few gardens of this size have such pungent and memorable atmosphere

PORTMEIRION
Gwynedd

Penrhyndeudraeth
LL48 6ET
2m SE of Porthmadog
Tel: 01766 770228
Fax: 01766 771331

Open: Daily 9.30–5.30

IN A WOODED COMBE overlooking the estuary of Traeth Bach towards the Harlech hills the architect Clough Williams-Ellis let rip with a fantasy Italianate village. He incorporated old architectural fragments into his buildings – cupolas, colonnades, statues and enough balconies to meet the needs of the world's population of Romeos and Juliets. Among these buildings there is interesting planting with a Mediterranean feeling – Chusan palms and Italian cypresses punctuate the scene, and cistus and artemisias flourish on the rocky slopes. Portmeirion has a mild microclimate so tender plants such as *Echium pininana* do particularly well. There is a hotel in the village and houses are available for rent.

POWIS CASTLE
Powys

THERE ARE FEW historic gardens that have so much to offer the gardener as Powis Castle. The place is historic because it preserves the splendid remains of a great formal garden of the 17th century – with grand terraces and immense old yews. But on these

Welshpool SY21 8RF
1m S of Welshpool by A483
Tel: 01938 554336

Owner:
The National Trust

Open: Apr to Jun, Sept to 3 Nov, daily except Mon and Tue 11–6; Jul to Aug, daily except Mon (open Bank Hol Mon) 11–6. 24 acres. Castle open

terraces the National Trust has laid out a brilliant series of borders, with wall plants and climbers forming a background to fortissimo displays of border perennials; these are designed to provide interest throughout the summer into early autumn. Another particular interest in the gardens is the exceptional collection of pots, beautifully planted with carefully judged combinations. A small woodland garden below the castle has great atmosphere, where a mysterious sculpture by Vincent Woropay of a disembodied foot lies in the grass.

THE PRIORY
Gloucestershire

Kemerton GL20 7JN
6m S of Pershore by B4080
Tel: 01386 725258

Owner: The Hon. Mrs Peter Healing

Open: Jun to Sept, Fri 2–6; also Suns 26 May, 23 Jun, 14 Jul, 4 Aug, 25 Aug, 8 Sept 2–6. 4 acres

THE HOUSE at Kemerton is an elegant Georgian box of Cotswold stone but the priory ruins are visible among the densely planted borders. On the south-facing slopes of Bredon Hill the garden has a protected site where Mrs Healing and her late husband devised brilliant borders in which colour harmony – some of it refreshingly bold – was the essential principle. Unusual plants chosen with an artist's eye fill these borders, and they flower over an extended period. Providing contrast are broad sweeps of lawn with beautiful ornamental trees (especially maples), yew hedges, a pergola of roses and vines. A nursery sells some excellent plants but there is no mail order.

RODMARTON MANOR
Gloucestershire

Rodmarton, nr Cirencester
GL7 6PF
In village of Rodmarton 6
miles SW of Cirencester by
A433
Tel: 01285 841253/841278

Owner: Mr and Mrs Simon
Biddulph

Open: 11 May to 31 Aug,
Sat 2–5; also by
appointment. 8 acres

THE ARCHITECT Ernest Barnsley started Rodmarton in 1909 and it became a shrine of the Cotswolds crafts movement. The grey, gabled house has an intricate garden, also designed by Barnsley, divided into 'rooms' and of a lively atmosphere. It is formal in spirit but the lavish planting has a cottage-garden informality. A flagged path separates double borders overflowing with old roses, peonies and campanulas, backed with stone walls and a yew hedge and enlivened with topiary of yew and box. Behind the house a pattern of enclosures separated by yew hedges and a pleached lime walk frames unspoilt views of the rural landscape.

RUSHFIELDS OF LEDBURY
Hereford and Worcester

Ross Road, Ledbury
HR8 2LP
1 1/2m SW of Ledbury by
A449
Tel: 01531 632004

Open: Wed to Sat 11–5
also by appointment

THIS IS A small nursery carrying a choice stock with an emphasis on herbaceous perennials. There are good collections of hardy geraniums, hostas, penstemons and interesting grasses. The very rare double-flowered sweet rocket is stocked, and there is a splendid selection of the exquisite hellebores cultivated by the legendary Helen Ballard. An informative catalogue is produced (s.a.e. A5 29p plus £1.00) but there is no mail order.

SEZINCOTE
Gloucestershire

nr Moreton-in-Marsh
GL56 9AW
1 1/2m W of
Moreton-in-Marsh by A44

Owner: Mr and Mrs D.
Peake

Open: Jan to Nov, Thur,
Fri and Bank Hol Mon 2–6
or sunset if earlier. 10
acres. House open

THE HOUSE at Sezincote was built in around 1810 by Sir Charles Cockerell and has a wonderful Indian character. At first the scene is quintessentially English – a sweeping drive and lovely parkland ornamented with exceptional cedars of Lebanon scarcely prepares the visitor for the exotic experience in store. Soon the drive runs over an Indian bridge surmounted by statues of bulls; below, a stream flows from a pool with an island bearing a curious column entwined with a three-headed snake. The banks of the stream are richly planted with hostas, rodgersias and skunk cabbage, relishing the moisture. On the far side of the bridge a figure of Souriya overlooks the temple pool. Old woodland spreads all around, studded with ornamental trees. Near the house a formal garden with a canal flanked by rows of soaring Irish yews is overlooked by a grand sweeping conservatory with minarets, ending in a domed pavilion. This heady mixture of subtle layout, excellent plants and orientalist decoration deep in the Cotswolds is a unique experience.

SNOWSHILL MANOR
Gloucestershire

Snowshill, nr Broadway
WR12 7JU
In village of Snowshill 3m
S of Broadway
Tel: 01386 852410

Owner:
The National Trust

Open: Apr and Oct, daily except Tue 1–5; May to Sept, daily exceot Tue 1–6. 2 acres. House open

CHARLES WADE, antiquarian and architect, was responsible for this extraordinary place where the garden was partly designed by the Arts and Crafts architect M.H. Baillie Scott. The house is a pretty stone-tiled Cotswold manor and the garden lies on steep west-facing slopes to one side. Wade terraced the slope and linked the separate spaces with stone steps and a bold descending avenue of Irish yews. Within the various garden enclosures Wade deployed a rich repertoire of garden ornaments – sundials, an armillary sphere, a gilt figure of George and the Dragon, pools, and benches painted in the distinctive 'Wade blue'. Flower beds and climbing roses look wonderful against the honey-coloured stone. The charm of this modestly sized garden lies in its different levels and endlessly shifting viewpoints.

SPETCHLEY PARK
Hereford and Worcester

nr Worcester WR5 1RS
3m E of Worcester by A422
Tel: 01905 345224/345213

Owner: Mr and Mrs R.J. Berkeley

Open: Apr to Sept, Tue to Fri and Bank Hol Mon 11–5, Sun 2–5. 25 acres

THE HEART of the garden is a maze of walks, borders and hedged enclosures which are so full of excellent plants that one's attention is repeatedly drawn by some lovely specimen, making it easy to lose one's orientation. The Berkeleys have been here a long time but, from the gardening point of view, the most important event was the marriage in 1891 of Robert Berkeley to Rose Willmott of Warley Place, the older sister of the famous gardener Ellen Willmott, who designed the fountain garden at Spetchley. Here a fountain lies at the centre of four large squares, enclosed in yew hedges and densely planted. Running along one side is an immense border in which roses, philadelphus and other shrubs are generously underplanted with herbaceous perennials – campanulas, delphiniums, geraniums and peonies. The suave stone Georgian mansion overlooks a park with lake and clumped trees. In July the woods on one side are filled with martagon lilies, plum-coloured and white, a fabulous sight. A new garden is being made in the walled garden but it is hoped that this will quickly assume the charmingly dishevelled look that is part of the place's allure. I know tidier and less weedy gardens but I know few of more irresistible character.

STANWAY HOUSE
Gloucestershire

Stanway, nr Cheltenham
GL54 5PQ
In the hamlet of Stanway,
11m NE of Cheltenham by
B4632 and B4077
Tel: 01386 584469

Owner: Lord Neidpath

Open: Jun to Aug, Tue and Thur 2–5. 20 acres

IN STRAIGHTFORWARD GARDENING terms it would be hard to justify the inclusion of this exquisite place. But the setting for the wonderful Elizabethan and Jacobean house is unforgettably beautiful. Behind it, well-wooded land slopes up towards a pyramid-like folly which in the 18th century was at the head of a spectacular cascade whose remains have recently been excavated and which it is hoped to restore. It is essential to walk up to the pyramid; the view is breathtaking and, on the way, an exhilarating cross vista through the woods is revealed. Everywhere there are exceptional trees: old cedars of Lebanon and sweet chestnuts by the pyramid; an exceptional tulip tree by the house; and a pair of ancient spreading oriental planes past the medieval tithe barn as you enter. It's not a place for fiddly borders but any gardener will love it.

STAPELEY WATER GARDENS
Cheshire

London Road, Stapeley,
Nantwich CW5 7LH
1m SE of Nantwich by A51
Tel: 01270 623868
Fax: 01270 624919

Open: Mon to Sat 9–6,
Sun and Bank Hol Mon
10–6.30; closes at 5 in
winter. 53 acres

THERE IS nothing at all quite like this anywhere in Britain. It is a tremendous celebration of water gardens and their plants. Although there is plenty of razzmatazz there is also nurserymanship of a high order and the gardens display the largest collection of hardy and tender water-lily varieties in the world – over 160 varieties are grown. There are also very many other water plants displayed in immense glasshouses and out-of-doors. A mail order service is provided and the well illustrated catalogue (£1.00) tells you probably all you need to know about making, stocking and maintaining a water garden.

STONE HOUSE COTTAGE
Hereford and Worcester

JAMES ARBUTHNOTT is a demon bricklayer and his wife Louisa a brilliant propagator. The garden, an old walled kitchen garden, now bristles with look-out towers, gazebos, arcades and other charming architectural geegaws which make ornaments as well as supports for the countless climbing, twining and

Stone, nr Kidderminster
DY10 4BG
2m SE of Kidderminster
by A448
Tel: 01562 69902

Owner: Major and the
Hon. Mrs Arbuthnott

Open: Mar to Sept, Wed
to Sat 10–5.30; also Suns
5 and 26 May and 9, 23
and 30 Jun 10–5.30. Oct
to Feb, by appointment
only. 3/4 acre

ramping plants that are a speciality of the garden. Hedges of yew and purple plum divide the space, and at the centre there is a pair of burgeoning borders culminating in a sundial. Ornamental trees and shrubs are planted in grass, and near the house raised beds contain alpines and smaller plants. There is an excellent nursery which specialises in wall plants, some very unusual, and some with reputations for dubious hardiness that have proved remarkably tough in this not very mild climate. A good catalogue (s.a.e.) is produced but there is no mail order. There is nothing like the Arbuthnotts' establishment – it's a remarkable achievement.

SUDELEY CASTLE
Gloucestershire

Winchcombe, nr
Cheltenham GL54 5JD
8m NE of Cheltenham by
B4075 and B4632
Tel: 01242 604357/602308
Fax: 01242 602959

Owner: Lord and Lady
Ashcombe

Open: Apr to Oct, daily
10.30–5.30. 10 acres. Castle
open

THIS IS a spectacular place with a grand late medieval castle with later additions, and a garden that takes full advantage of the architectural setting. Roses are the great thing at Sudeley and they look wonderful against the old stone walls. At the entrance a long lily pool runs in front of the ruins of the 15th-century great barn whose roof-less walls are draped with climbing roses and clematis. Beyond the castle, a recently replanted formal Victorian garden has a pool surrounded by L-shaped beds with old shrub roses underplanted with herbs. On either side are immense old tunnels of yew, and the surrounding lawns are studded with topiary shapes of golden and common yew. Old trees – walnuts, limes and a vast cedar of Lebanon – stand out superbly against the castle walls. In 1995 a knot garden was created to commemorate Queen Elizabeth I. A good nursery sells a general stock but has an especially distinguished collection of roses.

TATTON PARK
Cheshire

THE HOUSE was designed in the early 19th century for the Egerton family by Lewis Wyatt; he also had a hand in the gardens which have an exuberant 19th-century flavour. South of the house, on a terrace with grand views, a dapper parterre designed by

Knutsford WA16 6QN
3 1/2m N of Knutsford
signposted from the centre
of the town
Tel: 01565 654822
Fax: 01565 650179

Owner:
The National Trust

Open: Apr to Sept, daily
except Mon (but open
Bank Hol Mon) 10.30–6;
Oct to Mar, daily except
Mon 11–4. 60 acres.
House open

Joseph Paxton is brilliantly bedded out in summer. Her Ladyship's Garden, by the house, is a sunken garden with a pergola and rose-beds. Fine mixed borders with buttresses of yew are backed by the formerly heated walls of the kitchen garden. Nearby, a unique fernery designed by Wyatt houses tender ferns, and an orangery protects citrus plants and sub-tropical climbers. Both are newly restored, a splendid sight. On sloping land south of the house a long walk pierces well wooded lawns, with glimpses to the west of a serpentine network of lakes. Here is an exceptional Japanese garden, built in 1910 by Japanese gardeners, in which maples, moss-covered stones, an arched bridge and a Shinto temple make a convincing picture under a canopy of old trees.

TRETOWER COURT
Powys

OF THE VARIOUS ATTEMPTS to recreate a medieval garden, Tretower is quite one of the most attractive. The setting is a lovely one, beneath the windows and grey stone walls of the 15th-century manor house of the Vaughan family. Nothing is

Tretower, nr Crickhowell
In Tretower village, 3m
NW of Crickhowell by
A479
Tel: 01874 730279

Owner: Cadw: Welsh
Historic Monuments

Open: end Mar to endOct,
daily 9.30–6. 1 acre. House
open

known about the garden that existed here in the late
middle ages but what has been recreated is based on
historical knowledge of gardens of that period.
Lattice-work fences enclose beds planted with correct
plants of the period, and a tunnel arbour is richly
festooned with honeysuckle, roses and vines, with
shade-loving herbaceous plants at their feet. A
memorably atmospheric view of the garden is to be
had through the old glass of the leaded windows of
the first-floor rooms.

WATERWHEEL NURSERY
Gwent

Bully Hole Bottom, Usk
Road, nr Shirenewton,
Chepstow NP6 6SA
In the valley of Bully Hole
Bottom, 5m NW of
Chepstow by B4235; nr
Jnct 22 of M4
Tel: 01291 641 577

Open: Daily except Sun
9–6 (phone before making
a long journey)

DESMOND AND CHARLOTTE Evans's nursery always
has for sale some mouthwatering plant which
you certainly do not have in your garden. They carry
a large stock but, as Desmond puts it, they 'specialize
in not specializing'. Their range is wide, woody and
herbaceous, within which are some exceptional
groups – many euonymus (some you will find
nowhere else), several mahonias (including the new
M. pallida), unusual kinds of *Skimmia japonica* and
several viburnums. Among herbaceous plants are

many euphorbias, the best geraniums, ornamental grasses and some very pretty cultivars of periwinkle. There is a list, and mail order is available in autumn, but this is pre-eminently a place to nose around in.

WESTBURY COURT GARDEN
Gloucestershire

Westbury-on-Severn
GL14 1PD
9m SW of Gloucester by A48
Tel: 01452 760461

Owner:
The National Trust

Open: Apr to Oct, Wed to Sun and Bank Hol Mon 11–6 (closed Good Fri); also by appointment.
4 acres

THIS LATE 17TH-CENTURY formal water garden, for a house that was destroyed, survived by the skin of its teeth and has now been beautifully restored. It was created by Maynard Colchester and many of the original bills survive, giving a valuable record of exactly what plants he used. On low-lying land on the banks of the Severn formality is given by two parallel canals edged with yew hedges whose crests are decorated with yew and holly topiary. An elegant Dutch-style pavilion overlooks the head of one canal, and a boundary wall is covered in pre-1700 varieties of espaliered fruit. In one corner is a secret walled garden, overlooked by a charming little summer house, in which box-edged beds burgeon with plants in cultivation before 1700, and the paths are shaded by an arbour of honeysuckle and clematis. Nearby a parterre of box topiary and annuals has been recreated from an 18th-century print. On the way out keep an eye open for an unforgettable sight behind the pavilion – an immense holm oak (*Quercus ilex*), probably the oldest in the country.

WESTONBIRT ARBORETUM
Gloucestershire

Westonbirt, nr Tetbury
GL8 8QS
3m SW of Tetbury by the A433
Tel: 01666 880220
Fax: 01666 880559

Owner: The Forestry Commission

Open: Daily 10–8 or sunset if earlier. 600 acres

THIS IS ONE of the greatest collections of trees in the country but it is far more than just a collection. It was started in 1829 by Robert Holford who had a brilliant eye for arranging the huge quantities of trees which he so energetically collected. Planting has been continued by subsequent members of his family and, since 1956, under the ownership of the Forestry Commission. Today it is not only a marvellous place to learn about and admire trees and shrubs but it is also a landscape of rare beauty. The arboretum has the National Collections of *Acer japonicum* and of *A. palmatum* cultivars, and of

WOLLERTON OLD HALL
Shropshire

Wollerton, Market Drayton
TF9 3NA
1 1/2m NE of Hodnet by
A53; turn right immediately
after Wollerton sign;
garden 300 yards on left
Tel: 01630 685756
Fax: 01630 685583

Owner: John and Lesley
Jenkins

Open: 2 Jun to 30 Aug, Fri
and Sun 12–5. 3 acres

THE JENKINSES' GARDEN was started in 1984 and is a marvellous example of what can be done in a short space of time. It is a garden of compartments and crafty vistas, carried off with rare skill. Different parts show strikingly contrasting moods: a sunken garden of Arts and Crafts character has the calming sound of running water and a quiet colour scheme; Lanhydrock is an explosion of purple cordyline, rich red poppies, inky black aeoniums, and flaming hot pokers. The parts are harmoniously linked and the planting everywhere shows rare judgement. Many of the effects are dazzlingly simple – a shady walk of limes underplanted with a sea of purple sage, or the opening of a path marked by a pair of staddle stones emerging from clumps of hosta. This is a garden to be enjoyed – and to be plundered for inspiration.

THE
HEART
OF
ENGLAND

Derbyshire
Leicestershire
Northamptonshire
Nottinghamshire
Staffordshire
Warwickshire
West Midlands

Map

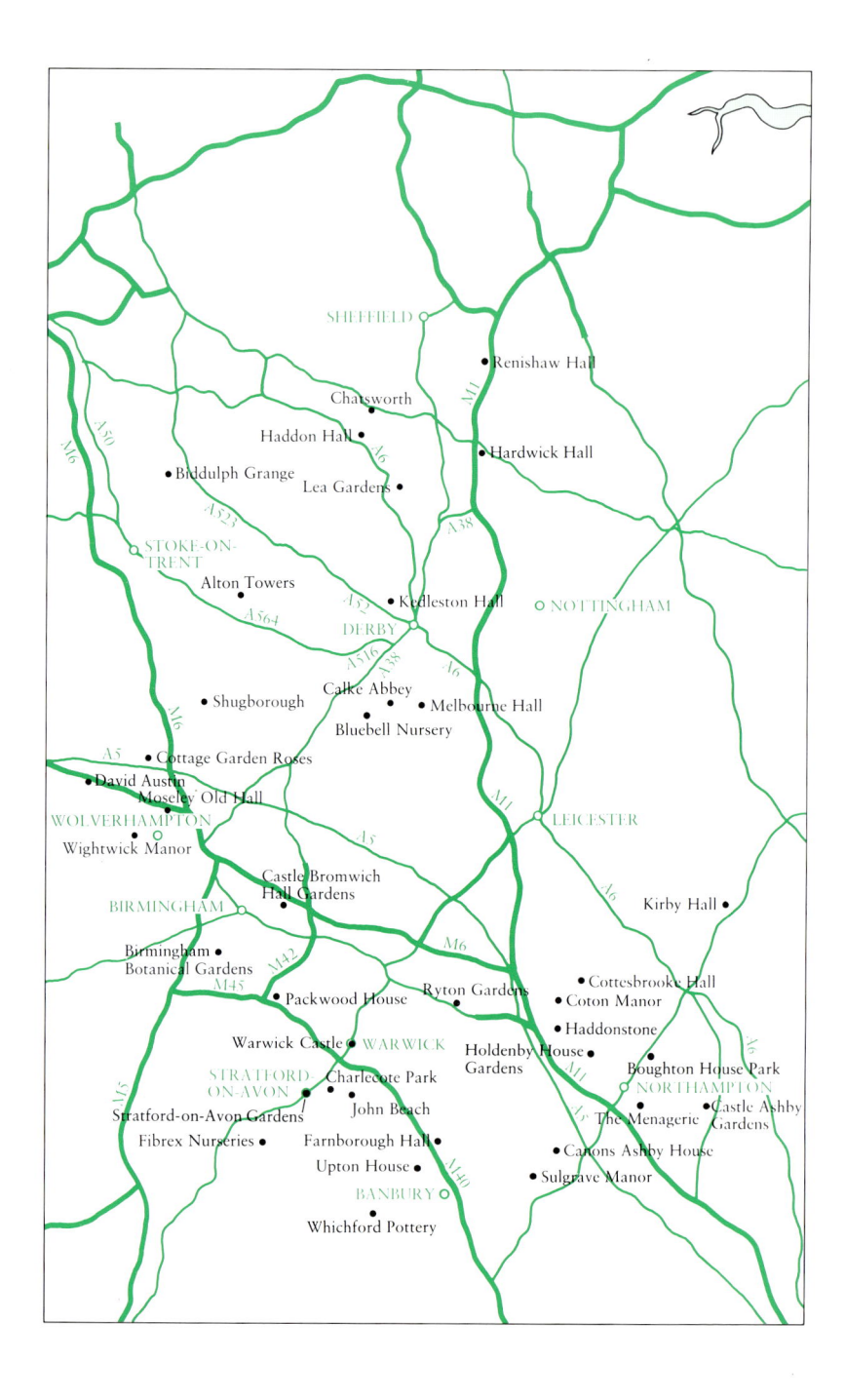

- SHEFFIELD
- Renishaw Hall
- Chatsworth
- Haddon Hall
- Hardwick Hall
- Biddulph Grange
- Lea Gardens
- STOKE-ON-TRENT
- Alton Towers
- Kedleston Hall
- NOTTINGHAM
- DERBY
- Shugborough
- Calke Abbey
- Melbourne Hall
- Bluebell Nursery
- Cottage Garden Roses
- David Austin
- Moseley Old Hall
- WOLVERHAMPTON
- Wightwick Manor
- LEICESTER
- Castle Bromwich Hall Gardens
- BIRMINGHAM
- Kirby Hall
- Birmingham Botanical Gardens
- Packwood House
- Ryton Gardens
- Cottesbrooke Hall
- Coton Manor
- Haddonstone
- Warwick Castle
- WARWICK
- Holdenby House Gardens
- Boughton House Park
- STRATFORD-ON-AVON
- Charlecote Park
- NORTHAMPTON
- Stratford-on-Avon Gardens
- John Beach
- The Menagerie
- Castle Ashby Gardens
- Fibrex Nurseries
- Farnborough Hall
- Canons Ashby House
- Upton House
- Sulgrave Manor
- BANBURY
- Whichford Pottery

ALTON TOWERS
Staffordshire

Alton ST10 4DB
18m E of Stoke-on-Trent
Tel: 01538 702200
Fax: 01538 704097

Owner: Madame Tussauds
Group of Companies

Open: Apr to Oct, daily
9–6 (open until 8 on some
summer evenings; check by
'phone). 200 acres

A RING-A-DING family leisure park, the busiest in Britain, is not a place where you would expect much by way of a garden. The gigantic house was designed for the 16th Earl of Shrewsbury in the first half of the 19th century by a bevy of architects of which the chief was A.W.N. Pugin whose wild gothic palace was said to sacrifice 'domestic comfort to showmanship'. The gardens were made on a similarly lavish scale. In a precipitous dell north of the house huge numbers of conifers clothe the slopes which are animated by exotic buildings, most of which were designed by Robert Abraham: a palatial mosque-like conservatory with many domes and beautiful stone work; a gothic prospect tower on the heights; a memorial to the 15th Earl; and, best of all, a fountain in a lake disguised as a Chinese pagoda. A shady terrace runs in front of the conservatory, with urns and a topiary tunnel of yew. J.C. Loudon thought the whole place was 'in excessively bad taste', and that is exactly what many people will love. The gardens are splendidly well cared for.

DAVID AUSTIN
West Midlands

ALTHOUGH DAVID AUSTIN grows other things (irises, peonies and daylilies, for example) he is overwhelmingly a rose specialist, and one of the very best in the country. He is known above all for old

Bowling Green Lane,
Albrighton,
Wolverhampton WV7 3HB
7m NW of Wolverhampton
by A41 and A464 nr Jnct 3
of M54
Tel: 01902 373931
Fax: 01902 372142

Open: Mon to Fri 9–5, Sat,
Sun and Bank Hol Mon
10–6

roses and his own 'English Roses' which combine the beauty of flower and form of the old varieties with the repeat flowering of the modern ones. In fact he does not disdain modern roses and has a carefully chosen selection of Hybrid Teas, some of which are now hard to find. Go, of course, in late June or July and be bowled over by the beauty and scent. He produces an excellent and informative catalogue and sells by mail order.

JOHN BEACH LTD
Warwickshire

9 Grange Gardens,
Wellesbourne CV35 9RL
(office); Tanworth Lane,
Henley-in-Arden (nursery)
1m N of Henley-in-Arden
by A3400 near Jnct 3a of
M40
Tel: 01789 840529
Fax: 01789 841520

Open: Mon, Wed, Fri, Sat
10.30–4.30 (or dusk in
winter)

THE BEST PART of John Beach's nursery is the marvellous collection of clematis – well over 150 different kinds, with a particularly good selection of the species and smaller-flowered varieties. An excellent catalogue (£1.50) has invaluable information on the care and cultivation of these sometimes tricky customers. Although clematis loom largest on Beach's list he also sells shrubs, trees and herbaceous perennials. Among these there are some interesting things, with unusual selections of, for example, fuchsias and hibiscus cultivars, and an unexpectedly good range of grape vines – for both wine and dessert. A mail order service is provided.

BIDDULPH GRANGE GARDEN
Staffordshire

Biddulph, nr
Stoke-on-Trent ST8 7SD
5m SE of Congleton by
A527
Tel: 01782 517999

Owner:
The National Trust

Open: 30 Mar to 31 Oct,
Wed to Fri 12–6 (closed
Good Fri), Sat, Sun and
Bank Hol Mon 11–6 ; 2
Nov to 22 Dec, Sat and
Sun 12–4 or dusk if earlier.
15 acres

GARDENS THAT ARE snatched from the brink of extinction always have a special attraction, and Biddulph is an exceptionally fine example. It was made by James Bateman and Edward Cooke over a long period from 1842, when tastes in garden design turned to the exotic and a flood of newly introduced conifers fuelled the gardening imagination.
A frightening rocky tunnel lit by a glimmer of candle-light leads suddenly into a glittering gold, scarlet and white interior of a Chinese pagoda overlooking a pool fringed with maples. Stone sphinxes and monumental clipped yews guard the mysterious entrance to Egypt. A sprightly dahlia walk marches up to a sombre avenue of deodars piercing deeply into the woodland. This has been superbly

restored by the National Trust; more work is still being done but the results already make Biddulph a truly exciting place. No other garden in Britain gives quite such a vivid impression of the exitement of 19th-century gardening.

BIRMINGHAM BOTANICAL GARDENS AND GLASSHOUSES
Birmingham

Westbourne Road,
Edgbaston B15 3TR
2m SW from city centre
Tel: 0121 454 1860

Owner: Birmingham Botanical and Horticultural Society Ltd

Open: Daily except Christmas Day 9 (10 on Sun)–8 or dusk if earlier. 15 acres

THERE IS a zip about the Birmingham Botanical Gardens. First, they are beautifully gardened – even the bedding schemes manage brilliantly to avoid municipal plodding. Second, although they call themselves botanical gardens, they are treated by locals, and those from farther afield, as a public park and there are plenty of horticultural diversions. They were founded in 1829 on an attractively undulating site which was landscaped by J.C. Loudon. Glasshouses of several different climates protect a very wide range of tender plants which includes a collection of warm climate 'economic' plants. Collections of particular groups of plants – introductions by E. H. 'Chinese' Wilson (who had been a student here), rhododendrons, rock and water plants, and modern roses, are all well displayed.

BLUEBELL NURSERY

Derbyshire

Illustration: Itea ilicifolia

Blackfordby, Swadlincote
DE11 8AJ
6m E of Burton-on-Trent
off the A50 in the village of
Blackfordby (behind the
Bluebell Inn). *Note:* A
move to a site nearby is
planned for 1996; phone
before making a special
journey
Tel: 01283 222091
Fax: 01283 218282

Open: Daily 9–5 (closed 25
Dec–2 Jan)

FOR SOME REASON most enterprising young nurseries have specialised in herbaceous plants. Robert and Suzette Vernon sell a few but their hearts and souls are in woody plants of which they offer one of the most mouth-watering selections in the country. From the very desirable but inexplicably overlooked (such as the lovely *Itea ilicifolia*) to rare cultivars of many shrubs and trees (*Quercus cerris* 'Argenteovariegata'!) it is a list bursting with a passion for plants. I defy any gardener to visit the Bluebell Nursery without finding some unfamiliar plant which *must* be bought. There is a mail-order service and an admirable catalogue is produced (£1 and two 1st-class stamps).

BOUGHTON HOUSE PARK

Northamptonshire

nr Kettering NN14 1BJ
3m NE of Kettering on A43
by the village of Geddington
Tel: 01536 515731
Fax: 0536 417255

Owner: The Duke and
Duchess of Buccleuch and
Queensberry

Open: May to Sept, daily
except Fri 1–5. 350 acres

THE GREAT HOUSE at Boughton has something decidedly French about it. It was started in the 1680s, an addition to a much older house, by the first Duke of Montagu who had been ambassador to Louis XIV. To his great palace the Duke added a formal garden of appropriate scale, designed by a Dutch gardener, Van der Meulen. In the 18th century the estate became a secondary residence of the Buccleuch family, and the formal garden was not kept up. Today visitors may wander in this vast park of wonderful trees, lakes and canals, and exhilarating views. Sheep graze on the terraces of the old formal garden, now covered in turf, and there are marvellous glimpses of the distant house. The character of the place today is essentially that of a landscaped park, but always visible, like the underpainting of an old master, are the smudged but distinguished traces of the earlier garden.

CALKE ABBEY
Derbyshire

Ticknall DE7 1LE
9m S of Derby by A514
Tel: 01332 863822/864444

Owner:
The National Trust

Open: 30 Mar to Oct, Sat to Wed 11–5.30 (closed Good Fri). Park only open throughout the year dawn–dusk. House open

THE EARLY 18th-century grey stone mansion seems almost like an after-thought when the visitor has traversed the many acres of wonderfully unspoilt ancient parkland that surrounds it. The garden, at some distance from the house, as was often the case in the 18th century, consists of a walled formal garden with a pattern of borders containing bedding schemes of Victorian appearance. In one corner a rare 'auricula theatre' – shelves on which to display auriculas in pots – is used for pelargoniums in summer. In the restored walled kitchen garden many old varieties of vegetables and fruit are grown. The charm of Calke Abbey is the beauty of its setting.

CANONS ASHBY HOUSE
Northamptonshire

Canons Ashby, Daventry
NN11 6SD
11m NE of Banbury by
A361, A422 and B4525
Tel: 01327 860044

Owner:
The National Trust

Open: 30 Mar to Sept, Sat to Wed 1–5.30 or dusk if earlier. 70 acres. House open

THE BEGUILING brick and stone house, the home of the Dryden family, was started in the 1550s and substantially rebuilt in the early 18th century. The essential layout of the garden as it is today is a rare survival from the same period. The Green Court by the west façade, with its decorative stone walls and gates, is ornamented with giant cones of clipped yew and a lead statue of a fluting shepherd boy which was probably made by John Van Nost. A door leads under a vast cedar of Lebanon to the garden proper in which terraces descend towards decorative gates. Here there has been much replanting with formal rows of Portugal laurels and ancient varieties of fruit trees. The Drydens were an old-fashioned family and rejected the late 18th-century craze for landscaping, so preserving the gentlemanly formality of an earlier period that may be seen today.

CASTLE ASHBY GARDENS
Northamptonshire

CASTLE ASHBY was built for the Compton family between 1574 and 1640 and it is still in their hands. The Marquess of Northampton has recently undertaken a strikingly successful restoration of house and garden. A Victorian terraced garden below the house has been brilliantly restored with scalloped fountains, ribbon carpet bedding and elaborate

Castle Ashby NN7 1LQ
5m E of Northampton by
A428
Tel: 01604 696696
Fax: 0604 696516

Owner: The Marquess of
Northampton

Open: Daily 10–one hour
before sunset. 25 acres.
Terrace garden by
appointment only

arabesques of gravel cut into the turf. Marvellous parkland to the south-west was laid out by 'Capability' Brown in 1761, and much replanting of trees has been carried out. The Italian garden has a glamorous conservatory designed by Matthew Digby Wyatt, overlooking formal gardens with a pond, yew topiary and terracotta urns. A path leads downhill to an arboretum with some fine trees, especially the specimens of weeping beech.

CASTLE BROMWICH HALL GARDENS
Birmingham

Old Chester Road, Castle
Bromwich B36 9BT
6m NE of city centre by
A47, near Jnct 5 of M6
(exit northbound only;
entry southbound only)
Tel: 0121 749 4100

Owner: Castle Bromwich
Hall Gardens Trust

Open: Easter to Sept, Mon
to Thur 1.30–4.30, Sat, Sun
and Bank Hol Mon 2–6.
10 acres

CASTLE BROMWICH HALL is a fine brick mansion built in the 17th century for the Bridgeman family. The gardens are an exciting survival from the heyday of English formal garden design of the late 17th and early 18th century and are in the process of restoration by a privately formed trust. Already much has been done and this is a very rare opportunity to see an authentic restoration of a garden of this period in a mavellous setting of old brick walls and fine garden buildings. The site is a west-facing slope divided down the centre by a holly walk – a broad path lined with regularly spaced variegated hollies – a replanting of the 'Gilded ever Green' mentioned in surviving records. One end of the walk is punctuated by an elegant pedimented brick orangery and the other by the corresponding recently restored music room. Above the walk is an area of 'wilderness', formal shubberies with winding walks, and below, kitchen gardens and a holly maze. Work on other features is going ahead and it will be fascinating to follow this restoration as it progresses.

CHARLECOTE PARK
Warwickshire

THE APPROACH to Charlecote – across an ancient park with grazing fallow deer – has wonderful atmosphere. The house, originally an Elizabethan mansion, was comprehensively done over in the 19th century. The garden has been revitalised in recent

Wellesbourne, Warwick
CV35 9ER
5m E of
Stratford-on-Avon by
B4086
Tel: 01789 470277

Owner:
The National Trust

Open: Apr to Oct, Fri to
Tue (closed Good Fri)
11–6. 30 acres. House
open

years by the National Trust, with lively mixed borders in the walled forecourt with its ornate turreted gate-tower. Charlecote has associations with Shakespeare – he is supposed to have poached here as a lad – and a border of flowers mentioned in his plays commemorates him. Behind the house the River Avon curves across flat parkland with avenues radiating into the distance. An admirable park walk of about one mile runs along the banks of the river, girdling the estate, and gives wonderful shifting views of the house and its lovely setting.

CHATSWORTH
Derbyshire

Bakewell DE4 1PP
4m E of Bakewell by A6 or
A619 and minor roads
Tel: 01246 582204
Fax: 01246 583536

Owner: Chatsworth House
Trust

Open: Easter to Oct, daily
11–5. 100 acres. House open

THE CAVENDISHES first made a garden at Chatsworth in the 16th century, and it was subsequently added to by many of the greatest garden designers and architects of the day. In the late 17th century London and Wise were called in; in the 18th century 'Capability' Brown landscaped the garden, undoing one of the greatest of all formal gardens; in the 19th century Joseph Paxton was head gardener, adding great conservatories and rockeries. Today, the garden is full of reminders of the past – a handsome formal scheme of lime walks and pools to the south; Paxton's 'conservative' wall; an exquisite orangery of 1698; the dazzling cascade house of 1703 over whose domed roof water pours as though off an umbrella. But this is not a museum and there are lively new borders in front of the orangery shop and the charming caprice of a miniature ornamental *potager*. The 1 1/2-acre working kitchen garden is now visitable, and the great yew maze planted in 1961 is once again open. Above all, views across the valley beyond the great house to exquisite pastoral scenery, provide an incomparable setting. Good plants are sold at the plant centre, and Chatsworth makes its own garden furniture which is of very high quality.

COTON MANOR

Northamptonshire

nr Guilsborough NN6 8RQ
10m NW of Northampton by A50
Tel: 01604 740219

Owner: Mr and Mrs Ian Pasley-Tyler

Open: Easter to Sept, Wed to Sun 12–8 (also Bank Hol Mon). 10 acres

THE GARDENS at Coton Manor are better than ever, with sparkling evidence of horticultural enterprise. The land sloping away from the gabled stone house is divided into areas of strikingly varied character – from sun-baked bed to woodland rill edged with moisture-loving plants. The paved terrace south of the house, full of plant interest and overhung with the rose 'Seven Sisters', leads to a fortissimo herbaceous border hedged in holly. At a distance from the house an entirely new development is a pretty formal herb parterre with gravel paths. Everywhere there are roses, and other excellent and unusual plants, and the garden is maintained to very high standards. There is an attractive plant-sales area in the shade of a handsome black walnut.

COTTAGE GARDEN ROSES
Staffordshire

Illustration: Rosa *'Souvenir du Docteur Jamain'*

Woodland House, Stretton, nr Stafford ST19 9LG
9m SW of Stafford by A449; 2m from Jnct 12 of M6
Tel: 01785 840217

Open: Daily 9–6

Illustration opposite: The borders at Cottesbrooke Hall

THIS NURSERY was formerly known under the delightful name of Roses du Temps Passé and specialised in the very best old and wild roses. To this original collection have been added modern roses of high quality, all possessing the virtues of beautiful flowers and lovely scent found in the older kinds. John Scarman, who runs the nursery, knows an immense amount about these plants and has produced one of the best catalogues ever assembled, beautifully illustrated in colour and with a great deal of background information about roses and their cultivation. He describes it as a selective guide to the most interesting and reliable roses. Roses may be bought in containers at the nursery or supplied bare-rooted by post. The Rose Garden School at the nursery runs attractive residential courses on practical rose gardening, with visits to other gardens.

COTTESBROOKE HALL
Northamptonshire

nr Northampton NN6 8PF
9m NW of Northampton by A50 (A14–A1M1 link road)
Tel: 01604 505808

Owner: Captain John Macdonald-Buchanan

Open: 8 Apr to 29 Sept, Wed, Thur, Fri and Bank Hol Mons, also Suns in Sept 2–5. 25 acres. House open

SOME GARDENS DESERVE to be better known and Cottesbrooke is a prime example. The beautiful early 18th-century brick and stone house has a garden which matches it for beauty and interest. It looks out over wonderful 18th-century parkland and a central vista is aligned on the distant spire of Brixworth church. The garden today is the result of many different influences – the present owner's mother, Lady Macdonald-Buchanan, the Arts and Crafts designer Edward Schultz, Dame Sylvia Crowe and Sir Geoffrey Jellicoe. Around the house there is a

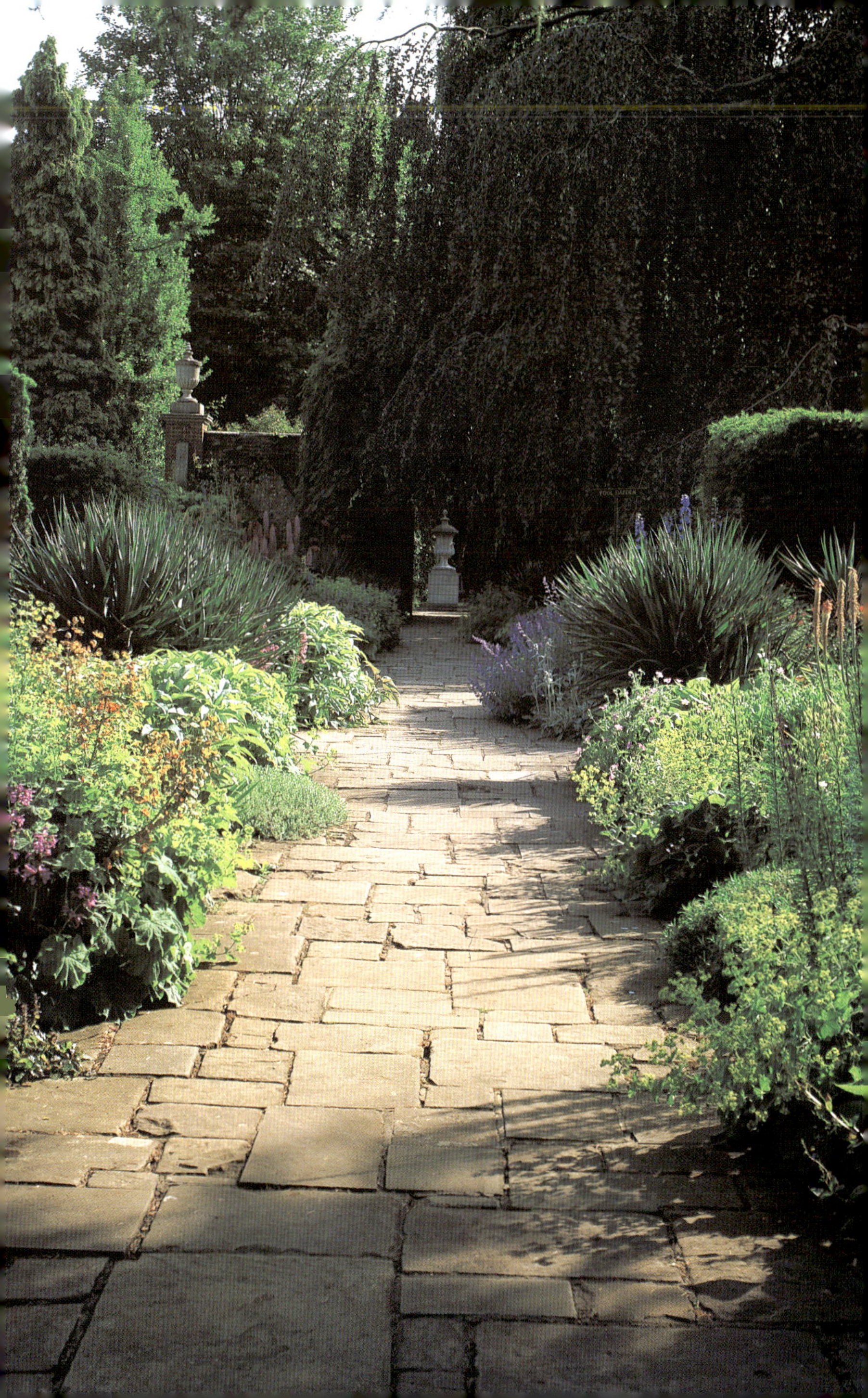

cornucopia of formal gardens: a pair of fortissimo herbaceous borders; a stately walk with yew hedges and wrought-iron gates with fine piers; enclosed gardens with pools and a pergola; and a south-facing terrace with statues and plantings of roses and agapanthus. All about is splendid parkland and countless good trees. At a distance from the house, the wild garden has a beautifully planted stream – arched bridges and many Japanese maples give an eastern atmosphere. There are few gardens anywhere with so much to admire and enjoy as Cottesbrooke.

FARNBOROUGH HALL
Warwickshire

nr Banbury, Oxfordshire
OX17 1DU
6m N of Banbury off A423
Tel: 01295 89 202

Owner:
The National Trust

Open: Apr to Sept, Wed and Sat 2–6; also 5 and 6 May 2–6. Terrace walk only, Thur and Fri 2–6. 16 acres

FARNBOROUGH is a very unusual intimate landscape garden laid out in the 18th century – delicate chamber music rather than resounding symphony. William Holbech inherited the estate with its handsome late 17th-century house in 1717 and, with the help of the elusive Sanderson Miller, laid out the grounds in the new landscape taste. Behind the house a half-mile long terrace of grass curves up a slope. Woodland presses in on one side and, on the other, there are occasional views of the countryside and parkland. The terrace is embellished with two pavilions, one of which is an unusual oval in section, with an open loggia, and the other in the form of a columned temple. Hidden in the woods a game-larder is built in the form of an exquisite temple. The very end of the terrace is marked by a slender obelisk. It is one of the most original and memorable landscape gardens in the country.

FIBREX NURSERIES LTD
Warwickshire

Illustration: Polystichum setiferum

Honeybourne Road,
Pebworth, nr
Stratford-upon-Avon
CV37 8XT
5m NW of Chipping
Camden by B4081 and
minor roads
Tel: 01789 720788
Fax: 01789 721162

Open: Jan to Mar, Sept to
Nov, Mon to Fri 12–5; Apr
to Aug, Tue to Sun 12–5;
closed Dec

THE NURSERY has four specialities, in each of which it offers marvellous collections. First, its pelargonium list is enormous, essential browsing for anyone with an interest in those plants. Second, there is a rich selection of ivies with, for example, over 200 different varieties of *Hedera helix*. Third, it has a particularly attractive collection of hardy ferns for which a good catalogue is issued with much valuable information. Lastly, there is a unique selection of very rare cultivars of *Helleborus orientalis*, known as the Raithby hybrids, with lovely and unusual colouring. Mail order is provided and lists (two 2nd-class stamps) of each speciality are published.

HADDON HALL
Derbyshire

Bakewell DE4 1LA
2m SE of Bakewell by A6
Tel: 01629 812855
Fax: 01629 814379

Owner: The Duke of
Rutland

Open: Apr to Jun, Sept,
daily 11–6; Jul and Aug,
daily except Sun 11–6. 6
acres. House open

HADDON HALL is an intensely romantic place: a vast castle, built between the 12th and 17th centuries, with turrets, crenellations and tracery windows. It is set in hilly wooded countryside and the garden still has some of the character of the formal gardens of the 17th century. The south garden, a series of terraces with balustrades, dates from the very early 17th century. Buttresses at the lowest level make an attractive and protected setting for roses and other flowering shrubs and climbers. There is a fountain and an immense collection of roses but the eye is constantly drawn to the old stone of the castle and to the river looping through the rural landscape below.

HADDONSTONE LTD
Northamptonshire

The Forge House, Church Lane, East Haddon, Northampton NN6 8DB
8m NW of Northampton off A428
Tel: 01604 770711
Fax: 01604 770027

Open: Mon to Fri 9–5.30 (closed Bank Hol Mon and 25 Dec)

GARDEN ORNAMENTS and buildings made of reconstituted stone have a long and honourable history. Haddonstone is one of the leading manufacturers and produces a very wide range of statues, urns, columns, garden buildings and architectural detailing. It also makes individual architectural pieces to customers' specifications. Many of the designs are faithful copies of surviving examples in historic gardens. A beautifully kept show garden displays many of the products in a setting planned to display their ornamental use. An elegant catalogue is produced and ornaments may be supplied by Haddonstone's own delivery service.

HARDWICK HALL
Derbyshire

Doe Lea, Chesterfield
S44 5QJ
6 1/2m W of Mansfield by A6175 and minor roads, nr Jnct 29 of M1
Tel: 01246 850430

Owner:
The National Trust

Open: 30 Mar to Oct, daily 12.30–5 or sunset if earlier (closed Good Fri). 7 acres. House open

BESS OF HARDWICK married successfully (four times) and this is her final architectural flourish, built in the late 16th century when she was in her seventies and Countess of Shrewsbury. She ornamented the parapet of her great house with her initials, E.S., carved in fretted stone against the sky. The gardens are disposed in the Elizabethan stone courts to the west and south of the house. The entrance court, with a fine old cedar of Lebanon on the lawn, has splendid new mixed borders in which colour and foliage have been cunningly chosen. Repeated plantings of the sprawling, elegant *Aralia elata* 'Aureovariegata', and in late summer of the arching plumes of miscanthus, give structure to a dashing colour scheme – hot reds, oranges and yellow near the house, and blues, whites and yellow farther away. The south court is divided into four by yew and hornbeam hedges. One of the divisions is a virtuoso herb garden in which pillars of golden and ordinary hop rise magnificently from a sea of angelica, lavender, sage, sweet cicely and thyme.

HOLDENBY HOUSE GARDENS
Northamptonshire

Holdenby, nr Northampton
NN6 8DJ
6 1/2m NW of
Northampton by A428 and
minor roads; signposted off
A428 and A50
Tel: 01604 770074
Fax: 01604 770962

Owner: Mr and Mrs James Lowther

Open: Easter to Sept, Sun 2–6 and Bank Hol Mon; Jul and Aug also open Thurs 1–5. *Note:* Entrance through falconry centre. 10 acres

HOLDENBY WAS BUILT in the 16th century by the Hattons who also owned Kirby Hall. In its day it was one of the great houses of England and had a spectacular garden of which tantalising traces remain today – two magnificent archways and grandiose terracing in the fields. The present house is Victorian although two magnificent Elizabethan stone arches survive in a field at a distance from the house. By far the best feature of the garden today is a dazzling little evocation of a 16th-century garden designed by Rosemary Verey. Enclosed in yew hedges, with a sundial at the centre, surrounding beds are decorated with lollipops of variegated box or holly, mounds of santolina and hedges of lavender and artemisia. In summer there are drifts of white, mauve or purple *Salvia viridis* and the surrounding beds are filled with culinary herbs. The whole is overlooked by a shady gazebo of clipped yew.

KEDLESTON HALL

Derbyshire

Derby DE6 4JN
5m NW of Derby by A52
and minor roads
Tel: 01332 842191

Owner:
The National Trust

Open: Garden: 30 Mar to
Oct, Sat to Wed 11–6;
Park: Apr to Oct, daily
11–6; Nov to 18 Dec, Sat,
Sun 12–4. 7 acres of
garden. House open

KEDLESTON is the grandest and possibly the prettiest of Robert Adam's houses, built for Nathaniel Curzon in the 1760s. Adam also had a hand in the park which forms a lovely approach for the house. To the north, a long serpentine lake is spanned by a three-arched bridge with a rocky cascade below it, and nearby, on the banks, a charming Fishing Room with a Venetian window is flanked by a pair of pedimented boathouses. Behind the house, in the well wooded old pleasure grounds, a circular garden of beds of roses radiating from a central pool is hedged in laurel and overlooked by a domed hexagonal temple. Shrubberies of dogwoods, rhododendrons and roses are embellished by a fine stone urn and, round a corner, the Medicean Lion rises up with a roguish grin.

KIRBY HALL

Northamptonshire

4m NE of Corby by minor
roads
Tel: 01536 203230

Owner: English Heritage

Open: Daily 10–6. 5 acres

THIS IS A GHOSTLY place on the edge of the industrial sprawl of Corby – the uninhabited remains of an exquisite late 16th-century palace built for one of Queen Elizabeth's favourite courtiers, Sir Christopher Hatton. In the late 17th century Charles Hatton made a great garden here, which was restored after excavations in the 1930s. But this was highly inauthentic – full of HT roses and with a jolly Victorian flavour. Hatton's garden is particularly well documented, including detailed lists of the plants. English Heritage is now in the process, rather slowly, of redoing it and it will be fascinating to see what it achieves. In the last two years the turf plats and gravel paths in front of the house have been re-made and a few old varieties of fruit trees planted. If what is eventually achieved is anything like as beautiful as the house it will be wonderful to see.

LEA GARDENS
Derbyshire

Lea, Matlock DE4 5GH
5m SE of Matlock by A6
and minor roads
Tel: 01629 534380
Fax: 01629 534260

Owner: Mr and Mrs J. Tye

Open: 20 Mar to 15 Jul, daily 10–7. 4 acres

THIS GARDEN, inspired by Bodnant and Exbury, although quite small by comparison, was started in 1935 by John Marsden-Smedley. It is a marvellous site, high up on south-facing wooded slopes that run down to the valley of the River Derwent. It makes a splendid setting for the excellent collection of rhododendrons which Marsden-Smedley built up. Subsequent owners have developed the garden even further and added many new trees and herbaceous plants. The nursery sells alpines, conifers, azaleas, rhododendrons and kalmias. A list is issued (s.a.e. and 30p) and there is a mail order service.

MELBOURNE HALL
Derbyshire

MELBOURNE IS a fascinating place. The house, of grey stone, presents its most glamorous façade, of 1744, to the garden which was laid out in the early 18th century. Giant steps of turf descend to the Great

Melbourne D73 1EN
9m S of Derby by A453
Tel: 01332 862502

Owner: Lord Ralph Kerr

Open: Apr to Sept, Wed, Sat, Sun and Bank Hol Mon 2–6. 16 acres. House open Aug only

Basin, a curved pool that crisply reflects the house. On one side is the 'Birdcage', Robert Bakewell's airy arbour of wrought-iron of exquisite delicacy. To the south lies a pattern of lime alleys, unchanged in almost 300 years, with grassy walks punctuated by urns and statues of marvellous quality, some of them by John Van Nost, the greatest maker of garden ornaments of the early 18th century. Of the same period, leading to the west, is an immense tunnel of yew between whose gnarled trunks the visitor may walk. On its south side are some very good new mixed borders, showing that the spirit of gardening at Melbourne is still alive and kicking.

THE MENAGERIE

Northamptonshire

Horton. Northampton
NN7 2BX
5m SE of Northampton off B526; entrance just S of the village of Horton
Tel: 01604 870957
Fax: 01604 870923

Open: Apr to Sept, Wed 10–4. 3 acres

THE MENAGERIE is an enchanting classical building of the 1750s designed by the mysterious architect and garden designer Thomas Wright, 'the wizard of Durham'. Gervase Jackson-Stops rescued it from dereliction, restored it impeccably and made it into a house. More recently he turned his mind to the garden and transformed it into a delicious *jeu d'esprit*. An avenue of limes runs away from the south front, flanked by radiating hornbeam alleys. Overlooking a round pool on each side is a thatched building – one suavely Gothic, the other crisply Classical. But in each case the facade that faces the wilder part of the garden is faced with rustic woodwork, encrusted with tormented oak boles. The borders by the south-facing terrace are finely planted with striking foliage – artichokes, delphiniums, eremurus, thalictrum – and subtle colours. At the entrance is the admirable Drywood Nursery selling a short but very choice range of plants. As we went to press Gervase Jackson-Stops died – The Menagerie is a wonderful memorial to him.

MOSELEY OLD HALL

Staffordshire

Moseley Old Hall Lane, Fordhouses, Wolverhampton WV10 7HY
3 1/2m N of Wolverhampton, between A460 and A449, S of M54
Tel: 01902 782808

Owner:
The National Trust

Open: 16 Mar to Oct, Sat, Sun, Bank Hol Mon and following Tue 1.30–5.30 (Bank Hol Mon 11–5); May to Oct, also Wed 1.30–5.30; Jul to Aug, also Tue 1.30–5.30. Nov to 22 Dec, Sun 1.30–4.30. 1 acre

AROUND AN UNASSUMING Elizabethan and 17th-century house the National Trust has made a little formal garden rich in the features of the 17th century. The old windows overlook a parterre with a geometric pattern of box hedges, coloured pebbles and lollipops of clipped box – all this was taken from a design of 1640. A nut walk leads to a paved path flanked by pairs of medlars, mulberries and quinces. Running down one side of the parterre is a 'carpenter's work' tunnel, festooned with purple-leafed vines and clematis, underplanted with aquilegias, geraniums and lavender. The enclosed front garden which has box topiary clipped into cones and spirals, and borders of period plants.

PACKWOOD HOUSE
Warwickshire

Lapworth, Solihull
B94 6AT
11m SE of Birmingham by A34
Tel: 01564 782 024

Owner:
The National Trust

Open: Apr to Sept, Wed to Sun and Bank Hol Mon (closed Good Fri) 1.30–6; Oct, Wed to Sun 12.30–4.30.
5 acres. House open

A SOLEMN GROUP of immensely tall clipped yews, known as the Multitude and the Apostles, surrounds a mount covered in box. A mysterious spiral path leads to the top which is crowned by a clipped parasol shape of yew. Some of these giant topiary pieces date back to the 17th century and have an unforgettable atmosphere. Nearer the house, a stately gabled brick mansion of the late 16th century, there is a completely different mood with a pronounced Arts and Crafts feel. A fine wrought-iron gate leads down into in a handsomely walled garden overlooked by a long terrace edged with flowery borders and with a gazebo at each end. A decorative sunken garden with a pool is hedged in yew and has lively summer bedding schemes.

RENISHAW HALL
Derbyshire

THIS IS ONE of the greatest, and most attractive, gardens in England. It is the creation of Sir George Sitwell who in the 1890s studied Italian Renaissance gardens (visiting over 200 of them), digested what he saw and came back to the family estate in Derbyshire determined to make an Italianate garden. On south-facing slopes, in an industrial area of England not much resembling Tuscany, he laid out

Illustration opposite:
Renishaw Hall

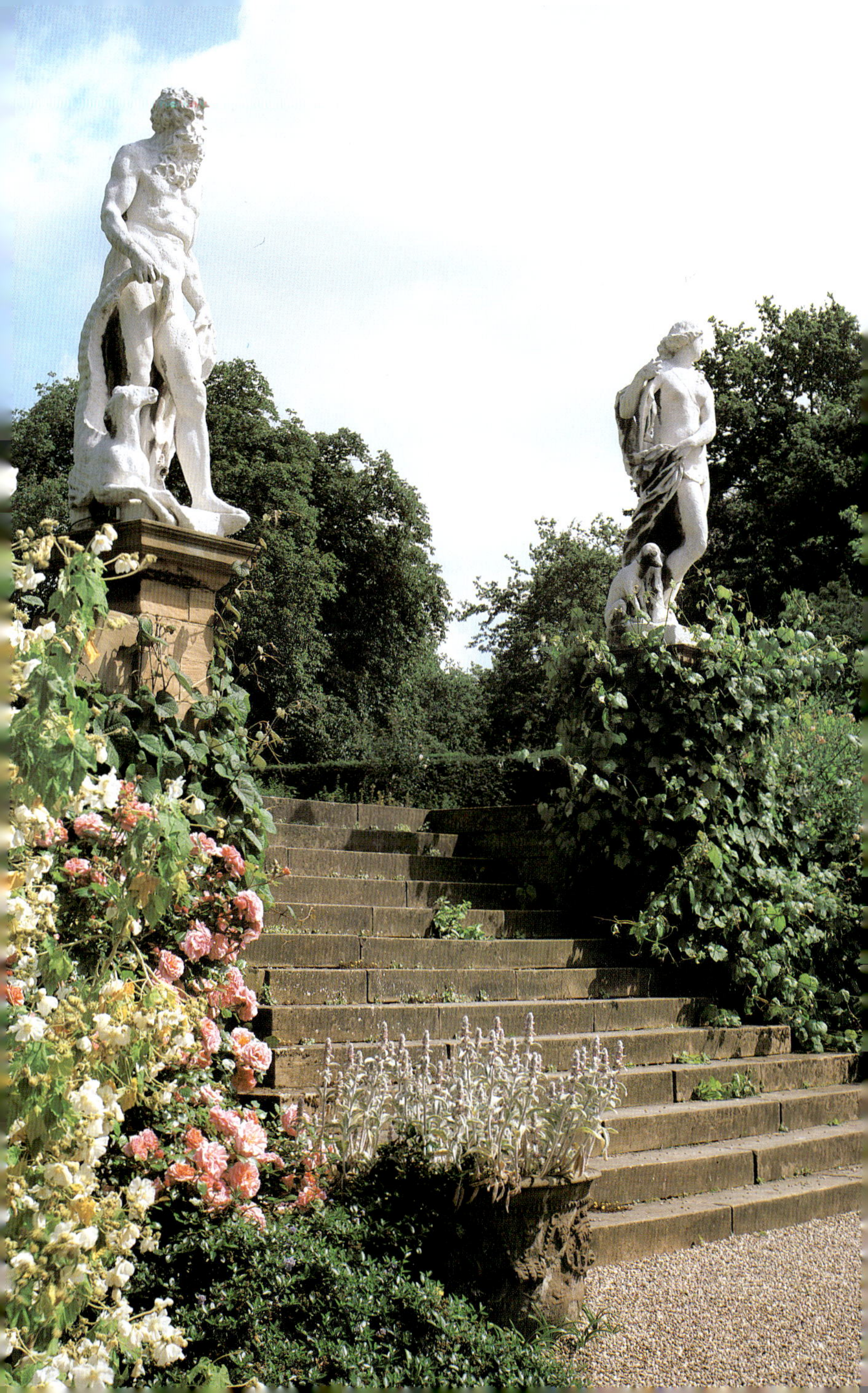

Renishaw,
Sheffield S31 9WB
On the edge of the village
of Renishaw, 1m NW of
Jnct 30 of the M1
Tel: 01246 432042/01777
860755

Owner:
Sir Reresby Sitwell Bt

Open: Easter to mid Sept,
Fri, Sat, Sun and Bank Hol
Mon 10.30–4.30

a series of yew-hedged terraces sparkling with statues, urns and fountains. Sir George regarded flowers with some contempt – 'such flowers as might be permitted . . . [should not] call attention to themselves by hue or scent.' The garden he made is beautifully cared for by the family today. However, there are now admirable borders, well judged colour associations and many floriferous fripperies which will delight modern visitors. There is an outstanding collection of shrub roses which reaches its climax in the lower terrace where in late June their scent, intermingled with that of *Buddleja alternifolia* and philadelphus, provides a delicious experience. Although 'hue and scent' are rather prominent here, it does not in the slightest detract from Sir George's extraordinary Renaissance vision.

RYTON ORGANIC GARDENS
Warwickshire

Ryton-on-Dunsmore,
Coventry CV8 3LG
5m SE of Coventry by A45
Tel: 01203 303517
Fax: 01203 639229

Owner: The Henry
Doubleday Research
Association

Open: Daily 10–5.30
(except Christmas holiday).
10 acres

THIS IS the home of the National Centre for Organic Gardening. As well as being the leading research centre of its subject, it is a fascinating display garden, showing the techniques of ecologically friendly gardening. Regarded by some until recently as the province of cranks, this is now seen to be the best way to garden, working with nature rather than zapping it with chemicals. At Ryton, demonstration areas show techniques of vegetable growing, how to make compost, how to control weeds and pests and many other things. A wildflower meadow is rich in native plants; a rose garden has varieties that are resistant to disease. This is not only muck and magic – there are also some attractively laid out pleasure gardens. Any gardener will learn from the insights of this unique place.

SHUGBOROUGH
Staffordshire

SHUGBOROUGH is a dream-like picturesque landscape garden in which marvellous ornaments and garden buildings float into view at every turn. From the house, largely built by Samuel Wyatt for Viscount Anson in the 1790s, a series of shallow

Milford, nr Stafford
ST17 0XB
6m E of Stafford by A513
Tel: 01889 88 1388

Owner:
The National Trust

Open: 23 Mar to 29 Sept, daily 11–5. 18 acres. House open

terraces descend to the River Sow, decorated with golden yew topiary and rose beds. A wild picturesque ruin designed in 1750 by Thomas Wright crouches on the water's edge. To one side a rose garden with an Edwardian flavour has roses trained on arches and pillars. A path now winds away into the informal heart of the garden where an arched scarlet Chinoiserie bridge leads to the pagoda-like Chinese house (1747). In the woods there is a mysterious Cat's Monument; the riddling Shepherd's Monument; a dapper Doric temple; and, in front of the house, handsome parkland with James 'Athenian' Stuart's Temple of the Winds.

STRATFORD-UPON-AVON GARDENS
Warwickshire

Illustration: The garden of Hall's Croft

STRATFORD IS, of course, thoroughly given over to the celebration of Shakespeare's life and work. Some of the various old houses associated with him in and around the town have gardens of considerable charm. **Shakespeare's Birthplace** (Henley Street. *Open:* Mar to Oct, daily 9–5.30 (Sun 10–5.30); Nov to Feb, daily 9.30–4 (Sun 10.30–4)). A lawn at the back is ornamented with trees such as a fig, hawthorn, medlar and quince, all of which are mentioned in the plays. A pair of pretty, mixed borders is planted to give interest throughout the year. **Hall's Croft** (Old Town. *Open:* Mar to Oct, daily 9.30–5 (Sun 10.30–5); Nov to Feb, daily 10–4

(Sun 1.30–4)). The garden is walled and has a splendid old mulberry and borders running from a sundial to the back of the half-timbered house. **New Place** (Chapel Lane. *Open:* Mar to Oct, daily 9.30–5 (Sun 10.30–5); Nov to Feb, daily 10–4 (Sun 1.30–4)). A knot garden follows Elizabethan patterns in its layout of low hedges of box, hyssop and santolina and its surrounding apple tunnels, but is planted in thoroughly 20th-century summer bedding. The Great Garden behind has topiary of box and yew and burgeoning herbaceous borders. **Anne Hathaway's Cottage** (in the village of Shottery, 1 1/4m NW of Stratford by A422. *Open:* Mar to Oct, daily 9–5.30 (Sun 10–5.30); Nov to Feb, daily 9.30–4 (Sun 10.30–4)). At the front a profusion of planting gives a vision of the English cottage garden.

SULGRAVE MANOR
Northamptonshire

Sulgrave, nr Banbury
OX17 2SD
7m NE of Banbury by
B4525
Tel: 01295 760205

Owner: The Peoples of England and America

Open: Apr to Sept, daily except Wed 10.30–1, 2–5.30 (closed 16 Jun); Oct, daily except Wed 10.30–1, 2–4; Nov, Dec and Mar, Sat and Sun 10.30–1, 2–4 (closed 25, 26, 27, 30 and 31 Dec).
2 acres. House open

GEORGE WASHINGTON'S ancestors lived here and the American connection is proudly emphasised, with the stars and stripes flying above the roof. The house is a 16th-century stone-tiled manor and the garden was designed in 1927 by Sir Reginald Blomfield, who laid out a crisply formal entrance of yew hedges. The entrance leads across an orchard with gravel walks, lawns decorated with topiary yew birds and herbaceous borders flanking the porch. A little herb parterre on a terrace above is shaded by an old walnut tree. A rose garden is edged in box and a sundial stands in the middle, fringed with lavender. There is no attempt at historical planting but the garden makes an attractive setting for the old house.

UPTON HOUSE
Warwickshire

Banbury, Oxfordshire
OX15 6HT
7m NW of Banbury by
A422
Tel: 01295 670266

Owner:
The National Trust

Open: Apr to Oct, Sat to
Wed 2–6. 19 acres. House
open

THE HOUSE, finished in 1695 and built of golden Hornton stone, lies on the edge of a steep combe; on its slopes the garden is spread like a patchwork quilt. Formal steps and a balustrade entwined with wisteria lead downwards towards areas enclosed in wavy old yew hedges – among them a marvellous vegetable garden. Sweeping down the hill are a pair of herbaceous borders with accents of hot red and a cool turf path running down between them to the pool at the bottom. A mile from the house is a delightful piece of landscape gardening dating from the 1760s – a lake and Doric temple (possibly by Robert Adam) deftly slipped into the countryside, the very essence of 18th-century elegance.

WARWICK CASTLE
Warwickshire

Warwick CV34 4QU
In the centre of Warwick
Tel: 01926 408000
Fax: 01926 401692

Owner: Pearsons plc

Open: Daily 10–6 (5 in winter); closed Christmas Day. 60 acres. Castle open

THIS SPECTACULAR CASTLE was until 1978 the home of the Earls of Warwick. In front of the orangery there is a Victorian parterre, with vivid contrasts of golden and common yew and blood-red roses. Peacocks preen and fit well with the mood of the place. The land falls steeply away and, framed by 18th-century cedars of Lebanon, is a fabulous view – 'Capability' Brown's breathtaking park sweeping down to a curve in the River Avon 200 feet below. The Victorian rose garden has been beautifully restored; old roses with irresistible names like 'Adélaïde d'Orléans' and 'Variegata di Bologna' are draped in festoons and rise in columns to produce unforgettably swoony scents in late June and July.

WHICHFORD POTTERY
Warwickshire

JIM KEELING, trained in the traditional craft of hand-throwing terracotta pots, now leads a team of potters making a very wide range of different styles. From plain flower pots to giant Florentine vases dripping with swags and foliage, all are

Whichford, nr
Shipston-on-Stour
CV36 5PG
22m NW of Oxford E of
A3400
Tel: 01608 684416
Fax: 01608 684833

Open: Mon to Fri 9–5, Sat
and Bank Hol Mon 10–4

beautifully made in local clay and are guaranteed frostproof. There is nowhere in Britain quite like this and it is very well worth visiting. Outside the pottery are displayed immense numbers of pots and planters, some beautifully planted up to show their effectiveness in the garden. An excellent catalogue is produced and pots may be delivered by carrier.

WIGHTWICK MANOR
West Midlands

Wightwick Bank,
Wolverhampton WV6 8EE
3m W of Wolverhampton
by A454
Tel: 01902 761108

Owner:
The National Trust

Open: Mar to Dec, Thur
and Sat, Bank Hol Mon
and preceding Sun
2.30–5.30. 10 acres. House
open

WIGHTWICK MANOR is a piece of ripe High Victoriana – a decorative Pre-Raphaelite mansion made for a paint millionaire – with a garden in keeping. It was laid out in 1887, partly by the watercolourist Alfred Parsons and partly by the architect and garden designer T.H. Mawson, who was responsible for the south terrace and the dramatic procession of great clipped drums of yew that marches purposefully away from it. On one side a 'writers' bed' is filled with plants from the gardens of Dickens, William Morris, Shelley and Tennyson. A formal garden of zig-zag yew hedges, yew topiary and rose beds leads to a walk of variegated holly.

**THE
EAST
OF
ENGLAND**
Bedfordshire
Cambridgeshire
Essex
Hertfordshire
Lincolnshire
Norfolk
Suffolk

CAISTOR
Potterton & Martin
A46
Valley Clematis
LINCOLN
Doddington Hall
Gunby Hall
SKEGNESS
Belton House
GRANTHAM
A1
A17
Norfolk Lavender
A149
Sheringham Park
CROMER
Felbrigg Hall
Sandringham House
Mannington Hall
Wolterton Park
Blickling Hall
KING'S LYNN
Hoecroft Plants
The Romantic Garden Nursery
A140
GREAT YARMOUTH
A47
Peckover House
NORWICH
Fairhaven Garden Trust
PETERBOROUGH
Oxburgh Hall
Ravningham Hall
Peter Beale's Roses
Reads Nursery
Somerleyton Hall
A11
Euston Hall
Blooms
Wootten's Plants
A10
Monksilver Nursery
Cambridge College Gardens
Hartshall Nursery Stock
Cambridge Botanic Gardens
BURY ST EDMUNDS
Park Green Nurseries
Fisks Clematis Nursery
A45
Anglesey Abbey
Ickworth
Crossing House
CAMBRIDGE
Haughley Park
Helmingham Hall
Wimpole Hall
Padlock Croft
BEDFORD
A12
The Swiss Garden
Docwra's Manor
Melford Hall
Notcutts
IPSWICH
Wrest Park
ROYSTON
Gannock Growers
Paradise Centre
M1
Audley End
R. Harkness
Benington Lordship
M11
B. & H.M. Baker
Saling Hall
COLCHESTER
LUTON
A120
Beth Chatto Gardens
Luton Hoo
Knebworth
A1(M)
Hopleys Plants
ST ALBANS
Hatfield House
CHELMSFORD
The Gardens of the Rose
M25
Hyde Hall
LONDON

ANGLESEY ABBEY AND GARDEN

Cambridgeshire

Lode, Cambridge CB5 9EJ
In the village of Lode 6m
NE of Cambridge by B1102
Tel: 01223 811200

Owner:
The National Trust

Open: 23 Mar to 7 Jul,
Wed to Sun and Bank Hol
Mon 11–5.30; 8 Jul to 8
Sept, daily 10–5.30; 11 Sept
to 3 Nov, Wed to Sun
11–5.30. 100 acres. House
open

ANGLESEY ABBEY was an Augustinian priory and its buildings, with many additions, form an alluring ornament at the heart of gardens that Lord Fairhaven started to lay out in 1930. He deployed a marvellous collection of statues and garden ornaments, giving them their full decorative presence in subtly contrived settings of alleys, vistas, hedged enclosures and distant prospects. Handsome parkland and some exceptional old trees – particularly limes – give his scheme a rich background. The statues and bold formal designs are what makes Anglesey famous, and walking among them is indeed an exciting experience. But contrasting with these grand formal schemes are more intimate areas – gardens devoted to dahlias and hyacinths, some exceptionally good borders in the herbaceous garden enclosed in a great horseshoe hedge of beech, and a river walk with grassy banks and a mill-house of rural atmosphere.

AUDLEY END

Essex

AUDLEY END is a much fiddled with Jacobean mansion set in splendid parkland designed by 'Capability Brown' from 1762 onwards. Shortly after this Robert Adam added various splendid buildings to the estate – a three-arched bridge over the Cam, a

near Saffron Walden
1m W of Saffron Walden
by B1383
Tel: 01799 522842

Owner: English Heritage

Open: Apr to Sept, Wed to Sun and Bank Hol Mon 12–6. 50 acres House open

Temple of Victory and Lady Portsmouth's Column. Newly restored is a great flower parterre east of the house, which was designed in 1832 by William Gilpin. A vast geometric pattern of beds spreads out below the windows of the house. The planting is a mixture of old shrub roses, herbaceous perennials and annuals; all the plants are known to have been available when the parterre was originally laid out.

B. & H.M. BAKER
Essex

Greenstead Green,
Halstead CO9 1RJ
6m NE of Braintree by
A131 and minor roads
Tel: 01787 476369/472900

Open: Mon to Fri 8–4.30, Sat to Sun 9–12, 2–4.30

THE BAKERS' SPECIALITY is fuchsias and their fuchsia-red list is a connoisseur's delight. There has been an explosion of new fuchsia cultivars in recent years and some of the best old varieties have been trampled to death in the rush to buy new ones. Baker's fascinating catalogue (20p plus stamp) lists varieties going back to the early 19th century and gives the dates of introduction and the names of their breeders. Many of these represent the best varieties of the past – very few are the latest. Most are, of course, the tender varieties but there is also a section devoted to hardy kinds as well as a very unusual list of species. No mail order service is available.

PETER BEALES ROSES
Norfolk

Illustration: Rosa '*Gruss an Aachen*'

PETER BEALES is the author of one of the best rose books of recent times, *Roses*, and here at Attleborough may be seen one of the best rose nurseries in Britain. It sells all kinds of roses but the heart of the business is old-fashioned, species and

London Road,
Attleborough NR17 1AY
15m SW of Norwich by
A11
Tel: 01953 454707
Fax: 01953 456845

Open: Mon to Fri 9–5, Sat
9–4.30, Sun 10–4

modern shrubs, of which it sells a staggering range. If you are searching for an old rose this is probably the best place to start with; a visit in late June will provide an unforgettable sight. A wonderful catalogue is produced, a model of such things, full of information about the history and cultivation of roses. Plants may be supplied by post.

BELTON HOUSE
Lincolnshire

Grantham NG32 2LS
3m NE of Grantham by
A607
Tel: 01476 66116

Owner:
The National Trust

Open: 30 Mar to Oct, Wed
to Sun and Bank Hol Mon
(closed Good Fri) 11–5.30.
Free access on foot to park
only, all the year from Lion
Lodge gates. 100 acres.
House open

BELTON HOUSE is an exquisite mansion dating from the 1690s. The park was landscaped in the late 18th century by William Emes in the style of 'Capability' Brown, but traces of an earlier formal garden survive – including a slender canal at the head of which is a pretty pedimented temple. Between the house and the church a grand conservatory designed by Sir Jeffry Wyatville in 1811 overlooks a formal garden with a circular pool and fountain surrounded by a low hedge of purple plum and pale pink roses. Columns of Irish yew, mounds of clipped box and stone urns give vertical emphasis. To the north of the house a walk of golden and common yew columns and mounds is backed by borders with a ghostly planting of white roses, cream petunias and lavender edging. This might have been a pompous and overwhelming setting for a very grand house but cheerfulness keeps breaking through.

THE EAST OF ENGLAND • 215

BENINGTON LORDSHIP
Hertfordshire

Benington, nr Stevenage
SG2 7BS
4m E of Stevenage by
minor roads; signposted
from Watton-at-Stone
Tel: 01438 869668
Fax: 01438 869622

Owner: Mr and Mrs
C.H.A. Bott

Open: Apr to Aug, Wed
12–5 and Sun 2–5; Jul and
Aug, also Thurs 12–5; Sept,
Wed 12–5. Easter, spring
and summer Bank Hol
Mon 12–5. 7 acres

AT BENINGTON the remains of a Norman castle, a neo-Norman gatehouse and a 1700 brick mansion give character that is in every way matched by the garden. The house looks across a gentle valley to lakes below, fed by a stream edged with acanthus, astilbes, ferns, geraniums and primulas. To one side, descending the slope, a pair of dazzling herbaceous borders has a colour scheme of cream, white, yellow and blue, with touches of orange and red. Beyond it, the walled kitchen garden has more borders, vegetables and a small nursery. On the other side of the house a formal garden has pink and white roses underplanted with irises, aquilegias and catmint.

BLICKLING HALL
Norfolk

BLICKLING HALL – turreted, gabled and irresistible – was built in around 1620 by Robert Lyminge. The chief part of the garden lies to the east of the house, where a parterre of four square herbaceous beds is

Blickling, Norwich
NR11 6NF
15m N of Norwich
Tel: 01263 733084

Owner:
The National Trust

Open: 23 Mar to 3 Nov,
daily except Mon and Thur
(open Bank Hol Mon)
11–6; Jul and Aug, daily
11–6. 46 acres. House open

brilliantly contrived: the planting rises towards the centre, giving, in late July, the shape of a pyramid. Colours are subtly graded – the beds near the house in yellow and cream, those farther away in blue, pink and red. Rounded cones and curious 'grand-piano' shapes of clipped yew, fine urns and a central fountain decorate the parterre. A pair of sphinxes starts a long gravel walk, backed by azaleas and woodland, leading to a classical temple, from which on either side oak avenues plunge into the woods.

BLOOMS OF BRESSINGHAM
Norfolk

Bressingham, nr Diss
IP22 2AB
3m W of Diss by A1066
Tel: 01379 687464
Fax: 01379 688034

Open: Daily 10–5.30

FEW FAMILIES choose their occupation to suit their name so happily as the Blooms of Bressingham. Although best known for a very wide range of herbaceous plants (more, probably, than any other nursery in the country) they also sell choice alpines, bamboos, hardy ferns, bamboos, conifers, grasses, rhododendrons, shrubs and heathers. Many varieties, especially of herbaceous plants, bear the name 'Bressingham' and give some idea of the liveliness and enterprise of this influential nursery. Although the nursery itself is primarily wholesale there is still plenty for individual gardeners to see, admire and buy. A very well planned catalogue is produced twice a year, packed with detailed information about the cultivation of the plants. New cultivars are constantly being added, particularly in the perennial department. Orders may be supplied by mail order.

BRESSINGHAM GARDENS
Norfolk

Bressingham, Diss
IP22 2AB
3m W of Diss by A1066
Tel: 01379 687386
Fax: 01379 688085

Owner: Alan Bloom

Open: Apr to Sept, daily 10–5.30. 6 acres

ALAN BLOOM has, through his nursery and his books, had a great influence on garden taste. In his own Dell garden, alongside the nursery, visitors may see these ideas put into practice. There is, of course, a huge range of herbaceous perennials grown in his famous sweeping island beds. Over 5,000 species and cultivars of herbaceous plants, including 200 or so new plants introduced by the nursery, are displayed in an informal setting. There are very few places where such a range of plants is to be seen and there is the added interest that most of them may be ordered from the nursery next door.

CAMBRIDGE BOTANIC GARDEN
Cambridgeshire

Cambridge CB2 1JF
3/4m S of city centre by Trumpington Road (A10)
Tel: 01223 336265
Fax: 01223336278

Owner: The University of Cambridge

Open: Daily 10–dusk (6 in summer, 4 in winter), closed 25 and 26 Dec. 35 acres

ALTHOUGH the primary purpose of botanic gardens is to provide material for study, many of them are both beautiful and instructive places for gardeners to visit. This is no exception, and at any time of the year there is much to be seen. Of special interest to gardeners are a particularly good rock garden in which plants are grouped according to country of origin; comprehensive collections of tulips and cranesbills; a huge collection of European species of saxifrage (of which the garden holds the National Collection); and glasshouses protecting different types of plant, from alpines to tropical food plants. There are beds of herbaceous plants and of shrubs, and everywhere there are fine trees, many rare, well displayed in the attractively laid out grounds.

CAMBRIDGE COLLEGE GARDENS
Cambridgeshire

CAMBRIDGE IS STRIKINGLY rich in planted space and the Backs running along the west bank of the Cam provide an exquisite setting for the great college buildings. Within the colleges there is some excellent

Illustration: New Court, St John's College

gardening, and in many cases these more intimate enclosures connect harmoniously with the larger landscape of the Backs. The garden at **St John's College** (St John's St; *Open:* Daily 10.30–5.30 but closed May and Jun) is approached through marvellous 16th-century courts, across the Wren Bridge which has the best view of the most glamorous Cambridge bridge, the Bridge of Sighs. Bold borders run along the gothic screen of New Court, and, in the distance, fine trees mark the Scholars' Garden hedged in yew with an old weeping ash, ornamental trees and mixed borders. **Clare College** (Trinity Lane; *Open:* 2–4) has large and varied gardens of which the best part is the Fellows' Garden, redesigned in 1947 by Professor Willmer. It lies off the Avenue, which has wonderful 18th-century wrought-iron gates, and its most spectacular feature is a dazzling pair of beautifully kept herbaceous borders in blue and yellow, with daylilies, delphiniums, thalictrum and verbascums. **Newnham College** (Sidgwick Avenue; *Open:* 9–4) has fine late-Victorian buildings by Basil Champneys and preserves gardens that are touched with the same atmosphere – yew hedges, lively borders and some excellent trees, among them several *Ailanthus altissima* and a fine *Sorbus latifolia*.

BETH CHATTO GARDENS

Essex

Elmstead Market,
Colchester CO7 7DB
1/4 mile E of Elmstead
Market by A133
Tel: 01206 822007
Fax: 01206 825933

Owner: Mrs Beth Chatto

Open: Mar to Oct, Mon to
Sat 9–5; Nov to Feb, Mon
to Fri 9–4

BETH CHATTO'S garden and nursery make a most attractive place to visit. Her nursery is particularly strong on herbaceous plants and plants with ornamental foliage. She also fully recognises the importance of a plant's natural habitat, as she has shown in her excellent books on the dry and the damp garden. The former car park has recently been transformed into a brilliant gravel garden. Beyond the nursery a series of pools runs along a hollow edged with moisture-loving plants. Farther up the slopes are sweeping beds containing immense numbers of bulbs and herbaceous perennials backed with shrubs and trees. No gardener could come here and fail to discover something seductive and unfamiliar. An informative catalogue (£2.50) is produced and plants are sold by mail.

CROSSING HOUSE

Cambridgeshire

THE URGE to make a garden can often be so overwhelming that the small matter of a railway line running through one's plot may easily be brushed aside. Mr Fuller was in charge of the railway crossing and Mrs Fuller made a garden, at first immediately

78 Meldreth Road,
Shepreth, Royston SG8 6PS
In Shepreth village 8m S of
Cambridge off A10
Tel: 01763 261071

Owner: Mr and Mrs
Douglas Fuller

Open: Daily, dawn–dusk.
1/4 acre

about the house, but increasingly along the railway line itself – which she is no longer allowed to tend. Although in general appearance a cottage garden, signs of serious plant collecting are soon detected. Here is an immense range of plants, many exceedingly rare and beautifully grown. Alpines are grown on raised beds and there are some excellent groups of particular plants – several varieties of witch hazel, for example. Winding paths and decorative ornaments and a yew arbour give the impression of space. The level of interest is unflagging and there are very many far bigger gardens in which there is much less to admire.

DOCWRA'S MANOR
Cambridgeshire

Shepreth, nr Royston
SG8 6PS
In Shepreth village 8m S of
Cambridge off A10
Tel: 01763 261473/260235

Owner: Mrs John Raven

Open: Mon, Wed and Fri 2–5; Apr to Oct, 1st Sun 2–5; Bank Hol Mon 10–5.
2 1/2 acres

COLLECTIONS OF PLANTS can be extremely boring to gardeners if they are not given a harmonious setting. Mrs Raven and her late husband took a particular interest in natural species, especially those from Mediterranean countries, and gave them a home in this cold but very dry part of England. Many of them flourished and the Ravens designed a layout which would provide both a satisfactory habitat for the plants and make an attractive garden for non-botanists. In this they were triumphantly successful. There is just enough formality, such as a decorative tunnel of pears and clematis, to prevent a mere jungle but there is no artificial regimentation of plants. Old outhouses and courtyards give protection from the wind on this flat and well drained site. An excellent nursery sells plants propagated in the garden.

DODDINGTON HALL
Lincolnshire

Doddington,
nr Lincoln LN6 4RU
5m W of Lincoln by B1190;
signposted off A46 Lincoln bypass
Tel: 01522 694308
Fax: 01522 682584

Owner: Mr and Mrs A.G. Jarvis

Open: Mar and Apr, Sun 2–6; May to Sept, Wed, Sun and Bank Hol Mon 2–6. 12 acres

ROBERT SMITHSON, the greatest Elizabethan architect, designed this lovely brick mansion which casts its spell over the gardens that surround it. Rare Elizabethan garden walls enclose the courts at back and front, making a wonderfully ornamental background to the varied planting that they enclose. The courtyard of the entrance front, has a simple pattern of lawns edged with box, mounds of clipped yew and borders flanking the porch. In the courtyard on the west side ebullient box parterres make a brilliant display, in which crown imperials and many irises are followed by roses, and where deep herbaceous borders line the walls. Beyond this a wild garden has excellent old trees, including some superb ancient sweet chestnuts, and many decorative incidents – a turf maze, an elegant Temple of the Winds and a water garden.

EUSTON HALL
Suffolk

EUSTON HALL was built by the Earl of Arlington in the 1670s, and in the early 18th century a pioneer landscape garden was laid out by William Kent; later in the century 'Capability' Brown was consulted by the 3rd Duke of Grafton. South of the house a formal terraced garden is ornamented with summer planting in urns, and a balustrade. To one side, the

Euston, Thetford IP24 2QP
3m S of Thetford by A1088
Tel: 01842 766366

Owner: The Duke and Duchess of Grafton

Open: 1 Jun to 28 Sept, Thur 2.30–5; also Sun 25 Jun and Sun 3 Sept 2.30–5. 70 acres. House open

King Charles Gate, a survival from the 17th century, leads out into the park, and in the far distance Kent's exquisite domed temple rises on an eminence. From the formal garden a beautiful wrought-iron gate leads through a high wall with a very successful mixed border. Beyond, to the west, the remains of a great lime avenue stretches out towards Kent's arched lodge. The present Duke has added new borders to the east of the house and contrived a charming setting for a wooden William Kent summer house.

THE FAIRHAVEN GARDEN TRUST
Norfolk

c/o G. Debbage, 2 The Woodlands, Pilson Green, South Walsham, Norwich NR13 6EA
9m NE of Norwich by B1140, E of the village of South Walsham
Tel: 01603 270449

Owner: The Fairhaven Garden Trust

Open: May to Sept, Tue to Sun 11-5.30 (Sat 2–5.30). 170 acres

WITH AN EXCEPTIONAL setting on the broads, this unique woodland garden was started in 1947 by Lord Fairhaven of the same family that made the garden at Anglesey Abbey. In marvellous old woodland of beech and oak, some of great age and beauty, exotic plantings are unostentatiously slipped into the scenery – azaleas, cherries, dogwoods, enkianthus and mahonias. In the spring immense spreads of bluebells are followed by candelabra primulas glittering along shady walks. Occasional glades and clearings give calm views of South Walsham Inner Broad. This is not a place for great rarities or fortissimo displays of flower power. But there is no other garden quite like it – where a lovely piece of natural landscape has been gently shaped by the restrained hand of the gardener.

FELBRIGG HALL
Norfolk

Roughton, nr Norwich
NR11 8PR
2m SW of Cromer by A148
and B1436
Tel: 01263 837444

Owner:
The National Trust

Open: 23 Mar to 3 Nov,
daily except Tue and Fri
11–5. Parkland open daily
except 25 Dec dawn–dusk.
1/2 acres. House open

A WINDY PLAIN surrounds the mansion at Felbrigg with its curious contrasting Jacobean and mid Georgian façades. Handsome parkland – dating from the 17th century and with some survivals from that time – is planted with beech, oak and sweet chestnut, but the object of chief interest is the magnificent old walled kitchen garden at a distance from the house. Gravel paths and low box hedges divide the area in which productive plants – vines, figs, pears and plums – are trained against the walls. Borders line the walls – peonies and lilies under shrub roses. An orchard is underplanted with spring bulbs and there is a collection of thorns planted in formal rows in grass. An octagonal dovecote with white doves stands in the centre of the north wall, forming an eye-catcher at the end of the central path. Of particular interest is the collection of colchicums of which Felbrigg has the National Collection.

FISKS CLEMATIS NURSERY
Suffolk

IT IS HARD to imagine any garden not possessing at least one or two clematis. Here at Jim Fisk's admirable nursery, which has its own display garden, the visitor can see an immense range of varieties. The large-flowered hybrids as well as the species and other small-flowered sorts are stocked in variety, and

Westleton, Saxmundham
IP17 3AJ
5m NE of Saxmundham by
A12 and minor roads
Tel: 01728 648263

Open: Mon to Fri 9–5; also
Sat and Sun summer only,
10–1, 2–5

many of them are rare – such as 'Louise Rowe' with frilly double and single mauve flowers. There is always something of interest flowering from spring to late autumn. A model catalogue (four 1st-class stamps), well illustrated in colour, gives much valuable information on cultivation. Fisks supply by mail order, with meticulous planting instructions.

GANNOCK GROWERS
Hertfordshire

Illustration: Lathyrus
latifolius

Gannock Green, Sandon,
Buntingford SG9 0RH
Turn SE off A505 towards
Sandon mid way between
Baldock and Royston.
Nursery is 2 1/3m from
A505 and 1/2m NW of
Sandon church
Tel: 01763 287386

Open: Mar to Oct, Tue to
Sat and Bank Hol Mon
10–4; also by appointment

GANNOCK GROWERS specialises in unusual hardy herbaceous plants. The range is wide, with many plants suitable for the border and some smaller items verging on alpines. Penny Pyle has several aquilegias, good campanulas, an unusual range of centaureas, species dianthus, eryngiums, one of the very best ranges of geraniums, lychnis, several species penstemons, a rare collection of silenes and some decorative sedges and grasses. There are countless individual plants, rarely seen in nurseries, that will seduce any gardener. Most plants are priced by pot size and prices are modest. A list is published (three 1st-class stamps) and plants are sold by mail order.

THE GARDENS OF THE ROSE
Hertfordshire

THOUSANDS OF ROSES, including well over 1,700 varieties, are displayed here, and although there is a strong emphasis on modern varieties there are also interesting reference collections of the main

Chiswell Green AL2 3NR
2m SW of St Albans by
B4630
Tel: 01727 850461

Owner: Royal National
Rose Society

Open: Mid Jun to mid Oct,
Mon to Sat 9–5, Sun and
Bank Hol 10–6. 25 acres

historic groups. The site is flat and windswept, and some vertical emphasis is given by Irish yews and pergolas on which the climbing roses are trained. Modern roses are generally arranged in large beds, often with a single block of one variety making a vast splash of colour. The Royal National Rose Society, one of the leading specialist plant societies, publishes a journal and provides advice to members.

GUNBY HALL
Lincolnshire

nr Spilsby PE23 5SS
7m W of Skegness by A158
Tel: 01909 486411

Owner:
The National Trust

Open: 30 Mar to Sept,
Wed and Thur (also Tue,
Thur and Fri by written
appointment) 2–6. 7 acres.
House open

GUNBY PRESENTS an elegant pastoral scene – the Georgian brick mansion looking out over serene parkland. In the old walled kitchen garden there is more excitement, with a rumpus of roses, burgeoning herbaceous borders, apples trained over arches and underplanted with irises, and a dinky domed gazebo painted a celestial blue. A second walled garden has beds of fruit and vegetables and old pear trees growing out of herbaceous borders. There is a rose walk, a bed of hydrangeas and, hidden behind a yew hedge, a stately walk of Irish junipers along a canal. On the far side of the house lawns are ornamented with specimen trees and there is a wild flower walk.

R. HARKNESS & CO LTD
Hertfordshire

HARKNESS SELL chiefly roses with the emphasis on modern cultivars, of which they are constantly making new introductions, but they also stock a worthwhile selection of old varieties. Immense

The Rose Gardens,
Hitchin SG4 0JT
On A505 between Hitchin
and Letchworth
Tel: 01462 420402

Open: Mon to Sat 9–5, Sun
and Bank Hol Mon 10–5

numbers of all these are available in containers at the nursery, but more energetic visitors are also allowed to visit the growing fields nearby. An especially informative and well produced catalogue is issued free; it includes, for example, information about the origin of every rose. A mail order service is provided, orders are sent between November and March.

HARTSHALL NURSERY STOCK
Suffolk

Hartshall Farm,
Walsham-le-Willows, Bury
St Edmunds IP31 3BY
1 1/2m SE of
Walsham-le-Willows off
Westhorpe road
Tel: 01359 259238

Open: Tue to Sat 10–4.30.
Closed Jul and all Bank
Hols

LIKE SOME MUCH-LOVED, but elderly, actress Hartshall keeps threatening to retire, but popular acclaim repeatedly brings it back from the brink. Trees and shrubs are the best part of the stock but it does carry carefully chosen examples of just about every kind of plant you would want for your garden. In the tree department it has notable ranges of birches, cherries, maples, oaks and willows. There is no mail order but in any case the chief merit of the nursery is the excitement of exploration and chance discoveries. Lists are issued (three 1st-class stamps).

HATFIELD HOUSE
Hertfordshire

Hatfield AL9 5NQ
In the centre of Hatfield
village, 20m N of London
by A1 and A1(M) Jnct 4
Tel: 01707 262823

Owner: The Marquess of
Salisbury

Open: 25 Mar to 8 Oct,
daily 11–6 (closed Good
Fri); East Garden Mon 2–5
(closed Bank Hol Mon). 30
acres. House open

HATFIELD HOUSE, a Jacobean extravaganza of pink brick, was started in 1607 by Robert Cecil, and the family has owned it ever since. There has always been a notable garden here, but over the last twenty years the present Marchioness of Salisbury has brought dazzling new life to it. Near the house there are formal gardens, most of which have ancient origins. By the Old Palace Lady Salisbury has made a new knot garden with old varieties of plants, including many of those introduced by John Tradescant the Elder who worked for the Cecils when the garden was started. The privy garden and the scented garden to the west of the house have been replanted, and in summer are very beautiful. The East Garden is decorated with formal rows of clipped holm oaks (*Quercus ilex*) and brimming box-edged beds of shrubs, especially roses, underplanted with herbaceous plants. Beyond are avenues of apple trees, a Victorian yew maze (alas, not open) and the New

Illustration opposite: The Privy Garden at Hatfield

Pond which is full of atmosphere. There are few great historic gardens that demonstrate so visibly the excitement of gardening. A shop, at the entrance, sells a few good plants.

HAUGHLEY PARK
Suffolk

nr Stowmarket IP14 3JY
4m NW of Stowmarket by A45
Tel: 01359 240205

Owner: R.J. Williams

Open: May to Sept, Tue 3–6. 8 acres plus woodland

THE GABLED HOUSE was built in 1620, with a pretty gothic wing added in 1820 and the whole restored by A.J. Williams after a fire in 1961. Handsome old woodland, with some exceptional individual specimens, makes a fine setting for the gardens which are almost entirely of the 20th century. North of the house a broad apron of grass opens out, edged with mixed borders, and, to one side, an immense hollow oak which is at least 1,000 years old. The vista is continued by an old lime avenue stretching across fields into the distance. A dell has shady walks fringed with hostas, and the woodland garden, ablaze with bluebells in spring, has many azaleas and rhododendrons planted among majestic beeches and Scots pines.

HELMINGHAM HALL
Suffolk

nr Stowmarket IP14 6EF
9m N of Ipswich by B1077
Tel: 01473 890363
Fax: 01473 890776

Owner: Lord Tollemache

Open: 28 Apr to 8 Sept, Sun 2–6. 10 acres

AT HELMINGHAM, house, parkland and garden together create an exceptional work of art. The brick house, with its romantic moat and drawbridge, is of several periods, starting in 1500, and has always been owned by the Tollemaches. It overlooks a deer park with a double avenue of oaks and, to one side, also moated, a walled kitchen garden has been turned to ornamental purposes. At the entrance a box-edged parterre with summer bedding is surrounded on three sides by borders of old roses and hedges of lavender. Winged horses cap the piers of the gates into the walled garden, which is divided into four parts by two superb double herbaceous borders running down and across. Leading off them are paths through tunnels of sweet peas, runner beans or gourds, and behind the ornamental borders fruit and vegetables grow in impeccable beds. On the banks of the moat a

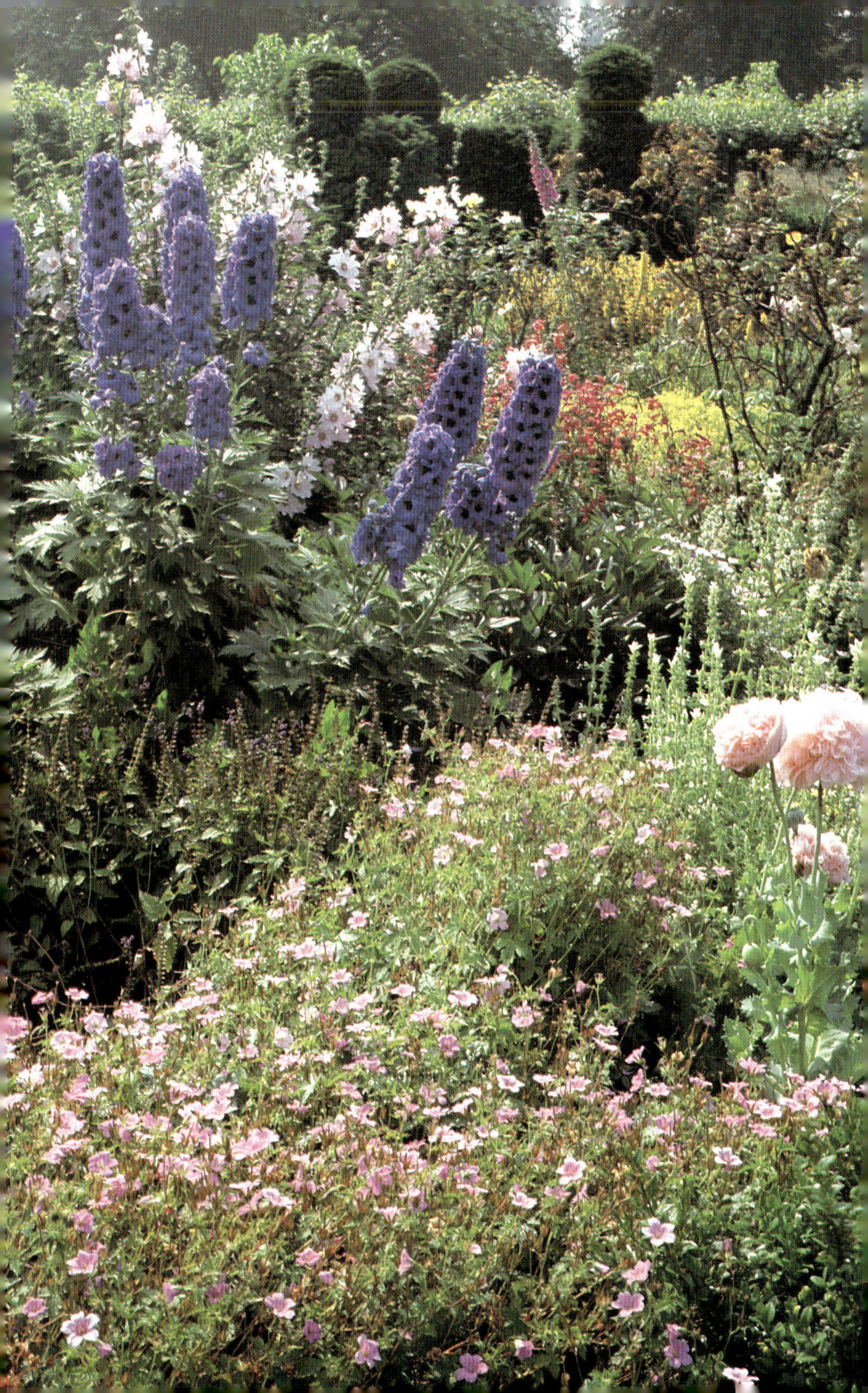

grassy walk with narrow borders encircles the walls. On the far, eastern, side of the house a herb and knot garden made since 1982 is hedged in yew. Within are low hedges of clipped box or lavender and several beds of old roses which are underplanted with bulbs and herbaceous perennials. Few great historic houses have gardens so exquisite as those at Helmingham.

HOECROFT PLANTS
Norfolk

Severals Grange, Holt Road, Wood Norton, Dereham NR20 5BL
6m E of Fakenham by A1067 and B1110
Tel: 01362 860179/844206

Open: May to Sept, Mon, Wed and Sat 10–4

THIS ADMIRABLE NURSERY used to be near Bath but has now reappeared, with rekindled vigour, in Norfolk. Margaret Lister sells wonderful ornamental grasses, and plants with especially distinguished foliage – both herbaceous and woody. It is the grasses, though, that are the special excitement of her list. These are really valuable border plants, mixing easily with any other plantings. Hoecroft carries a very wide range, some of which you will scarcely find

in any other nursery in the country. Over 160
varieties include reeds, sedges and bamboos. The
catalogue (£1.00) is outstanding, with much valuable
information on the garden use of the plants.

HOPLEYS PLANTS
Hertfordshire

Illustration: Paeonia
mlokosewitschii

High Street, Much
Hadham SG10 6BU
5m SW of Bishop's
Stortford by B1004
Tel: 01279 842509
Fax: 01279 843784

Open: Mon to Sat (closed
Tue) 9–5, Sun 2–5; closed
Jan

YOU WOULD HAVE to be a gardener of steely resolve
to avoid buying something at Hopleys. They have
introduced into commerce some of the most
successful new garden plants of recent years –
including, for example, *Potentilla* 'Red Ace' and
Lavatera 'Barnsley'. Their list ranges widely and
every year new and exciting plants – hardy and
non-hardy – are offered. Some groups are especially
well represented (for example, salvias) but the
striking quality of Hopleys is the very careful choice
of particular cultivars of a single species (e.g. 14
different varieties of *Argyranthemum frutescens*). The
beautifully kept 4-acre garden, alongside the nursery,
is open to visitors. There is an impeccable catalogue
(£1.20) and a mail order service in the autumn only.

HYDE HALL
Essex

WHEN THE ROBINSONS came here to farm in 1955
there was no garden, merely a handful of trees
on top of a famously windswept hill in one of the
driest parts of the country. The garden they made is
now enormous, full of wonderful plants in diverse

Rettendon, nr Chelmsford
CM3 8ET
7m SE of Chelmsford by
A130
Tel: 01245 400256
Fax: 01245 401363

Owner: The Royal
Horticultural Society

Open: 26 Mar to 29 Oct,
Sat, Sun, Wed, Thurs and
Bank Hol Mon 11–6.
24 acres

habitats – a brilliant tribute to their gardening skill.
An immensely wide range of plants is grown –
daylilies, irises, peonies, roses, snowdrops and
countless ornamental trees and shrubs. Hyde Hall has
two National Collections: of crab apples (*Malus*) and
of viburnums. This is not merely a plant collection,
for many parts of the garden have carefully worked
out colour harmonies – e.g. a gold garden and a
series of herbaceous borders with hot or cool
schemes. No gardener could come here without being
informed and delighted. A nursery sells excellent
plants but there is no mail order. Hyde Hall is now
owned by the RHS and it is hoped that the charm of
the Robinsons' style will survive intact.

ICKWORTH
Suffolk

Horringer, Bury St
Edmunds IP29 5QE
3m SW of Bury St
Edmunds by A143
Tel: 01284 735270

Owner:
The National Trust

Open: Jan to 22 Mar, daily
10–4; 23 Mar to 3 Nov,
daily 10–5; 4 Nov to Mar
1997, daily 10–4. Park open
daily throughout year 7–7.
33 acres. House open

THERE IS no house like Ickworth – a dumpy,
domed cylinder with curving wings designed in
the late 18th century by Francis Sandys with help
from his patron, the Earl of Bristol, Bishop of Derry.
The garden is influenced by the shape of the house.
At the front, a sweeping herbaceous border, echoing
the wings, is well planted in blues and purples –
acanthus, campanulas, geraniums and sage – with
clumps of purple-leafed cotinus. Behind the house
there is a more formal arrangement, again related to
the shape of the house, with a curved terrace and
box-hedged alleys. A marvellous walk about the
estate of Ickworth affords splendid views back to the
house and to the Earl's obelisk in the distance. The
park is a wonderful combination of ancient
woodland and the tactful hand of 'Capability' Brown.

KNEBWORTH
Hertfordshire

Knebworth SG3 6PY
28m N of London by
AI(M) Jnct 7
Tel: 01438 812661
Fax: 01438 811908

Owner: Lord Cobbold

Open: 29 Mar to 15 Apr, daily 11–5.50; 20 Apr to 19 May, Sat, Sun and Bank Hol Mon 11–5.30; 25 May to 3 Sept, daily 11–5.30; 7 Sept to 29 Sept, Sat and Sun 11–5.30. 25acres. House open

THE LYTTONS have lived here since the late Middle Ages and the house, a wild and woolly gothic fantasy, was partly designed by Bulwer Lytton, the best-selling Victorian novelist. Edwin Lutyens married a Lytton daughter and between 1907 and 1911 he simplified the immensely complicated Victorian garden. From the façade of the house a pair of cool pleached lime walks leads to a formal rose garden flanked by herbaceous borders. Beyond a screen of clipped yew, with statues half-embedded in niches, a circular pool has gold borders on either side and a path leads to a garden of old roses underplanted with artemisias, catmint and lamb's ears. To one side of the house an attractive little herb garden has been recreated from a Gertrude Jekyll design of interlocking circles.

LUTON HOO
Bedfordshire

THE MANSION at Luton Hoo was designed by Robert Adam in 1764 and revised by Sir Robert Smirke in 1827. It is a palatial affair and the terraced gardens which lie below it to the south are appropriately glamorous. At the upper level, lawns on either side of the path have fine stone urns which in summer are filled with pale pink petunias and helichrysum; behind them are mixed borders of pale colours. In the middle of the lower terrace, hedged in

Luton LU1 3TQ
1 1/2m SE of Luton by
A6129; Jnct 10 of M1
Tel: 01582 22955
Fax: 01582 34437

Owner: The Luton Hoo
Foundation

Open: Easter to mid Oct,
Fri, Sat and Sun and Bank
Hol Mons 12–6; Tue, Wed
and Thurs open to groups
by appointment only. 10
acres. House open

yew, a circular water-lily pool has a central fountain with a bronze boy and dolphin on a rock. Box-edged rose beds surround it, ornamented with box topiary cones and spirals. On either side domed temples mark the corners, and splendid old cedars of Lebanon rise up behind. At some distance from the house a romantic rock garden has a series of pools overhung with fine old Japanese maples, planted round about with conifers and rhododendrons. The cascades are now working again after 30 waterless years. The superb park at Luton Hoo is the work of 'Capability' Brown who dammed the River Lea to make two lakes and planted huge numbers of trees.

MANNINGTON HALL
Norfolk

nr Saxthorpe NR11 7BB
18m NW of Norwich by
B1149 and minor roads
Tel: 01263 874175

Owner:
Lord and Lady Walpole

Open: Easter to Oct, Sun
12–5; Jun to Aug, also
Wed to Fri 11–5. 20 acres

MANNINGTON HALL, with its moat, towers and crenellations, has a wildly romantic air. It dates from the late 15th century but was much changed in the 19th century. The moat is splashed with water-lilies and walled with yew on the inner bank. Behind the hedges are beds of modern roses and stone busts on plinths surveying the scene. Lawns and specimen trees – some fine cedars of Lebanon – lie on the far side of the moat, and a classical pavilion with a statue of Diana gives architectural contrast to beds of shrub roses. In a large walled garden a little distance from the house, the Heritage Rose Garden has a very large collection of roses of all the representative types, trained on pergolas or walls and

in beds. Part of the garden is laid out to show the
use of roses in different period styles. A visit at rose
time is a heady experience but the beauty of house
and setting is worth seeing at any time. A nursery
sells a good selection of roses.

MELFORD HALL
Suffolk

Long Melford, Sudbury
CO10 9AH
In village of Long Melford
4m N of Sudbury by A131
Tel: 01787 880286

Owner:
The National Trust

Open: Apr, Sat, Sun
2–5.30; May to Sept, Wed
to Sun (except Fri) 2–5.30;
Oct, Sat and Sun 2–5.30. 9
acres. House open

IF IT WERE NOT for the gazebo at Melford Hall the
garden would only just be worth visiting – but
what a gazebo! It is octagonal, built of brick, and it
bristles with pediments and finials. Gertrude Jekyll
visited it and, recognizing its architectural distinction,
criticised it for being smothered in ivy. Today it is
revealed in its full eccentric glory. Steep steps lead up
to it, and from tall sash windows there are views on
one side over the dry moat and on the other of the
garden with its curving herbaceous borders, old
weeping ash and mulberry, and a pretty little herb
parterre planted with low hedges of yew and patches
of purple sage, germander, lavender and rue.

MONKSILVER NURSERY
Cambridgeshire

Illustration: Centaurea
macrocephala

HERE IS ONE of the most fascinating collections of
herbaceous plants that you will find anywhere.
The Monksilver list (six 1st-class stamps) is the sort
you take to bed on a winter's evening for a long,
happy and richly inspiring browse. There are rare
plants here, some exceedingly rare, but there are also

Oakington Road,
Cottenham CB4 4TW
In the village of Cottenham
4 1/2m N of Cambridge by
B1049
Tel: 01954 251555

Open: Apr to Jun, Fri and
Sat 10–4. Also open for the
National Gardens Scheme
from Apr to Oct, on the
second Sat of each month
10–4

countless more common (or garden) things that should not be overlooked. The catalogue describes the plants well, and in terms of naming and botanical precision has the highest standards. National Collections of *Galeobdolon*, *Lamium* and *Vinca* are held at the nursery. Chiefly a mail order business, the nursery has fairly restricted opening times. Prices are very fair, although in a few cases, for extreme rarities, they do not quote a price, but invite bids (of money or *even rarer plants*). Do not miss the chance of a visit to this unique place.

NORFOLK LAVENDER
Norfolk

Caley Mill, Heacham
PE31 7JE
13 1/2m N of King's Lynn
on A149
Tel: 01485 570384
Fax: 01485 571176

Open: Daily 10–5 (closed
23 Dec to 14 Jan)

LAVENDER USED to be very widely grown on a commercial scale in southern England but Norfolk Lavender is the only remaining lavender farm in England and it holds a National Collection (55 different species and varieties). Display beds show vividly the variations in foliage and flower, and in late summer fill the air with their scent. Many lavenders, and a few other plants, are sold in a small nursery, and a mail order service is provided.

NOTCUTTS NURSERIES LTD
Suffolk

NOTCUTTS is an institution and carries an immense general stock. In every department gardeners will find excellent things. New introductions are constantly being made and medals relentlessly won at the best shows. A mail order service is provided and

Ipswich Road, Woodbridge
IP12 4AF
Tel: 01394 383344
Fax: 01394 385460

Open: Mon to Sat
8.45–5.30, Sun 10–5

the oustanding catalogue is a valuable gardening reference book, 300 pages long and very detailed. The main section, called 'Plants for a Purpose', gives lists of plants grouped under every imaginable heading. Apart from the Woodbridge branch there are also centres in the east of England at Orton Waterville, nr Peterborough (01733 234600); Smallford, St Albans (01727 853224), Ardleigh, Colchester (01206 230271); and Daniel's Road, Norwich (01603 53155). All these have similar opening times to the main branch.

OXBURGH HALL
Norfolk

Oxborough, nr King's
Lynn PE33 9PS
In Oxborough 9m E of
Downham Market by
A1122 and A134
Tel: 01366 328258

Owner:
The National Trust

Open: 23 Mar to 3 Nov,
daily except Thur and Fri
12–5.30. 18 acres. House
open

RISING FROM its moat, the 15th-century manor house is wonderfully romantic. It was built by the Bedingfields who gave it to the National Trust in 1952. To the east of the hall a splendid Frenchified parterre was made in the 19th century after the Bedingfields saw a similar one on a visit to France in 1845. Against a background of gravel, swirling beds hedged in box are filled with a permanent planting of rue and santolina, which is enlivened by summer bedding of ageratums, marigolds and pelargoniums. Parterres of this sort were intended to be viewed from above, as this one can be from the windows of the hall or from the terrace to one side. A yew hedge separates a very handsome long mixed border from the parterre. A 19th-century brick-walled kitchen garden has been planted with a formal orchard of medlars, mulberries and different varieties of plum, with clematis and roses trained on the walls.

PADLOCK CROFT
Cambridgeshire

Illustration: Campanula punctata *'Pallida'*

19 Padlock Road, West Wratting, nr Cambridge CB1 5LS
14m SE of Cambridge by A1307, A604 and minor roads
Tel: 01223 290383

Open: Apr to Oct, visitors welcome at most times except Sun but please phone first. 1 acre

SUSAN AND PETER Lewis are famous for campanulas, of which their garden houses the National Collection; their splendid list (four 2nd-class stamps) leads with no less than fifteen pages of them, and nearly 300 different kinds may be seen growing in the garden. In addition they hold National Collections of the related genera of adenophora, platycodon and symphyandra; other species of the Campanulaceae family are also stocked. Garden and nursery blend indistinguishably at Padlock Croft, forming a maze of alpine troughs, glasshouses and packed beds. Alpines and smaller border plants are the speciality of the nursery, and there are very good collections. In every part of the list there are desirable things – a visit is especially rewarding to see the many unlisted plants growing in the garden.

PARADISE CENTRE
Suffolk

Twinstead Road, Lamarsh, Bures CO8 5EX
In village of Lamarsh 4m S of Sudbury by minor roads
Tel and Fax: 01787 269449

Open: Sat, Sun and Bank Hol Mon 10–5; also by appointment

THE HEART of this unusual nursery garden is its collection of bulbs and herbaceous perennials. Among the bulbs are exceptionally long lists of alliums, crocuses, erythroniums, many fritillaries and species narcissi and tulips. Among the herbaceous plants are excellent groups of epimediums, a good range of ferns, hardy geraniums, hostas, a wonderful list of primulas and several saxifrages. All the plants are well chosen and are available by post from an

Illustration: Anemone nemorosa

attractive and informative catalogue (four 1st-class stamps). As with many small and interesting nurseries, there are always excellent plants available at the nursery which have not been listed. The nursery is, in effect, the owners' own garden – made by them from virtually nothing – and it is delightful.

PARK GREEN NURSERIES
Suffolk

Wetheringsett, Stowmarket
IP14 5QH
6m NE of Stowmarket
E of A140
Tel: 01728 860139 and mobile 0860 122069

Open: Mar to Oct Thur to Mon 10–5.30

RICHARD AND MARY Ford grow over 150 different species and varieties of hosta, and there are few garden sites for which an appropriate and beautiful specimen cannot be found. Many of the plants are hard to come by, and some are available only here. As well as their chief speciality, the Fords also have a choice collection of astilbes, of which they have many named varieties of both tall and dwarf kinds. Plants are sold by mail order and are despatched from October to March when dormant. A good catalogue (three 1st-class stamps) is produced, with excellent descriptions of the plants. Seeds are also sold and, as hostas cross-pollinate with abandon, you may well germinate something new and interesting yourself.

PECKOVER HOUSE
Cambridgeshire

WHEN YOU HAVE got over the surprise of finding a garden as big as this behind an elegant town house in the middle of Wisbech, you can get down to admiring its distinctive charms. Lawns slope away

North Brink, Wisbech
PE13 1JR
In the centre of Wisbech
Tel: 01945 583463

Owner:
The National Trust

Open: Apr to Oct, daily except Thur and Fri 2–5.30. Parties at other times by arrangement with tenant. 2 acres. House open

from the back of the house, with many substantial specimen trees of a Victorian character, and a rustic summer house adds to the period flavour. To one side of the main lawn, hidden behind brick walls, a pair of mixed borders leads up to a pool and an elegant little gazebo. The borders are ornamented with slender metal pillars with roses and clematis, and a pair of topiary yew peacocks. In a separate part of the garden a conservatory houses oranges, daturas and other tender plants, and there is an unusual 19th-century fern house.

POTTERTON & MARTIN
Lincolnshire

Moortown Road,
Nettleton, Caistor
LN7 6HX
18m NE of Lincoln by A46 and B1205
Tel and Fax: 01472 851792

Open: Daily 9–5

POTTERTON & MARTIN call themselves 'The Cottage Nursery', which is misleading. In fact they sell a wide range of alpine plants, dwarf bulbs, ferns and orchids, with interesting excursions into such oddities as carnivorous plants, some of which are hardy and make good plants for the edges of ponds. There is generally a strong emphasis on species and forms, with an exceptionally good list of anemones; dozens of crocuses; virtually every species of cyclamen that is hardy out-of-doors (and some that are not), including some of the forms with especially pretty foliage; a good collection of the smaller irises; an excellent range of primulas; a long and interesting selection of saxifrages; and all sorts of other tempting things of the smaller kind. Catalogues are issued (50p stamp), and a mail order service is provided.

RAVENINGHAM HALL GARDENS
Norfolk

Raveningham, nr Norwich
NR14 6NS
14m SE of Norwich by
A146 and B1136
Tel: 01508 548222
Fax: 01508 468958

Owner:
Sir Nicholas Bacon Bt

Open: Garden: mid Mar to mid Sept, Wed 1–4, Sun and Bank Hol Mon 2–5; *Nursery, conservatory, arboretum and vegetable garden:* Mon to Fri 9–5; Mar to Oct, also Sat 9–5; mid Mar to mid Sept, also Sun 2–5

THE NURSERY attached to the garden has an excellent general stock, very largely propagated from the plants in the garden. Many of these are unusual without being modish – exactly the kind that give so many old-established country house gardens their distinctive character. There is a good range of agapanthus, several ceanothus, cistus, euphorbias, many hardy geraniums and snowdrop cultivars (some hard to come by). There is a catalogue (three 1st-class stamps) and mail order service. The garden itself, lying mostly to the south of the gentlemanly 18th-century brick mansion, has many grey and tender things such as *Buddleja crispa* doing surprisingly well in this part of the world. A rose garden is enclosed in brick walls and hedges of yew, a long deep herbaceous border runs along the outside of the walled kitchen garden.

READS NURSERY
Norfolk

Hales Hall, nr Loddon
NR14 6QW
10m SE of Norwich by
A146
Tel and Fax: 01508 548395

Open: Tue to Sat 10–1, 2–5 or dusk if earlier; May to Oct, also Sun and Bank Hol Mon 2–5

THIS OLD-ESTABLISHED (1890) nursery specialises in fruit, especially citrus fruits, of which the Reads have the largest selection commercially available in Britain – not just oranges and lemons but all sorts of exotics like mandarins and kumquats. They also sell desert and wine grapes, several different varieties of figs, mulberries and tender climbing plants. The nursery the National Collections of cultivars of the fig (*Ficus carica*). Reads occupies a particularly attractive group of buildings – the potting shed is housed in the largest medieval brick barn in England. A very informative catalogue (four 1st-class stamps) is produced and plants are supplied by post.

THE ROMANTIC GARDEN NURSERY
Norfolk

The Street, Swannington, Norwich NR9 5NW
In the village of Swannington, 9m NW of Norwich by A1067 and minor roads
Tel: 01603 261488

Open: Wed, Fri and Sat 10–5

THE ROMANTIC GARDEN NURSERY swarms with ready-made topiary – a menagerie of animals clipped of box. More unusual are many standard-trained and mop-headed plants – *Arbutus unedo*, bay, holly, privet and others. Plants for the conservatory, including oleanders with three-part trunks prettily plaited together, and a range of hand-thrown frost-proof Italian terracotta pots are sold. A list is produced (four 1st-class stamps) and there is a mail order service.

SALING HALL
Essex

Great Saling, nr Braintree CM7 5DT
6m NW of Braintree by A120
Tel: 01371 850141
Fax: 01371 850274

Owner: Mr and Mrs Hugh Johnson

Open: May to Jul, Wed 2–5. 12 acres

SOME GOOD GARDENS fall too easily into genteel ossification but at Saling Hall there is a constant buzz of horticultural activity. The present owners came in 1971 and found an old garden already full of interest surrounding the long, curvaceously gabled brick house of the early 17th century. They redefined the best parts (including a very pretty walled garden west of the house and a decaying water garden) and expanded boldly into the woodland with new ventures. Here is an excellent collection of trees, many rare, skilfully deployed with vistas and ornaments (including a recently made Tuscan Temple of Pisces), and a deft sketch of a Japanese garden with a stream, billowing mounds of clipped box and a snow-lantern. If you don't like what you see here you have probably lost interest in gardening.

Illustration opposite: The arboretum at Saling Hall

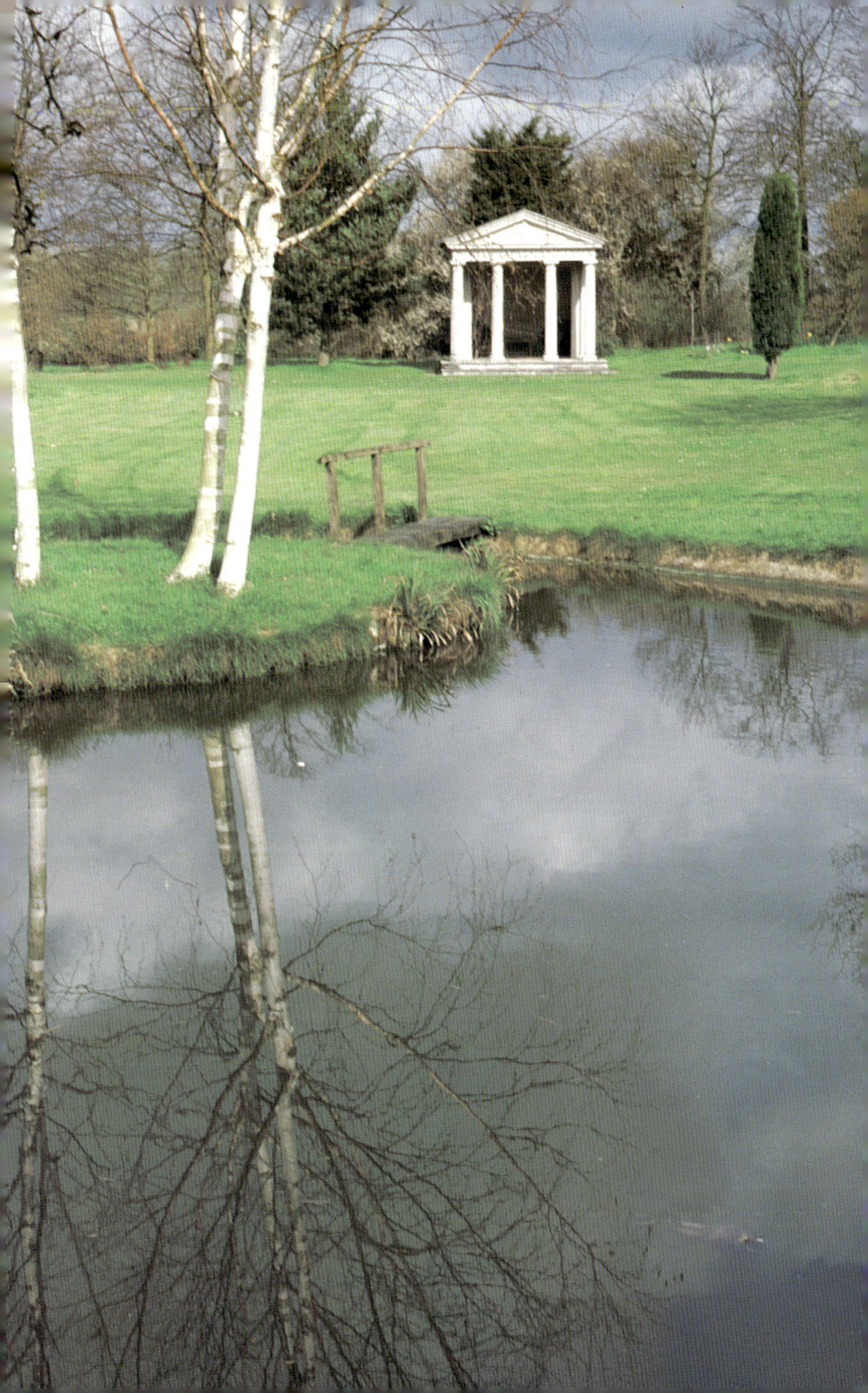

SANDRINGHAM HOUSE
Norfolk

Sandringham, King's Lynn
PE35 6EN
9m NE of King's Lynn by
B1440
Tel: 01553 772675
Fax: 01485 541571

Owner: H.M. The Queen

Open: Easter to late Jul,
early Aug to Oct, daily
10.30–5. House open

THERE ARE NOT many gardens belonging to the Royal Family that are regularly open to the public so this is one of the very few places where its taste in gardening may be seen. First, it is on a huge scale and the chief impression is one of immense and impeccable lawns punctuated with specimen trees, many of which are 19th-century plantings of conifers. On this sandy, acid soil rhododendrons do well and they flourish in the protection of the trees. Nearer the house there is an attractive formality with pleached lime walks, hedges of yew and a series of herbaceous beds enclosed in tall box hedges. On the other side of the house a stream feeds two lakes whose fringes are richly planted with conifers, maples and other ornamental trees and shrubs.

SHERINGHAM PARK
Norfolk

Upper Sheringham
NR26 8TB
2m SW of Sheringham by
A148
Tel: 01263 823778

Owner:
The National Trust

Open: Daily dawn–dusk.
90 acres

HUMPHRY REPTON was the genius behind this place of woods and rambling walks around a shallow combe by the sea. It was commissioned by Abbot Upcher's family, for whom Repton also built a new house between 1812 and 1819 in a more picturesque position embowered by trees – many of them marvellous 18th-century oaks – on one side of the valley. In the woods across fields to the south of the house is a collection of rare rhododendrons started by Abbot Upcher's son Henry who helped finance plant-hunting expeditions to the Himalayas. Many of these rhododendrons have grown to great size in the sheltered combe. In 1975 Thomas Upcher built an arcaded temple to Repton's design, on an eminence with lovely views to the house and the sea beyond.

SOMERLEYTON HALL
Suffolk

nr Lowestoft NR32 5QQ
5m NW of Lowestoft by B1074
Tel: 01502 730224
Fax: 01502 732143

Owner: Lord and Lady Somerleyton

Open: Easter Sun to Sept, Thur, Sun and Bank Hol Mon 12.30–5.30; Jul to Aug, also Tue and Wed 12.30–5.30. 12 acres. House open

SOMERLEYTON HAS a big, bold Victorian house and a garden to suit. The garden entrance leads through the former kitchen garden which now has a spanking pair of herbaceous borders marching down the middle. The well maintained glasshouses were designed by Joseph Paxton, and on the outside south walls of the kitchen garden there are rare peach cases awaiting restoration. Wellingtonias and monkey puzzles on the lawn beyond the kitchen garden were part of the 19th-century layout but among them are much older trees, including some superb sweet chestnuts. From the Victorian parterres by the house, planted with roses and columns of clipped yew, there are views of the remains of an ancient avenue of limes disappearing towards the horizon. There is also a hedge maze of yew built in 1846 and a magnificent winter garden of the same date in which the tea-room is now housed. Few places give such a vivid idea of the entire world of gardening at the height of the Victorian period.

THE SWISS GARDEN
Bedfordshire

Old Warden,
nr Biggleswade
2 1/2m W of Biggleswade by minor roads; signposted from A1 and A600
Tel: 01767 627666
Fax: 01234 228921

Owner: Managed by Bedfordshire County Council

Open: Mar to Sept, Sat, Sun and Bank Hol Mon 10–6, Mon, Wed, Thur, Fri 1.30–6; Jan, Feb and Oct, Sun 11–4. 9 acres

IN THE EARLY 19th century there was a fashion for everything Swiss, and here at Old Warden the Lord Ongley made an enchanting 'Swiss' garden full of rustic thatched houses, precipitous rocky descents and picturesque views. The site, well wooded and gently undulating, has interconnected ponds with ornamental islands, and paths wind about, revealing views of garden houses, delicate iron-work arched bridges, a kiosk with stained glass, statues and urns, a grotto and a fernery. All around are excellent trees and the garden has been beautifully restored by the county council. There is, surely, nothing like this in Switzerland but it is a great entertainment.

VALLEY CLEMATIS
Lincolnshire

Illustration: Clematis *'Perle d'Azur'*

Willingham Road, Hainton
LN3 6LN
17m NE of Lincoln, S of Hainton on the road to South Willingham
Tel: 01507 313398

Open: Daily 10–5 (closed 24 Dec to 1 Jan)

OTHER NURSERIES sell clematis, but none with quite the panache of Keith and Carol Fair. They win medals at all the best shows and have an outstanding range of plants for sale – including several unique to them. Over 350 varieties are grown, although not all of these will be available at any one time. The illustrated list (£1.00) is a delight, not only for the exceptional plants but also for the valuable suggestions for cultivation and the use of clematis in the garden. A mail order service is available.

WIMPOLE HALL
Hertfordshire

Arrington, Royston
SG8 0BW
8m SW of Cambridge by A603
Tel: 01223 207257

Owner:
The National Trust

Open: 16 Mar to 3 Nov, daily except Mon and Fri 10.30–5 (open Bank Hol Mon). 20 acres. House open

ON THIS WINDY, open site on the borders of Hertfordshire and Cambridgeshire the 18th-century house rises on a slight eminence, commanding wide and distant views. In the very early 18th century there had been a great formal garden here, and an immense avenue of elms, planted by Charles Bridgeman in the 1720s, survived until it was killed by the elm disease; it has now been replanted in limes. In the 1750s the formal garden began to be dismantled, and later both 'Capability' Brown and Humphry Repton worked here, naturalising the landscape even further. In recent years the National Trust has restored some of the formality (including parterres on the north side) but has respected the different layers of garden style that give Wimpole its interest.

WOLTERTON PARK
Norfolk

nr Erpingham NR11 7LY
2m N of Aylsham by A140
Tel: 01263 874175
Fax: 01263 761214

Owner: Lord and Lady Walpole

Open: 9–5 or dusk if earlier. 100 acres

WOLTERTON PARK is a handsome house of orange brick and stone built in the 1730s for Horatio Walpole. It has remained in the family but was abandoned in the 19th century, lived in once again in the 20th century and badly damaged by fire in 1952. Now the present Lord Walpole has taken it in hand and a programme of restoration is under way. The visitor starts with a wonderful rural amble, skirting fields and woods, passing a romantically ruined church tower and eventually emerging in a vast open space dotted with exceptional oaks. The south front of the house is then revealed, embowered in trees, overlooking in the far distance a great lake. Hedges and trees are being replanted in the park. The formal gardens south of the house, glimpsed from the park, are open only on occasional Sundays (advertised in the local press).

WOOTTEN'S PLANTS
Suffolk

MICHAEL LOFTUS STARTED his nursery in 1991 and already it has a distinctive, and distinguished, character. He sells chiefly herbaceous plants, not all hardy, and what makes the nursery different is the meticulous choice and the care with which they are

THE EAST OF ENGLAND • 247

Blackheath, Wenhaston,
Halesworth IP19 9HD
3m SE of Halesworth by
A144 and minor roads
Tel: 01502 70258
Fax: 01502 70258

Open: Daily 9.30–5. Closed
25 Dec–2 Jan

grown. The plants are regularly potted on and all visitors will be struck by their size and vigour. Here are many campanulas, diascias, euphorbias, geraniums, lychnis, penstemons, salvias and countless other things such as large daturas in pots, and the very finest pelargoniums. An excellent catalogue (£2.00) is produced. Virtually everything in it is desirable but you will have to go to the nursery, for there is no mail order. Michael Loftus's own very attractive garden alongside is occasionally open.

WREST PARK
Bedfordshire

Silsoe MK45 4HS
3/4m E of Silsoe by A6
Tel: 01525 860152

Owner: English Heritage

Open: Apr to Sept, Sat,
Sun and Bank Hol Mon,
10–6. 80 acres

THE GARDEN at Wrest Park has only fragments – but they are wonderfully attractive. The de Grey family had lived at Wrest since the 13th century but the present palatial house was built in the 1830s in the French style. A Frenchified parterre south of the house dates from the same time and has bedding schemes and fine classical statues. Of the elaborate formal garden of the early 18th century all that remains is a slender canal and a swagger domed classical pavilion designed by Thomas Archer in 1710. Between the pavilion and the canal is a lead figure of William III. A garden of woodland vistas and a serpentined pool has a pretty Chinese gazebo and traces of 'Capability' Brown who worked here from 1758 to 1760. One of the charms of the place is the mixture of his informal landscaping overlaid on the fine survivals of the earlier formal garden.

**THE
NORTH
OF
ENGLAND**

Cumbria
County Durham
Humberside
Lancashire
Northumberland
Yorkshire

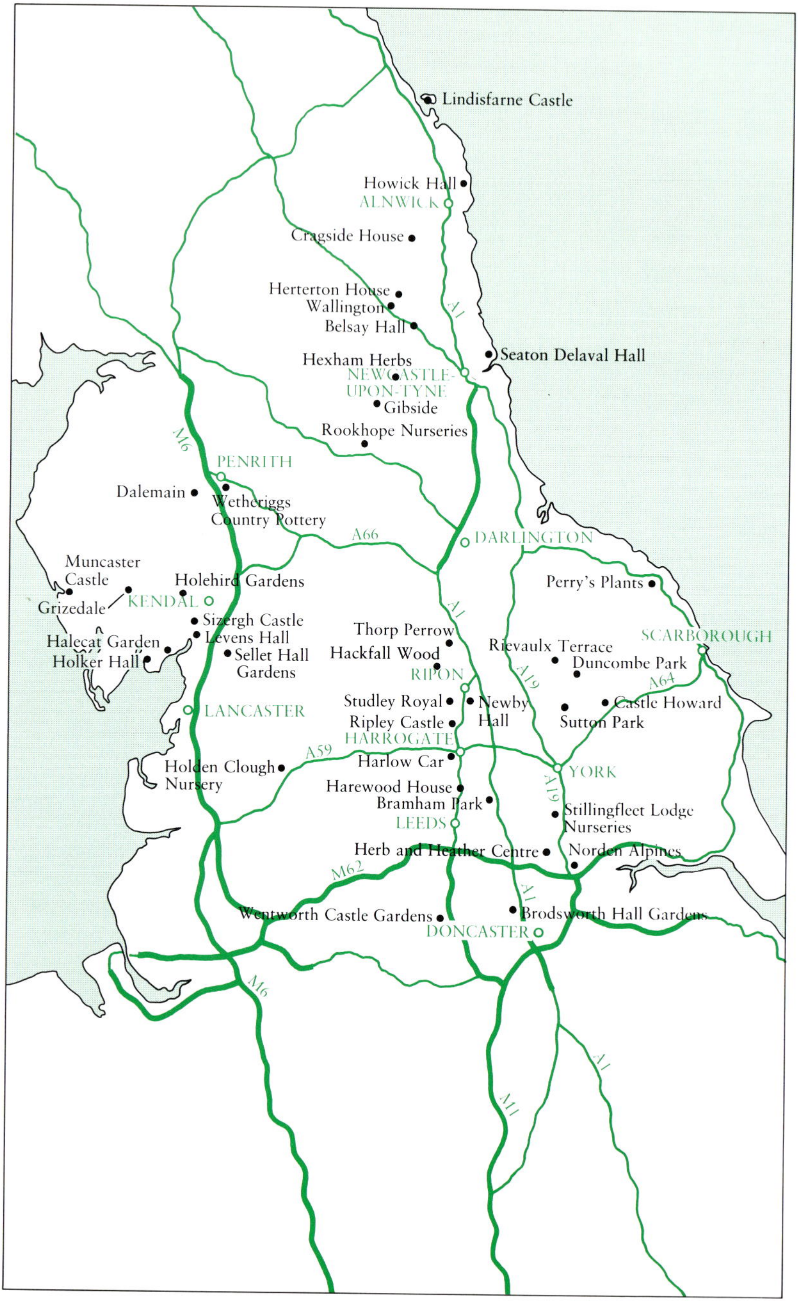
Lindisfarne Castle
Howick Hall
ALNWICK
Cragside House
Herterton House
Wallington
Belsay Hall
A1
Seaton Delaval Hall
Hexham Herbs
NEWCASTLE-
UPON-TYNE
Gibside
Rookhope Nurseries
M6
PENRITH
Dalemain
Wetheriggs
Country Pottery
A66
DARLINGTON
Muncaster
Castle
Holehird Gardens
Perry's Plants
Grizedale
KENDAL
Sizergh Castle
Levens Hall
Thorp Perrow
Halecat Garden
Holker Hall
Sellet Hall
Gardens
Hackfall Wood
A1
Rievaulx Terrace
SCARBOROUGH
Duncombe Park
RIPON
A19
A64
Studley Royal
Newby
Hall
Castle Howard
LANCASTER
Ripley Castle
Sutton Park
HARROGATE
A59
Holden Clough
Nursery
Harlow Car
YORK
Harewood House
Bramham Park
A19
Stillingfleet Lodge
Nurseries
LEEDS
Herb and Heather Centre
Norden Alpines
M62
A1
Wentworth Castle Gardens
Brodsworth Hall Gardens
DONCASTER
M6
A1
M1

BELSAY HALL
Northumberland

Belsay, nr
Newcastle-upon-Tyne
NE20 0DX
14m NW of Newcastle by A696
Tel: 01661 881636
Fax: 01661 881043

Owner: The Belsay Trust. In guardianship of English Heritage

Open: Apr to Oct, daily 10–6; Nov to Mar, daily 10–4 (closed Christmas Day, Boxing Day and New Year's Day). 50 acres. House open

THE NEO-CLASSICAL brown stone mansion at Belsay was built to the design of its owner, Sir Charles Monck, in the early 19th century. The stone was quarried on the site and the resulting rocky hollows and ravines were made by Sir Charles into an unforgettable wild and romantic garden. The planting is boldly appropriate to the setting, with the striking foliage of Chusan palms, the larger-leafed rhododendrons, *Gunnera mannicata* and the handsome angelica tree (*Aralia elata*) looking wonderful against the cliffs and outcrops. A path winds gently upwards between the walls of stone fringed with ferns, and emerges in meadows above the quarry. Here is a surprise – the substantial remains of 14th-century Belsay Castle rising up in the long grass. Near the house formal terraced gardens with yew hedges overlook woodland of conifers with a large collection of rhododendrons, and an unusual 'winter garden' is planted with different kinds of heathers for winter colour.

BRAMHAM PARK
West Yorkshire

Wetherby LS23 6ND
5m S of Wetherby by A1
Tel: 01937 844265
Fax: 01937 845923

Owner: Mr and Mrs George Lane Fox

Open: Easter weekend, spring Bank Hol weekend, May Day weekend 1.15–5.30; 16 Jun to 1 Sept, Sun, Tue, Wed and Thur and Bank Hol 1.15–5.30. 100 acres. House open

A GARDEN LIKE BRAMHAM is an exciting place, giving unique and special pleasure. There are borders and rose beds but the really wonderful thing here is the great formal garden with its immense alleys of clipped beech, distant views of lonely statues, exquisite garden buildings commanding wide views, and refreshing vistas out into the surrounding countryside. It was designed in the very early 18th century for Robert Benson, the 1st Lord Bingley, who probably masterminded the building of the beautiful house as well as the making of the garden. On the Grand Tour he had seen the latest French gardens and wanted to make something of the sort for himself. The garden he made has a definite French accent – but with an attractively playful English irregularity. It is certainly grand, but never solemn. Still owned by descendants of its maker, Bramham is maintained to wonderfully high standards; of its kind, there is nothing in England to touch it.

BRODSWORTH HALL GARDENS
South Yorkshire

Brodsworth, nr Doncaster
BN5 1TG
5 1/2m NW of Doncaster
by A1(M) or A638 and
B6422, in the village of
Brodsworth
Tel: 01302 722598

Owner: English Heritage

Open: Apr to Oct, daily
1–6. 15 acres. House open

THE HALL is a swagger Italianate mansion built in the 1860s with splendid views to the south over rural landscape. The garden is a romantic Victorian affair with great character. The flower gardens west of the croquet lawn are a knickerbocker glory of bedding schemes, ivy ribbons, cast-iron vases, soaring monkey puzzles and a gushing fountain. In the woods beyond, the quarry garden is a rocky ravine with a long archery lawn; at one end is a classically ruinous eyecatcher and at the other the delicious Palladian Gothic Swiss Cottage style Archery House. Beyond it an imense iron rose pergola curves round flower beds edged in box. English Heritage have breathed new life into this rare place and continue to do so.

CASTLE HOWARD
North Yorkshire

BIG IS THE WORD for Castle Howard but the garden gives pleasures that are both grand and intimate. Vanbrugh's gigantic early 18th-century palace is set in dramatic country that is matched for drama by the

nr York YO6 7DA
14m NE of York by A64
Tel: 01653 648444
Fax: 01653 648462

Owner: The Hon. Simon Howard

Open: Mid Mar to late Oct, daily 10–5. Castle open

house. To the south a vast formal arrangement of clipped yew hedges surrounds a fountain with a figure of Atlas supported by Tritons, designed by W.A. Nesfield in 1850. To one side, in a secluded walled garden, yew hedges and screens of hornbeam divide rose beds edged in dwarf box, lavender and purple berberis. The very large collection of roses – old and new – is beautifully arranged, underplanted with grey and silver artemisias, phlomis, pinks and santolina. On the slopes far beyond the house a completely different atmosphere reigns. Ray Wood is an immense woodland garden with winding walks and a marvellous collection of trees and shrubs.

CRAGSIDE HOUSE
Northumberland

Rothbury, Morpeth
NE65 7PX
13m SW of Alnwick by B6341
Tel: 01669 20333/20266

Owner:
The National Trust

Open: Garden: 2 Apr to Oct daily exccept Mon (open Bank Hol Mon) 10.30–6.30; *Grounds:* open same days as garden 10.30–7 and 2 Nov to 15 Dec Tue, Sat and Sun 10.30–4. 1,000 acres. House open

CRAGSIDE WAS DESIGNED by Norman Shaw for the industrialist Lord Armstrong and built in 1870. The very name makes one think of a Grimm fairy tale, and the appearance of the house rising high above a rocky bluff overlooking the Debdon Valley has more than a touch of Wagner. This is no place for genteel borders, and below the house a precipitous rockery cascades down the slopes. Giant steps lead down to a sombre and beautiful pinetum spreading along the banks of the river below. spanned by an elegant steel bridge. On the way down there are views of marvellous trees, the fern-fringed stream below and the wild house rearing on the cliff above. Recently the National Trust has acquired additional parts of the garden by the house including glasshouses with hydraulically-driven turntables to allow tender fruit to ripen evenly. These have been beautifully restored, as well as one of the grandest bedding schemes in the north of England.

DALEMAIN
Cumbria

ON ONE SIDE of the handsome 18th-century house at Dalemain a broad gravelled terrace, fringed with tumbling shrub roses, looks out over fields. Behind the house a knot of box-edged compartments is filled with artemisias, astilbes, campanulas,

Illustration opposite: The Doric rotunda at Duncombe Park

nr Penrith CA11 0HB
3m SW of Penrith by A66 and A592
Tel: 01768 486450
Fax: 01684 86223

Owner: R. Hasell McCosh

Open: Sun before Easter to first Sun in Sept, daily except Fri and Sat 11.15–5. 10 acres. House open

penstemons and violas, and in summer pots of lilies are arranged about a pool. A gravel walk with a border of shrub roses leads under old fruit trees to a door. Beyond this is Lob's Wood where a wild woodland walk follows the banks of the Dacre beck. On the other side of the beck the wild garden is occasionally revealed, with azaleas, rhododendrons and ornamental trees. This is the kind of garden, unpretentious and filled with good plants, that many think of as quintessentially English.

DUNCOMBE PARK
North Yorkshire

Helmsley YO6 5EB
On the W edge of Helmsley, 12m E of Thirsk by A170
Tel: 01439 770213
Fax: 01439 771114

Owner: Lord Feversham

Open: Apr and Oct, Wed and Sun 11–4.30; May to June, also open Thur to Sat 11–4.30; July to Sept, daily 11–4.30. 485 acres

THE STORY of Duncombe Park is a splendid reversal of fortune. The great early 18th-century house had been leased for over 60 years to a girls' school when Lord Feversham took it back as a private residence. He has also restored the garden with its exquisite views. To capitalise on its unique setting Thomas Duncombe created in the 18th century a great boomerang-shaped terrace giving views over the ancient castle and rooftops of Helmsley and of the sparkling waters of the curving river Rye below. The terrace is ornamented by two fine temples – at one end a rotunda by Sir John Vanbrugh, at the other a domed Doric temple by an unknown architect. A long, slow walk to absorb the Arcadian scenery is one of the greatest treats that any garden can offer. It was Thomas Duncombe who was also responsible for the terrace at Rievaulx nearby (see page 267).

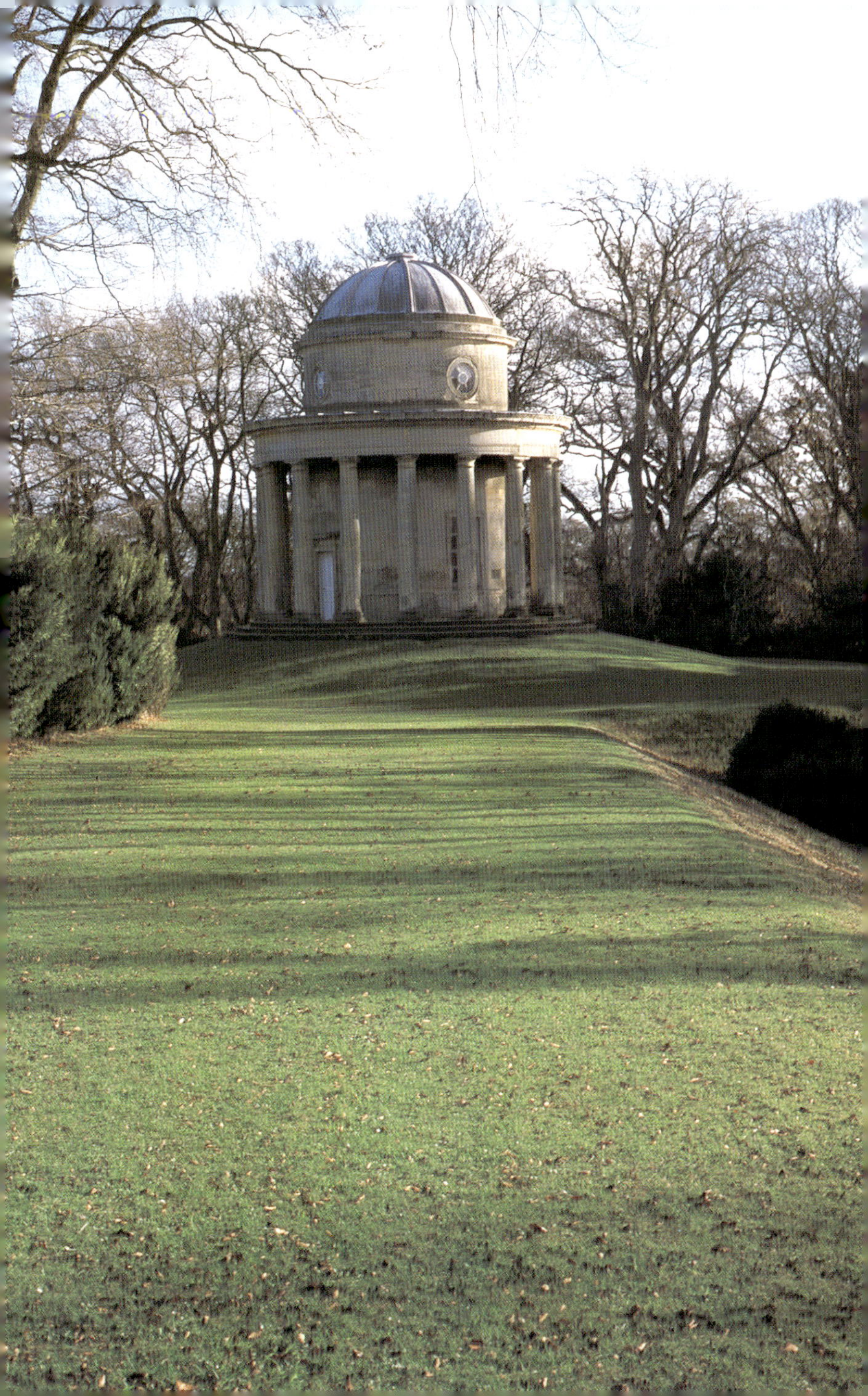

GIBSIDE
Tyne and Wear

nr Rowlands Gill,
Burnopfield,
Newcastle-upon-Tyne
NE16 6BG
6m SW of Gateshead; the
entrance is on the B6314
between Burnopfield and
Rowlands Gill
Tel: 01207 542255

Owner: The National Trust

Open: 2 Apr to Oct, daily
except Mon (open Bank
Hol Mon) 11–5

THIS IS THE SEDUCTIVE fragmentary remains of a splendid landscape park – spacious, calm and dramatic. Gibside was the home of the Bowes family which, in the 18th century, embarked on ambitious landscape schemes by the Derwent Valley – 'one of the grandest idylls of the 18th century' as Christopher Hussey called it. The house is now a shell but the essence of the place survives with James Paine's exquisite Palladian chapel at one end of a vast avenue of oaks leading towards an immense Column of Liberty. To one side winding paths lead through the woods towards the lovely Gothic Banqueting House. This is in the separate ownership of The Landmark Trust and it may be rented for holidays (01628 825925).

GRIZEDALE
Cumbria

Grizedale, nr Hawkshead,
Ambleside LA22 0QJ
3m S of Hawkshead by
B5285
Tel: 01229 860373

Owner: Forestry
Commission

Open: Daily dawn to dusk.
9,000 acres

GRIZEDALE FOREST lies between Coniston and Windermere, at the heart of some of the most beautiful scenery in the Lake District. It is an ancient place – the name is Norse for 'valley of the pigs' – and rich in trees. The Forestry Commission has opened it up for walking or biking, with over nine miles of pathways. The Grizedale Society had the bright idea of enriching the forest with splendid sculptures made of fallen timber, brushwood, slabs of stone and roughly hewn wood. Many of these are made by distinguished artists such as Sue Berger, Andy Frost, Andy Goldsworth and several others. Most are ephemeral and new ones are added from time to time. To the gardener they are of intense interest for they show vividly the power of such things to animate the scene.

HACKFALL WOOD
North Yorkshire

Grewelthorpe, nr Ripon
1/2m NW of the village of Grewelthorpe, 6 1/2m NW of Ripon

Owner: Woodland Trust

Open: Daily, dawn to dusk. 112 acres

THIS WONDERFUL WILD landscape garden was conjured out of a piece of dramatic country by William, son of John Aislabie of Studley Royal, between 1730 and 1750. A natural wooded gorge, 100 metres deep, overlooks a lovely loop of the River Ure. Aislabie added buildings, paths, waterfalls and rills to animate the woods of beech and oak. Today you may wander at will, pushing through thickets of bracken, and marvel at the romantic prospects within the woods or high above them from the crest of the gorge. A famous beauty spot until the 1930s, it fell into decay; rediscovered by local enthusiasts, it is now cared for by the Woodland Trust and accessible to all. It has a secret atmosphere and its present state of controlled dishevelment seems perfectly in tune with its exceptional character. Its charms yield themselves only gradually and are the more memorable for it. It is certainly not a place for a hurried visit – a protracted leisurely amble is needed, perhaps with a picnic at the banqueting house.

HALECAT GARDEN NURSERIES
Cumbria

Witherslack,
Grange-over-Sands
LA11 6RU
5m NE of
Grange-over-Sands by
B5277 and A590
Tel: 01539 552229

Open: Mon to Fri 9–4.30,
Sun 2–4

HALECAT HOUSE is an early 19th-century mansion looking south over terraced gardens and fields to exquisite, far-reaching views of Arnside Knott. This private garden is open to visitors, which gives an additional reason for coming to the very good nursery. Stone-paved terraces run along the south side of the house and a path skirts an unadorned lawn edged on two sides with generously planted mixed borders. A handsome gothic gazebo designed by Francis F. Johnson clings to the slope and provides an eye-catcher for a pair of borders with many shrub roses and a background of dark purple cotinus. In the nursery, on the far side of the house from the garden, an especially choice collection of over 60 varieties of hydrangea is the star of the list but there are many good things, herbaceous and woody, in other departments. A well produced catalogue is issued but there is no mail order.

HAREWOOD HOUSE
West Yorkshire

Harewood, Leeds
LS17 9LQ
7m N of Leeds and 7m S
of Harrogate by A61
Tel: 0113 2886331
Fax: 0113886467

Owner: The Earl and
Countess of Harewood

Open: 16 Mar to 27 Oct,
daily 10–5. 36 acres. House
open

HAREWOOD HOUSE is a palatial mansion designed by John Carr of York and Robert Adam, and built in the 1760s. In the 19th century there were many changes by Sir Charles Barry who also laid out the Italianate south terrace which survives today and has recently been replanted according to his original designs. A parterre with arabesques filled with sempervivums, stone urns and cones of clipped yew is embellished with a recent statue by Astrid Zydower – a nobly proportioned bronze figure of Orpheus with a leopard draped over his shoulders and standing on a black marble plinth veiled with falling water. But the view from the terrace over 'Capability' Brown's landscape park is the most beautiful thing at Harewood. A lake is masked by trees and the land rises and falls with belts and clumps of trees alternating with meadows in which cattle graze. No building or ornament is visible and the simplicity of it is a splendid foil to the imposing house. Barry's terrace is cheerful but coarse in comparison with Brown's Elysian scene. The restoration of a rock garden has also recently been completed.

HARLOW CARR BOTANICAL GARDENS
North Yorkshire

Crag Lane, Harrogate
HG3 1QB
1 1/2m W of Harrogate by
B6162
Tel: 01423 565418

Owner: The Northern
Horticultural Society

Open: Daily 9.30–6 or dusk
if earlier. 68 acres

THIS IS THE NORTHERN equivalent of Wisley Gardens and is crammed with the same sort of garden attractions. The site is a very handsome one, a shallow valley with a stream and well wooded on its south-western slopes. There are sections devoted to particular groups of plants, such as a bulb garden and an arboretum. Display areas have three different kinds of rockeries – peat, limestone and sandstone – and a winter garden. Much space is devoted to vegetables and a fruit cage. Something different is arranged for each season in the trial gardens, with displays of new cultivars. A seasonal leaflet is produced, giving background information about what is going on in the season in question, and about the plants displayed.

HERB AND HEATHER CENTRE
North Yorkshire

West Haddlesey, nr Selby
YO8 8QA
4m SW of Selby by A19
Tel: 01757 228279

Open: Daily except
Christmas week 9.30–5.30
(dusk in winter)

HERB GARDENS spring up all the time and vary considerably in their interest. Carole Atkinson's is a particularly good one, and apart from herbs she sells a wide range of heathers (over 200 varieties) and a good collection of conifers. All her plants are raised organically, and most may be seen in the adjacent display gardens which contain over 500 varieties of herbs and a National Collection of cotton lavender (*Santolina*). A list (£1.50) is issued and orders are supplied by mail order.

HERTERTON HOUSE GARDENS AND NURSERY
Northumberland

Hartington, nr Cambo
NE61 6BN
2m N of Cambo by B6342
Tel: 01670 774278

Owner: Frank and
Marjorie Lawley

Open: Apr to Sept, daily
except Tue and Thur
1.30–5.30. 1 acre

FEW GARDENS so small give so much pleasure and interest as Herterton. Stone outhouses and beautifully made walls frame a series of enclosed gardens, each with distinctive character. A flower garden has hedges of box and yew, and beds edged in stone, filled with unstaked herbaceous plants, giving generous informality to the ordered design of the layout. A physic garden, overlooked by an arcaded loggia, has a great clipped drum of silver pear at the centre, surrounded by beds edged in London pride or thrift. On the road side of the house the formal garden has topiary of yew and of box, and square box-edged beds brim with different varieties of dicentra. The important thing throughout the garden is the strength and simplicity of the design. The nursery sells only herbaceous perennials and although the stock is not large the choice is fastidious.

HEXHAM HERBS
Northumberland

IN LOVELY COUNTRY hard by Hadrian's Wall Hexham Herbs has found a happy home in a 2-acre walled former kitchen garden. Here are gravel paths, ebullient box-edged borders and, beautifully displayed on a sloping gravel bed, the National

Chollerford, nr Hexham
NE46 4BQ
On the W edge of
Chollerford, 4m NW of
Hexham by A6079
Tel: 01434 681483

Open: Easter to Oct, daily
10–5; phone for winter
opening hours

Collection of thymes – over 120 species and cultivars. A formal pool has recently been added and a knot garden, laid out from a design in William Lawson's *The Country Housewife's Garden* (1617). Indeed the garden is now so attractive that it is best to think of it as both a nursery *and* a garden. The nursery sells herbs, herbaceous plants and native species of wildflowers. There is no mail order but a catalogue is available (£1.50).

HOLDEN CLOUGH NURSERY

Lancashire

Holden,
Bolton-by-Bowland,
Clitheroe BB7 4PF
7m NE of Clitheroe by
A671, A59 and minor roads
(turn off at Sawley)
Tel: 01200 447615

Open: Mar to Sept, Mon
to Thurs 1–5, Sat 9–5 (also
open Sun in Apr and May
2–5); Oct to Feb, daily 9–5
but weather or shows can
interfere – best to phone
first

THIS IS an outstandingly good nursery, specialising in alpines above all but with many other worthwhile plants. The alpine department will excite even veteran fans with its splendid collections of, for example, gentians (over 20 species and cultivars), very many saxifrages, dozens of sedums and so on. New plants are constantly being added. If you are on the look out for the Central American *Weldenia candida* you can find it here. Apart from these there are some excellent ornamental grasses and a connoisseur's selection of ferns, heaths, herbaceous perennials, shrubs and climbers. The 160-page catalogue (£1.20) is exceptional. A mail order service is provided.

HOLEHIRD GARDENS
Cumbria

Patterdale Road,
Windermere LA23 3JA
1m N of Windermere by
A592
Tel: 015394 46238

Owner: The Lakeland
Horticultural Society

Open: Daily, dawn to
dusk. 3 1/2 acres

IN A WELL WOODED position on slopes above the eastern shore of Lake Windermere, Holehird has a marvellous site. The garden owes much of its present interest to William Groves who, in the early years of the 20th century, sponsored the plant-hunting expeditions of Reginald Farrer and William Purdom to north-west China. The Lakeland Horticultural Society took over in 1969 and is responsible for the impeccable upkeep and high level of plant interest that visitors may enjoy today. The soil is acid, and rainfall is famously high, giving excellent conditions for azaleas, ferns, heathers, Himalayan poppies, maples and rhododendrons. These are decoratively disposed on slopes intricately laced with winding walks. A fine walled garden, recently restored, gives protection to many surprisingly tender plants – callistemon, carpenteria, diascia and *Eucryphia glutinosa*. Holehird has National Collections of astilbes – probably the largest in the world – hydrangeas and polystichum ferns. The plants are handsomely displayed in well planned borders.

HOLKER HALL
Cumbria

Cark-in-Cartmel, nr
Grange-over-Sands
LA11 7PL
4m W of Grange-over-Sands
Tel: 01539 558328
Fax: 01539 558776

Owner: The Lord
Cavendish of Furness and
Lady Cavendish

Open: Apr to Oct, daily
except Sat 10.30–6.
25 acres. House open

SOME OF THE most worthwhile gardens manage to juggle very different ingredients with complete success, and Holker Hall is a prime example. The late 16th-century house has a splendid neo-Elizabethan wing built in 1871 after a disastrous fire. Inventive formal gardens near the house provide secluded sitting places and much to admire: an alley of glistening Portugal laurels, herbaceous borders with well judged colour harmonies, stately gravel walks, yew hedges and elegant thorns (*Crataegus orientalis*) set in squares of box hedging. A gate pierces the wall and leads to a newly made meadow garden, a brilliant contrast to the formal enclosures by the house. To one side gardens of a woodland character spread out; eucryphias, hoherias, magnolias, rhododendrons and stewartias ornament a background of venerable beeches and oaks. Among the trees an ornamental staircase, with cascades of water on either side, leads to a 17th-century Italian figure of Neptune. Everywhere there are distinguished plants and the garden will give pleasure in any season, not least for the inspiringly high standard of upkeep. The garden holds the National Collection of Styracaceae. This genus of plants sounds vaguely forbidding but it includes such exquisite trees as *Styrax japonica* which is possibly the most beautiful of all smallish trees for the garden. Holker Hall is a admirable source of inspiration and knowledge.

HOWICK HALL
Northumberland

Alnwick NE66 3LB
6m NE of Alnwick by B1340 and minor roads
Tel: 01665 577285

Owner:
Howick Trustees Ltd

Open: Apr to Sept, daily 1–6. 14 acres

HOWICK, very near the wild Northumbrian coast, has a secluded and romantic air. The grand late 18th-century house overlooks a series of balustraded terraces linked with steps. Thickets of *Choisya ternata* and *Carpenteria californica* flank the steps leading down from the uppermost terrace to a pool and to mixed borders rich with roses and lavender with, in late summer, great waves of blue agapanthus. Beyond the last terrace a meadow, brilliant in spring with narcissi and tulips, is planted with maples, birches and shrub roses. Although this is limestone country, part of the garden at Howick has acid soil and here, between the wars, an excellent woodland garden was made with azaleas, camellias, outstanding magnolias and rhododendrons under a canopy of old oaks, beeches and sweet chestnuts. Later in the season eucryphias, hydrangeas and viburnums continue interest, and in the autumn there is brilliant colour from cercidiphyllums and maples.

LEVENS HALL
Cumbria

Kendal LA8 0PD
5m S of Kendal by A591 and A6
Tel: 01539 560321

Owner: C.H. Bagot

Open: Apr to Sept, daily except Fri and Sat 11–5. 3 acres. House open

A MYSTERIOUS FRENCHMAN, Guillaume Beaumont, came to Levens Hall in 1690 and by 1694 had laid out an exotic formal garden – a forest of topiary and cool beech alleys – which still survives in splendid old age. Fanciful shapes of yew, both golden and common, and of box, many billowing and misshapen with age, are scattered about. Among them, bedding plants make blocks of colours, their brilliance going well with the monumental topiary. Rising above all this is the grey stone house with its great square pele tower. On one side, behind castellated yew hedges, are excellent new borders, a herb garden and an ornamental *potager*. Beaumont's extraordinary beech alley opens out into a giant circle and a path leads to a field with a ha-ha – the first in England – and an avenue of sycamores.

LINDISFARNE CASTLE
Northumberland

Holy Island, Berwick-upon-Tweed TD15 2SH
11 1/2m SE of Berwick-upon-Tweed by A1 and causeway at low tide; it is essential to phone the number below to check tide times, which are also posted at each end of the causeway
Tel: 01289 89244

Owner: The National Trust

Open: Apr to Oct, daily except Fri (open Good Fri) 1–5.30

EDWIN LUTYENS RESTORED the castle as a holiday home for Edward Hudson, the famous editor of *Country Life*; Lytton Strachey thought it 'very dark, and nowhere to sit'. A garden by Gertrude Jekyll was an essential accompaniment, and she laid out a little walled enclosure, at some distance from the castle across sheep pastures. It survives today; aquilegias, irises, Jacob's ladder, lady's mantle and lamb's ears spread among stone flags, and roses are trained on walls and wooden frames. It is so surprising, and such an appropriately simple layout, that any gardener will enjoy seeing it in this remote and wonderfully beautiful setting.

MUNCASTER CASTLE
Cumbria

MUNCASTER IS a wonderfully romantic place. Rising over ravines near the wild Cumbrian coast is a granite medieval castle, rebuilt by Anthony Salvin in 1862. From the entrance lodge the drive

Ravenglass CA18 1RQ
1m SE of Ravenglass by A595
Tel: 01229 717614
Fax: 01229 717010

Owner: Mrs P. Gordon-Duff-Pennington

Open: Daily 11–5. 77 acres. Castle open

plunges down towards the castle, and marvellous old rhododendrons line the way. Many of these were planted by Sir John Ramsden who financed some of Frank Kingdon-Ward's plant-hunting expeditions in the 1920s. Near the castle a grassy terrace walk snakes along the valley, giving unforgettable views of the Esk and the mountains beyond. The slopes above the terrace are richly planted with cherries, magnolias, maples, rhododendrons and other ornamental trees and shrubs. Along the other side of the walk a box hedge has regularly spaced topiary piers of golden and common yew; on the precipitous slopes below, are marvellous trees, including probably the biggest sweet chestnut you will ever look down on.

NEWBY HALL GARDENS
North Yorkshire

NEWBY HALL has one of the best private gardens in England, with outstanding collections of plants beautifully arranged and cared for. The gardens lie to the south of the house on a magnificent site that slopes gently down to the River Ure. Giant double

THE NORTH OF ENGLAND · 265

Ripon HG4 5AE
4m SE of Ripon by B6265
Tel: 01423 322583
Fax: 01423 324452

Owner: R.E.J. Compton

Open: Apr to Sept, daily except Mon (but open Bank Hol Mon) 11–5.30. 25 acres. House open

herbaceous borders, hedged on either side in yew, sweep down to the river edge, and paths lead off enticingly to other formal enclosures or into the surrounding woodland. Among the formal parts are a dramatic 19th-century statue walk; striking seasonal gardens designed specifically for spring and autumn; an excellent garden of old roses; and Sylvia's Garden in which herbs and grey-leafed plants flourish round paved paths. In the woodland are many excellent trees, especially maples, birch and dogwoods (a National Collection). Although full of rarities, this is a garden that can be relished even by those who cannot tell a dandelion from a daffodil. Intensely visited in the summer months, it is big enough to absorb the numbers and provide all kinds of intimate corners where the visitor may be virtually alone.

NORDEN ALPINES
Humberside

Hirst Road, Carlton, nr Goole DN14 9PX
8m W of Goole by A614 and A1041
Tel: 01405 861348

Open: Mar to Sept, Sat, Sun and Bank Hol Mon 10–5; also by appointment

THIS NURSERY is, in the words of the owners, the result of a hobby that got out of hand. It sells only alpines of which it has a dazzling selection: over 2,500 varieties, with marvellous groups of campanulas, dianthus, gentians, irises, primulas, saxifrages (well over 70 varieties), sedums and violas, all propagated on the premises, often in quite small quantities. There is a catalogue (four 2nd-class stamps) and a mail order service. Unusually, the nursery offers bed and breakfast for visitors.

PERRY'S PLANTS
North Yorkshire

River Gardens, Sleights, Whitby YO21 1RR
2 1/2m SW of Whitby on B1410
Tel: 01947 810329

Open: Easter to Oct, daily 10–5

PATRICIA PERRY specialises in herbaceous perennials with a few woody plants, and has charming gardens on the River Esk – Victorian tea-gardens with all sorts of amusements of the time: croquet, putting and, of course, tea. The nursery has a fine selection of anthemis, good hebes, excellent lavateras, mallows, and a very choice range of perennial wallflowers (erysimums). An intriguing group of euphorbias includes the splendidly named *E. characias* 'Winter Blusher' which sounds like an essential plant. A list is issued (large s.a.e.) but there is no mail order.

RIEVAULX TERRACE
North Yorkshire

Rievaulx, Helmsley
YO6 5LJ
2 1/2m NW of Helmsley by
B1257
Tel: 01439 798340

Owner:
The National Trust

Open: 30 Mar to 3 Nov,
daily 10.30–6 or dusk if
earlier. 15 acres

IT WAS ONE of the new ideas of 18th-century landscape gardening to make a terrace from which to admire fine views of the countryside and other beauties. At Rievaulx, high above the exquisite remains of the 12th-century abbey, a grassy terrace curves through woodland, giving wonderful views of the abbey, the valley and distant countryside. At each end of the terrace a little temple provides a punctuation mark;: the plain round Tuscan temple has a simple interior but the Ionic temple is sumptuously furnished, with a table laid for a feast, and decorated with a noble painted ceiling. All this was made in the late 1750s by Thomas Duncombe, an early exercise in picturesque landscape design that still has the power of enchantment. Modest in scale, it is the perfect place to grasp the genius of the 18th-century landscape revolution.

ROOKHOPE NURSERIES
County Durham

Rookhope, Upper
Weardale DL13 2DD
22 1/2m NW of Bishop
Auckland by A68 and A689
Tel: 01388 517272

Open: Apr to Oct, daily
9–5; Nov to Mar, times
vary, please phone

KAREN AND ALAN Blackburn's nursery on the Upper Pennine moors is over 1,000 feet up, and, among other things, provides a tough hardiness test-ground for garden plants. The most extensive part of the list is a representative collection of alpines, with many good campanulas, erodiums, gentians, the smaller geraniums, helianthemums, saxifrages, thymes and violas. In addition, there are dwarf conifers and heathers, and a good range of herbaceous perennials

Illustration opposite: Seaton Delaval Hall

and of shrubs. The adjacent garden shows what may be done in this cold, windy place which has regular heavy snowfalls. If you garden in similar conditions a visit is especially instructive. A catalogue (three 1st-class stamps) is issued and there is a limited mail order service.

SEATON DELAVAL HALL
Northumberland

Seaton Delaval, Whitley Bay, NE26 4QR
9m NE of Newcastle-upon-Tyne on the A190
Tel: 019 2373040/371493

Owner: Lord Hastings

Open: May to Sept, Wed, Sun and Bank Hol Mon 2–6

THE HOUSE AT Seaton Delaval is one of Vanbrugh's ripest confections, with a memorably dramatic position on the Northumberland coast, frequently veiled in sea mist. A few traces survive of the original garden (including bastions of a Vanbrughesque kind) but the present scheme has been almost entirely made by the present Lord Hastings who, in 1947, commissioned from James Russell a new formal garden to the west of the house. He laid out a splendidly theatrical arrangement of yew hedges and topiary, with lively patterns of box hedges, to which fine urns and a fountain were later added. On one side of the house a box parterre is planted with roses making a lovely patchwork in late June. Nearby, a pair of mixed borders sweeps round a wonderful old weeping ash. Behind yew hedges Lady Hastings has added a lily pond and a laburnum tunnel leading towards the Norman church. Everywhere the eye is caught by Vanbrugh's lovely swaggering house, a dramatic contrast to the light-hearted decorativeness of the garden.

SELLET HALL GARDENS
Lancashire

nr Kirkby Lonsdale
LA6 2QF
1m SW of Kirkby Lonsdale on the Low Biggins road
Tel: 01524 271865

Open: Mar to Oct, daily 10–5

THE LUNE VALLEY is one of the most beautiful parts of England, and Sellet Hall takes full advantage of its setting. It is a nursery, specialising in herbs, and a very attractive garden disposed in rooms linked by enticing vistas. Yew hedges and walls of the fine local stone divide the spaces, some of which are laid out as flowery parterres. Apart from a wide range of herbs, the nursery also sells trees (especially maples), shrubs, bamboos, many herbaceous perennials and a choice selection of auriculas.

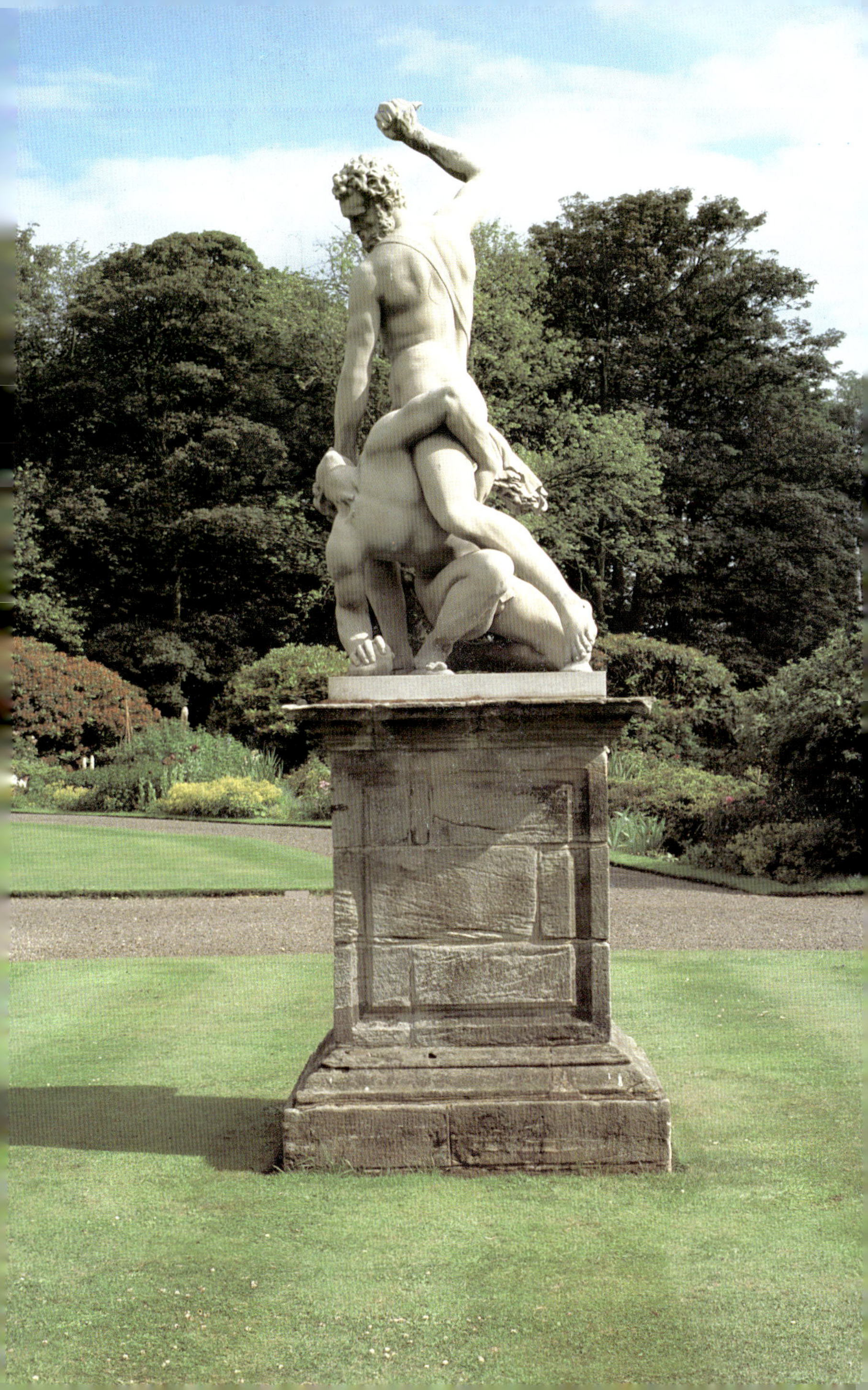

SIZERGH CASTLE
Cumbria

nr Kendal LA8 8AE
3 1/2m S of Kendal by A591
Tel: 015395 60070

Owner:
The National Trust

Open: Apr to Oct, Sun to Thur 12.30–5.30.
14 acres. House open

THE GREAT THING at Sizergh, in the shadow of the late medieval stone castle, is one of the best rock gardens in England. It was laid out in 1926 by a local firm, T.R. Hayes & Son of Ambleside, and is now a densely planted jungle of conifers and Japanese maples, laced with winding walks and a splashing stream and underplanted with a marvellous collection of hardy ferns – over 100 species and varieties. South of the castle steps lead down to an ornamental lake and to the west an avenue of rowans leads through a rose garden with species and shrub roses.

STILLINGFLEET LODGE NURSERIES
North Yorkshire

Illustration: Iris douglasiana

Stillingfleet, York
YO4 6HW
7m S of York by A19 and B1222; in the village, turn opposite the church
Tel: 01904 728506

Open: Apr to mid Oct, daily except Mon, Thur and Sun 10–4

VANESSA COOK specialises in herbaceous perennials, although she also sells some of the more versatile of the woody plants such as artemisias, cistus, daphnes, hebes, and lavenders. Mrs Cook's selection of herbaceous plants is particularly attractive, with good euphorbias, a long list of hardy geraniums, a superb selection of irises, penstemons, primulas, pulmonarias (of which she holds a National Collection) and veronicas. There are also several interesting grasses, or grass-like plants. Vanessa Cook's list is specially rich in those smaller ornamental items which find a decorative home in odd corners of the garden and immensely add to its character. A catalogue is issued (five 1st-class stamps), from which plants may be supplied by post.

STUDLEY ROYAL
North Yorkshire

Fountains, Ripon
HG4 3DZ
4m W of Ripon by B6265
Tel: 01765 608888/601005

Owner:
The National Trust

Open: Daily except Fri in Nov, Dec and Jan and 24 and 25 Dec; Apr to Sept 10–7 (closes at 5 on 5, 6 and 27 Jul); Oct to Mar 10–5 or dusk if earlier. 900 acres

JOHN AISLABIE was Chancellor of the Exchequer in 1720 when the South Sea Bubble collapsed, and subsequently he retired to his Yorkshire estate to lick his wounds and make a garden. In the wooded valley of the River Skell he laid out a great water garden ornamented with statues of lead and stone, and, in the woods above, built a banqueting house, an octagonal tower, a Temple of Piety and a Temple of Fame. John Aislabie's son William later acquired the ruins of the nearby Cistercian Fountains Abbey, and these were incorporated into the landscape scheme – suddenly revealed round a curve of the river, like a gigantic and exquisite garden ornament.

SUTTON PARK
North Yorkshire

Sutton-on-the-Forest, York
YO6 1DP
8m N of York by B1363
Tel: 01347 810249

Owner:
Mrs N.M.D Sheffield

Open: Easter to Oct, daily 11–5.30. 8 acres

THE APPROACH TO the garden at Sutton Park is oblique, through groves of ornamental trees, with the very pretty garden façade of the 18th-century brick and stone house gradually revealed. A series of terraces, filled with decorative planting, leads down from the house. The second terrace has a geometric pattern of beds, with standard roses underplanted with *Alchemilla mollis*, artemisia, catmint and rue, with a weeping silver pear in each corner. Vertical emphasis is given by a series of soaring cypresses and the last terrace has a long, calm lily pond. Across a lawn a beech hedge dips down in the middle to reveal the peaceful countryside beyond.

THORP PERROW ARBORETUM
North Yorkshire

Bedale DL8 2PR
2m S of Bedale off B6268
Tel: 01677 425323

Owner: Sir John Ropner Bt

Open: Daily dawn–dusk.
85 acres

THIS WAS STARTED by Colonel Sir Leonard Ropner in 1931 as a private plant collection. Old trees, especially conifers planted in the 1840s, provided both protection and a fine sombre background to the more colourful ornamental trees. Only a complete list would give a full idea of the range and depth of the woody plants represented here; it is a vast collection, with great rarities and excellent specimens of individual trees. For the gardener there are excellent collections of flowering shrubs and of the smaller ornamental trees such as cherries and crab-apples.

WALLINGTON
Northumberland

Cambo, Morpeth
NE61 4AR
12m W of Morpeth
Tel: 01670 774283

Owner:
The National Trust

Open: Apr to Oct, daily 10–7; Nov to Mar, daily 10–4 (or dusk if earlier). 100 acres. House open

THE HOUSE at Wallington looks out over a ha-ha and parkland. The pleasure garden lies at some distance from the house, hidden in woodland across the road. Overlooking a pond there remains from the 18th century the handsome Portico House, a classical gardener's cottage. In the heart of the woods an immense walled garden bursts into view – long and narrow, irregularly shaped and built on a slope. A high terrace is planted with a long white and silver border, and its retaining wall is crested with lead statues. From the gravelled terrace walk there are views over grassy paths sweeping between mixed borders in the lavishly planted gardens spread out like an intricate patchwork quilt below.

WENTWORTH CASTLE GARDENS
South Yorkshire

Illustration opposite: The Portico House at Wallington

SANDWICHED BETWEEN the ghastly M1 to the east and surprisingly unspoilt rural scenes to the west Wentworth Castle is caught between past and present. The Wentworth family built the great house in the early 18th century and laid out an elaborate garden, at first following the formal style of the day but, later in the century, becoming increasingly

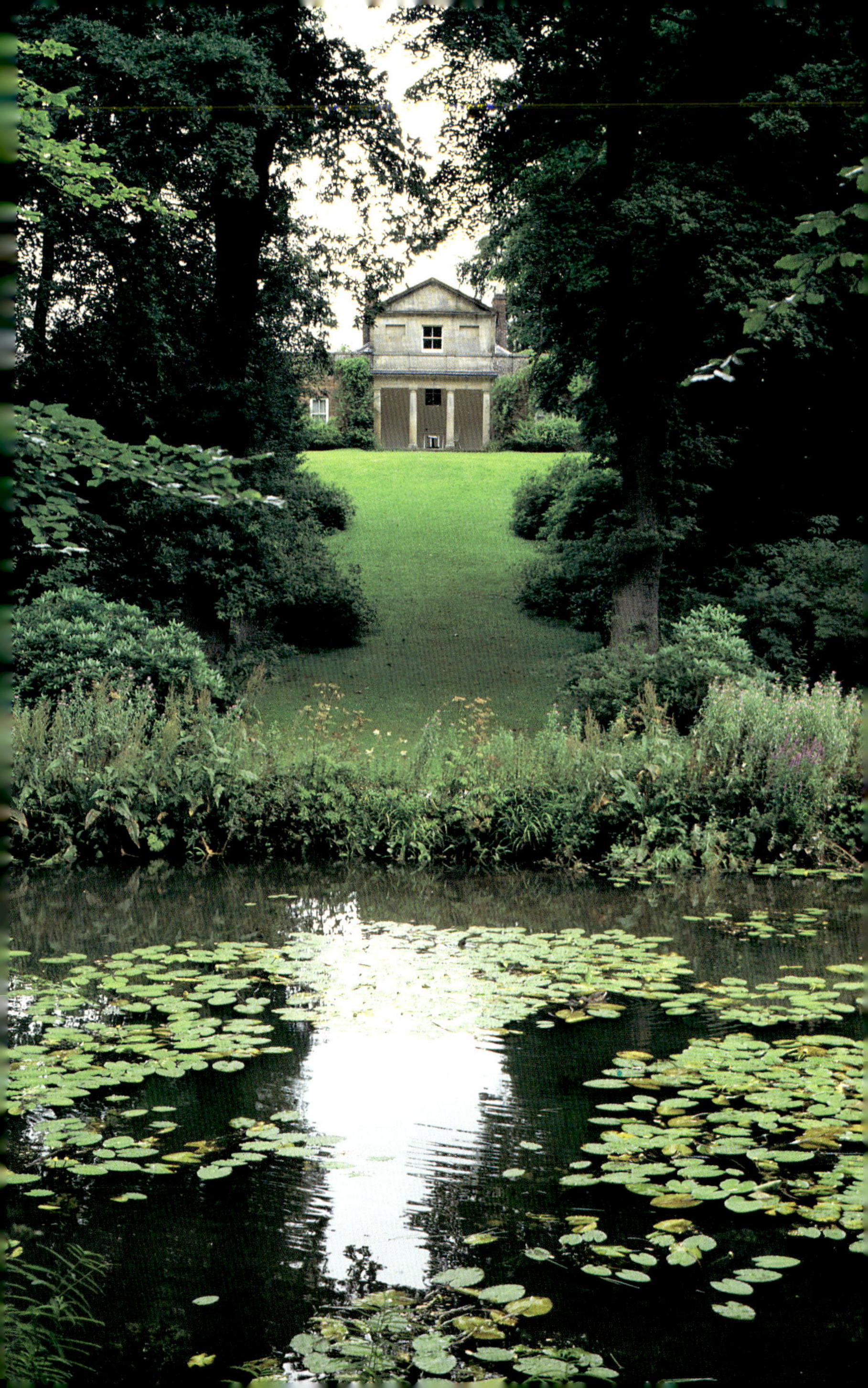

Stainborough, Barnsley
S75 3ET
4m SW of Barnsley on the
W side of the M1 between
Jncts 36 and 37
Tel: 01226 285426
Fax: 01226 284308

Owner: Barnsley
Metropolitan District
Council

Open: May and Jun, Thurs
2 pm, meet in car park for
conducted tour; group
visits by appointment at
other times

informal. The early 18th-century parterres are now a car-park but behind the house, where the land sweeps uphill, are fine surviving features. A memorial obelisk to Lady Mary Wortley Montagu (who introduced innoculation against small-pox in 1720) stands out on the skyline and to one side is the splendid Gothic folly of Stainborough Castle – dating from the late 1720s and one of the earliest Gothic garden buildings in the country. In the surrounding woodland there are fine trees and shrubs and the garden holds the National Collection of Falconera rhododendrons. Restoration is in progress in this potentially marvellous landscape and visitors will follow it with interest.

WETHERIGGS COUNTRY POTTERY
Cumbria

Clifton Dykes, Penrith
CA10 2DH
1 1/2m S of Penrith turning
E of A6 after Eamont
Bridge
Tel: 01768 892733
Fax: 01768 892722

Open: Daily 9–8 (summer),
10–5 (rest of year). Closed
25 and 26 Dec, 1 Jan

WETHERIGGS APPEARED in earlier editions of this book but went out of business a couple of years ago. Now it is back, looking healthier than ever. The pottery was founded in 1855 and preserves much of its original machinery which is still in use. Excellent garden pots are made, some based on 19th-century Wetheriggs patterns. Tableware and other kinds of pottery are made but it is the traditional garden pots that gardeners will find of special interest. The process of their manufacture – from clay-pit to kiln – may also be followed.

SCOTLAND

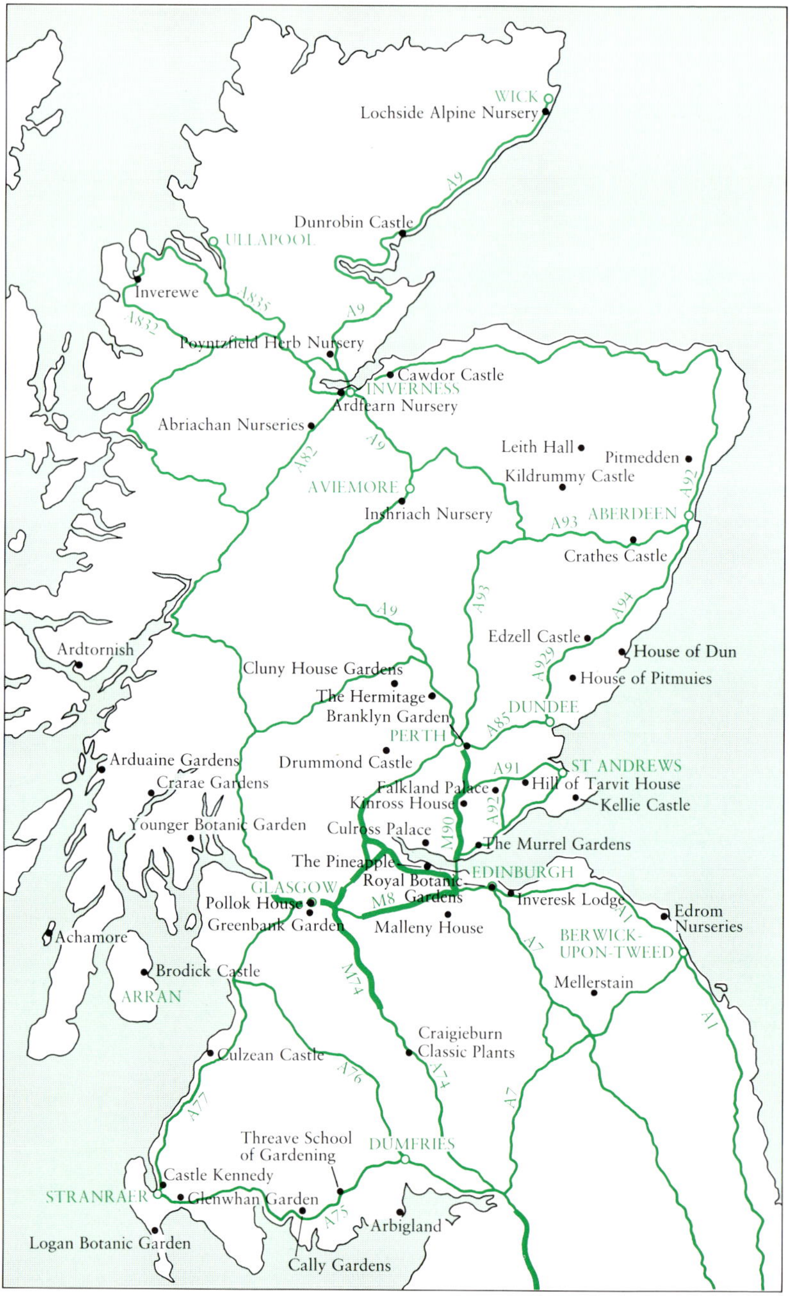

WICK
Lochside Alpine Nursery
A9
Dunrobin Castle
ULLAPOOL
Inverewe
A835
A832
A9
Poyntzfield Herb Nursery
Cawdor Castle
INVERNESS
Ardfearn Nursery
Abriachan Nurseries
A9
A82
Leith Hall
Pitmedden
Kildrummy Castle
A92
AVIEMORE
Inshriach Nursery
ABERDEEN
A93
Crathes Castle
A93
A94
A9
Edzell Castle
House of Dun
A929
House of Pitmuies
Ardtornish
Cluny House Gardens
The Hermitage
Branklyn Garden
DUNDEE
A85
PERTH
Drummond Castle
Arduaine Gardens
A91
ST ANDREWS
Crarae Gardens
Falkland Palace
Hill of Tarvit House
Kinross House
Kellie Castle
A92
Younger Botanic Garden
Culross Palace
M90
The Murrel Gardens
The Pineapple
EDINBURGH
GLASGOW
Royal Botanic Gardens
Pollok House
M8
Inveresk Lodge
A1
Edrom Nurseries
Greenbank Garden
Malleny House
Achamore
A7
BERWICK-UPON-TWEED
M74
Brodick Castle
Mellerstain
ARRAN
A1
Craigieburn Classic Plants
Culzean Castle
A76
A74
A77
A7
Threave School of Gardening
DUMFRIES
Castle Kennedy
STRANRAER
Glenwhan Garden
A75
Arbigland
Logan Botanic Garden
Cally Gardens

ABRIACHAN NURSERIES
Highland

Loch Ness Side IV3 6LA
9m SW of Inverness
on A82
Tel: 0146 386 232

Open: Feb to Nov, daily 9–7

ON THE VERY BANKS of Loch Ness, Abriachan Nurseries has an enviable south-facing sloping site. Here are grown a good range of plants of which herbaceous perennials and alpines are the strongest suits. Among the herbaceous plants there are excellent foxgloves, a very good range of hardy geraniums, several meconopsis and an immense collection of primulas. In the alpine department are gentians, helianthemums, lewisias, the smaller phlox and a large number of saxifrages. Well planted beds surround the nursery, and paths entice the visitor uphill to a further garden area. An attractive catalogue is produced (three 1st-class stamps) and plants are supplied by mail order.

ACHAMORE GARDENS
Strathclyde

Isle of Gigha PA41 7AD
Off west coast of Kintyre;
ferry from Tayinloan
Tel: 01583 505267/505254

Owner: Derek Holt

Open: Daily dawn–dusk.
50 acres

GIGHA IS a small island in the Inner Hebrides. Here Sir James Horlick came in 1944 and started to make a woodland garden, his new plantings protected by evergreens and old broad-leafed trees. Rhododendrons now reign supreme, constituting one of the best collections in Scotland, with the aristocratic, large-leafed species such as *R. falconeri* and *R. macabeanum* growing to exceptional size and beauty in this mild climate of high rainfall. Apart from the rhododendrons there is much else to admire, not least the rich underplanting of herbaceous and bulbous plants and the very wide range of ornamental trees and shrubs with excellent camellias, magnolias, mahonias, many shrub roses, viburnums and rare, tender trees such as the New Zealand Christmas tree, *Metrosideros umbellata*, and other very unusual things from the southern hemisphere. The wide range of plants growing in such a climate means that something interesting is happening in the garden on any day of the year.

ARBIGLAND
Dumfries and Galloway

Kirkbean DG2 8BQ
14m SW of Dumfries by A710
Tel: 01387 880283

Owner: Captain and Mrs J.B. Blackett

Open: May to Sept, daily except Mon (open Bank Hol Mon) 2–6. 20 acres

SOME GARDENS provide the thrill of exploration and discovery, gradually unlocking their charms to the visitor. Arbigland, with its elegant mid-Georgian house handsomely framed in fine trees, does not at first reveal signs of any particular garden interest. But behind the house the Broad Walk plunges down through woodland towards the hidden sea. From this central axis enticing paths lead to Japan – a bosky water garden; to a hidden rose garden built on the site of old Arbigland Hall; and to glades planted with ornamental trees and shrubs that flourish in this climate of high rainfall and mild winters. There are wonderful rhododendrons such as the tender, giant *R. sino-grande*; beautiful old maples; eucryphias grown to great size; and very fine conifers giving shelter from the coastal winds. The cry of seagulls and the sound of unseen waves provide a curious further dimension to the delights of this rare garden.

ARDFEARN NURSERY
Highland

Bunchrew IV3 6RH
4m W of Inverness by A862
Tel: 01463 223607
Fax: 01463 711713

Open: Daily, 9–5

JAMES SUTHERLAND and his son Alasdair have established this relatively new nursery as one of the best sources of alpine plants. A courtyard of old cow byres makes an attractive setting for the plants, many of which are displayed in beautifully planted raised beds and troughs. Over 1,000 species and varieties are available, and there is a constant stream of new introductions – some from the wild by plant-hunting expeditions to which the nursery subscribes – and even expert alpinists will find unfamiliar things. For the non-alpinist there is a good range of herbaceous perennials and shrubs. An alpine catalogue is produced (four 2nd-class stamps) in September and orders are fulfilled by post between October and March. There remains plenty for visitors to buy – but rarities are snapped up quickly.

ARDTORNISH
Highland

Morvern, by Oban
PA34 5XA
30m SW of Corran by A861 and A884; the Corran ferry joins the A828 from Oban to the A861
Tel: 01967 421288
Fax: 01967 421211

Owner: Mrs John Raven

Open: Apr to Oct, daily 10–5

THE ARDTORNISH ESTATE lies in one of the most beautiful parts of Scotland, in the south-western part of the Morvern peninsula, looking south-west across the Sound of Mull. The house and garden command splendid views from the head of Loch Aline. The garden was largely the creation of the present owner, her late husband John Raven, and her parents. Its character is informal and its great strength is the admirable collection of acid-loving trees and shrubs – cercidiphyllums, enkianthus, eucryphias, hoherias, maples, rhododendrons and many others. There are also many herbaceous perennials and underplantings of bluebells, colchicums, daffodils and snowdrops. The keen gardener will rent one of the flats or cottages on the estate, all of which give free access to the gardens. John Raven's excellent book *A Botanist's Garden*, now back in print, vividly describes the planting here and at the Ravens' other garden near Cambridge, Docwra's Manor (see page 221).

ARDUAINE GARDENS
Strathclyde

Kilmelford PA34 4XG
20m S of Oban by A816
Tel: 01852 200366

Owner: The National
Trust for Scotland

Open: Daily 9.30–sunset.
18 acres

THE GARDEN AT ARDUAINE was started in 1897 by James Arthur Campbell, a tea planter, and friend of Osgood Mackenzie the maker of Inverewe. It is a splendid site which slopes gently down towards the shores of Loch Melfort. At first the garden is fairly open, with many smaller azaleas and rhododendrons planted in island beds, and enlivened by a stream and pools. There is rich underplanting of superb Himalayan poppies, groves of gunnera, hostas and trilliums. Paths lead up the hill and the visitor soon experiences the full Himalayan effect. Immense rhododendrons are at their most impressive against a backdrop of coniferous planting. It is essential to keep going to the top of the hill where a viewpoint gives an exquisite panorama of the calm waters of Loch Melfort below.

BRANKLYN GARDEN
Tayside

Dundee Road,
Perth PH2 7BB
On the eastern edge of
Perth by A85
Tel: 01738 625535

Owner: The National
Trust for Scotland

Open: Mar to 23 Oct, daily
9.30–sunset. 1 3/4 acres

JOHN AND DOROTHY Renton started this garden in 1922. On a south-facing slope with acid soil they built up a wonderful collection of appropriate plants – smaller rhododendrons, maples, daphnes, magnolias and many woodland plants such as erythroniums, fritillaries, meconopsis and trilliums. Narrow paths of turf wind along the contours of the land, bringing the visitor nose-to-nose with all kinds of distinguished plants beautifully grown. The combination of woody plants underplanted with spring bulbs and later herbaceous plants is executed with brilliant aplomb.

BRODICK CASTLE
Strathclyde

BRODICK CASTLE occupies a splendid position, well protected from westerly winds and looking east across the Firth of Clyde. The castle with its castellated towers is partly medieval but rebuilt in the early 17th century and in 1844. The present garden dates from 1923 when the Duchess of Montrose

Isle of Arran KA27 8HY
2m from Brodick Ferry
Tel: 01770 302202

Owner: The National
Trust for Scotland

Open: Daily 9.30–sunset.
80 acres. Castle open

started an ambitious woodland garden with a
collection of rhododendrons, many of them recent
introductions from the great plant hunters, in
particular George Forrest; among them the
huge-leafed *R. macabeanum* and *R. sino-grande*.
From the castle paths wind downhill towards the
seashore, and in a shady place there is a fernery and
a delightful Bavarian summer house embellished with
rustic work and lovely inlaid panels of pinecones. In
spring the woodland, with meconopsis and primulas
flourishing about the ornamental shrubs, is a brilliant
sight. A walled garden, dated 1710, has been restored
with Victorian-style carpet-bedding, and mixed
borders on three sides prolong the flowering interest
to the very end of the summer.

CALLY GARDENS

Dumfries and Galloway

Gatehouse-of-Fleet,
Castle Douglas
DG7 2DJ
E of Gatehouse on
Dumfries Road
Tel: None

Open: Apr to Sept, Sat
and Sun 10–5.30

A 3-ACRE WALLED GARDEN is the setting for this
treasure trove of plants. Michael Wickenden has
around 3,000 different species and varieties, of which
about 500 are in stock at any one time. His sources
are exchanges with other collectors, seeds from
botanic gardens, and his own finds on
plant-collecting trips. The catalogue (three 1st-class
stamps) is therefore a moveable feast, but a feast
nonetheless, and you may always find something
unfamiliar and extremely desirable. He also sells
some beautiful terracotta pots from Crete. A mail
order service is provided but a visit is essential, to
inspect the stock, much of which is handsomely
displayed in deep, well filled borders against the walls.

CASTLE KENNEDY
Dumfries and Galloway

Rephad, Stranraer
DG9 8BX
5m E of Stranraer by A75
Tel: 01776 702024
Fax: 01776 702024

Owner: The Earl and
Countess of Stair

Open: Easter to Sept,
daily 10–5

MANY GARDENS seem interesting enough at the time but later fade in the memory to a blur of borders. Castle Kennedy is a vast place, a piece of heroic landscaping with intimate moments, that would be hard to forget. The garden lies between two castles – 15th-century Castle Kennedy and the 19th-century Lochinch Castle which make splendid eye-catchers to vistas through woods and up hills. North of the old castle are the rare remains of the early 18th-century formal gardens – extraordinary terraces and turf mounds sculpted in the ground. Woodland is embellished with an immense collection of distinguished trees and shrubs: many very large conifers, exceptional rhododendrons and eucryphias which grow to vast size. By the old castle a walled garden has excellent borders and, to its south, an avenue of eucryphias and embothriums plummets down to the shores of the loch.

CAWDOR CASTLE
Highland

CAWDOR, with its outlook towers, crow-steps, drawbridge, dungeons and courtyards, is exactly what a Highland castle should be. To one side of the castle ancient stone walls enclose a flower garden; here a broad grass path runs down the middle between a pair of excellent herbaceous borders with old apple trees rising behind. A rose garden, its oval

Cawdor IV12 5RD
11m NE of Inverness by
A96 and B9090
Tel: 01667 404615
Fax: 01667 404674

Owner: Countess Cawdor

Open: May to 13 Oct,
daily 10–5.30

beds edged in lavender, is given height by soaring columns of common and golden yew. There are some beautiful pieces of formal planting: a long rose tunnel, a peony walk and, in late summer, a virtuoso pair of beds brimming with *Galtonia candicans* and pale orange lilies. On one side of the walled garden a gate leads to a wild woodland garden on the slopes below, and, on the other side of the castle, a large holly maze and herbaceous borders are laid out in the old walled kitchen garden.

CLUNY HOUSE GARDENS
Tayside

by Aberfeldy PH15 2JT
3 1/2m NE of Aberfeldy.
From Aberfeldy go W to
bridge over Tay and turn
right at Weem–Strathtay
road
Tel: 01887 820795

Owner: Mr J. and Mrs W.
Mattingley

Open: Mar to Oct, daily
10–6

THIS PART of Perthshire, 600ft above the River Tay, has an alpine character, and the name Cluny means in Gaelic 'meadow place'. The house is a pretty, early 19th-century mansion with gothic touches, and the garden is disposed on the slopes below it. Here are many shrubs and trees relishing the acid soil and high rainfall, but its greatest glory is the range of herbaceous plants. The National Collection of Asiatic primulas, well over 100 species, is kept here, and many of these exquisitely delicate plants line the paths that thread their way through the woods. Apart from these there are lovely crocuses, fritillaries, gentians, spectacular examples of the giant lily *Cardiocrinum giganteum*, narcissi and trilliums. This is very much a garden to explore, and gradually, as you get your eye in, you will discover more and more – many of the best things are tucked away in odd corners. A small nursery has some admirable, and often rare, plants for sale.

CRAIGIEBURN CLASSIC PLANTS
Dumfries and Galloway

FEW THINGS ARE MORE exciting to gardeners than new nurseries and new gardens. Craigieburn started in 1991 and already Bill Chudziak and Janet Wheatcroft have built up an excellent collection of plants and made a solid start on restoring the exquisite woodland garden. Behind the house the

Craigieburn House, by
Moffat DG10 9LF
2m E of Moffat by A708
Tel: 01683 21250

Open: Mid Apr to Oct,
daily except Mon and Tue
12.30–8

Craigie Burn plummets down a spectacular ravine
with wooded slopes crowding in all about. Bill is a
former computer programmer who saw the light and
has made himself an expert on Himalyan poppies;
the nursery sells the finest range of *Meconopsis*
commercially available. The emphasis is on
herbaceous perennials, particularly species and forms,
with lovely aquilegias, digitalis, primulas and violas.
An excellent catalogue (four 1st-class stamps) is
produced and a mail-order service is provided.

CRARAE GARDENS
Strathclyde

Crarae, by Inveraray
PA32 8YA
10m S of Inveraray by A83
Tel: 01546 886614

Owner: The Crarae Garden
Charitable Trust

Open: Summer, daily 9–6;
winter, daily dawn–dusk.
50 acres

CRARAE GARDENS have a marvellous site in a
precipitous glen on the north-west bank of Loch
Fyne. The garden was given to the trust that now
owns it by Sir Ilay Campbell Bt, whose grandparents
had come to live here in 1904. It was his father, Sir
George, a cousin of the great plant-hunter Reginald
Farrer, who had the greatest influence on the garden.
At the very centre of it lies the glen, a romantic
wooded ravine, stuffed like a good plum pudding
with plenty of rich fruit: the great Asiatic flowering
shrubs – azaleas, camellias, magnolias and
rhododendrons – are well represented but there are
choice collections of many other groups: several
species of the southern beech, *Nothofagus*, excellent
rowans, some lovely examples of styrax and much
else. Paths girdle the glen which is occasionally

traversed by wooden bridges giving exquisite views of the magnificent plants and rocky burn below. Crarae is worth visiting in any season, and there is always the piquant contrast of exotic introductions in a natural Scottish setting of special beauty.

CRATHES CASTLE
Grampian

nr Banchory AB31 3QJ
3m E of Banchory and 15m SW of Aberdeen by A93
Tel: 01330 844525

Owner: The National Trust for Scotland

Open: Daily 9.30–sunset. 92 acres. Castle open

ALTHOUGH THE BONES of this garden are old – the superb yew hedges were planted in about 1700 and the romantic tower house dates from the 16th century – the garden is almost entirely of the 20th century. Sir James Burnett of Leys inherited the estate in 1926, and he and his wife started a new garden much influenced by the Hidcote tradition of lavish plantings of often unusual plants within a firmly disciplined plan of enclosed areas. The Burnetts made a series of magnificent borders, some with single colour schemes, and one of the finest herbaceous borders in Britain. Gardeners from farther south will note that herbaceous plants, because of the much longer daylight hours at this northern latitude, grow exceptionally well. All this is maintained impeccably,

CULROSS PALACE

Grampian

Culross KY12 8JH
In the centre of Culross,
14m SE of Stirling by A907
and B9037
Tel: 01383 880359

Owner: The National Trust
for Scotland

Open: Good Fri to Sept,
daily 11–5. 1/4 acre

THE LITTLE TOWN of Culross is one of the most enchanting survivals in Scotland – a cluster of wonderfully preserved 17th- and 18th-century houses in a surprisingly isolated position hard by the banks of the Firth of Forth. The Palace has no royal associations, it was a grand merchant's house of the 17th century. The National Trust for Scotland recently completely restored it and had the excellent idea of recreating a period garden on the terraced slopes behind. The early 18th century was an important moment in Scottish garden history, when gardens were becoming increasingly cultivated for ornamental purposes. Period plants, culinary and ornamental, are arranged in a pattern of raised beds and an arbour is covered with pleached mulberry and vines. The 'herbers', rough lawns, are cut with a hook to give them the true shaggy texture of their time. It is a triumphant success. The most memorable views of the garden are from the old leaded windows on the north side of the house.

---

and visitors will learn much about practical gardening as well as enjoying an exceptionally beautiful garden. It its day the garden at Crathes was a pioneer; today, it preserves its freshness and its power to inspire gardeners.

CULZEAN CASTLE
Strathclyde

Maybole KA19 8LE
4m SW of Maybole and
12m S of Ayr by A719
Tel: 01655 760274

Owner: The National
Trust for Scotland

Open: Daily 9.30–sunset.
120 acres. Castle open

ROBERT ADAM'S gothic castle – towered, turreted and irresistible – occupies a suitably dramatic site on the very brink of cliffs, looking north-west across the sea to the Isle of Arran. To the south of the castle, terraces with fine borders overlook a pool and fountain, and, in the walled former kitchen garden at some distance from the castle, are glasshouses and a peach-house . Fruit is still grown here and there are excellent borders of old roses and herbaceous perennials. The benign coastal climate allows many tender plants to flourish – cabbage palms, mimosa, myrtles, olearias and pittosporums. But the real excitement is the woodland with its marvellous 19th-century conifers and, in spring, immense numbers of bluebells, narcissi and snowdrops.

DRUMMOND CASTLE GARDENS
Tayside

Muthill, nr Crieff
PH7 4HZ
2m S of Crieff by A822
Tel: 01764 681257
Fax: 01764 681550

Owner: Grimsthorpe and
Drummond Castle Trust

Open: May to Oct, daily
2–6. 15 acres

THE CASTLE is of different periods – chiefly a late medieval keep and a fine 17th-century house. Backed by old woodland, it sits at the top of a slope below which spreads one of the most extraordinary formal gardens in Britain. Inspired by 17th-century garden taste, it was laid out in the 1830s when garden makers looked to the past for inspiration. A huge rectangle is divided by paths forming a St Andrews cross, with a magnificent multi-facetted sundial at the centre, and within the areas formed by this division an intricate symmetrical pattern of ornament and planting is laid out. Box-edged parterres are filled with roses, bedding schemes or gravel, and height is given by a profusion of clipped cones of yew, Portugal laurels and purple Japanese maples. These varied ingredients are given order by the firm underlying pattern of the design, and the place has an exuberant and festive air.

DUNROBIN CASTLE GARDENS
Highland

Golspie KW10 6RR
1m N of Golspie by A9
Tel: 01408 633177/633268
Fax: 01408 633800

Owner:
The Sutherland Trust

Open: Daily 10.30–5.30.
Castle open

DUNROBIN is the ancient estate of the earls and dukes of Sutherland, and at its centre is a wonderful early 19th-century fantasy castle with a touch of the Loire and a dash of Bavaria, rising cheerfully on the slopes above the Dornoch Firth. Sir Charles Barry rebuilt the house in its present form, and almost certainly laid out the formal gardens on terraces that descend to the sea. The first terrace wall gives shelter to a long border with bold mixed plantings. Below this, a circular parterre in Barry's full-blown formal style has box-edged compartments planted with roses, geraniums and potentillas, and clipped domes of yew rising above them.

EDROM NURSERIES
Borders

Illustration: Roscoea
cautleyoides

THIS IS NOT a large nursery but it has a very carefully chosen list of excellent plants, some of which are rarely found for sale. The great speciality is alpines, but there are a few rhododendrons and

Coldingham, Eyemouth
TD14 5TZ
12m NW of
Berwick-upon-Tweed by
A1 and A1107
Tel: 01890 771386

Open: Mar to Sept, Mon
to Fri 10–4.30, Sat and Sun
2–5

various oddities that have caught the nursery's fancy
(like *Zaluzianskya ovata* from Lesotho). In the alpine
department there are androsaces, marvellous gentians,
lewisias, several meconopsis and one of the most
fastidiously selected collections of primulas you will
find anywhere. There is an excellent catalogue from
which mail orders are fulfilled.

EDZELL CASTLE
Tayside

Edzell, nr Brechin
DD9 7UE
7m N of Brechin by A94
and B966
Tel: 01356 648631

Owner: Historic Scotland

Open: Apr to Sept, daily
9.30–6 (Sun 2–6); Oct to
Mar, daily except Fri
9.30–4 (Thurs 9.30–2 and
Sun 2–4). 1 acre

IN THE EARLY 17th century the now ruined castle of
the Lindsays had a fine ornamental garden, or
'pleasaunce', enclosed in walls carved with the
Lindsay arms and all kinds of symbolic motifs
representing virtues, the arts and planetary deities.
To this rare and beautiful survival was added in the
1930s a box-edged parterre, of vaguely 17th-century
character – a pretty sight viewed from the upper
rooms of the castle and towers of the garden walls.

FALKLAND PALACE
Fife

HIDDEN BEHIND stone walls in the centre of
Falkland, the gardens still have the feeling of a
royal 'privy' garden. The 16th-century palace of the
Kings of Scotland, formerly a Stewart hunting lodge,
gives immense character to what is an almost entirely

Falkland KY7 7BU
11m N of Kircaldy by A912
Tel: 01337 857397

Owner: The National Trust for Scotland

Open: Apr to 23 Oct, Mon to Sat 11–5.30, Sun 1–5.30. 7 acres. Palace open

20th-century garden. Large areas of lawn are broken by island beds lavishly planted with shrubs and ornamental trees – a scheme designed by Percy Cane in the 1950s. These beds are straight where they run along the perimeter walls but curved where they face each other across the lawn, giving a lively, sinuous walk between them. A giant mixed border almost 500 feet long faces west across the lawn to a blue and white herbaceous border and a dazzling new border of delphiniums. At the southern extremity of the lawn, monumental yew hedges shelter a lily pond, and at an upper level there is a formal arrangement of yellow ('Allgold') and scarlet ('Frensham') roses – the heraldic colours of the Stewarts – underplanted with lavender and silver *Brachyglottis greyi* and given emphasis with pyramids of golden yew.

GLENWHAN GARDEN

Dumfries and Galloway

HIGH ABOVE the main road to Stranraer, Glenwhan Garden spreads out over a windy hilltop with marvellous views of Luce bay and the Mull of Galloway. Since 1979 the Knotts have made a very

Dunragit, by Stranraer
DG9 8PH
7m E of Stranraer by A75
Tel: 01581 400222

Owner: Mr and Mrs
William Knott

Open: Apr to Sept, daily
10–5. 12 acres

large, interesting and individual garden that is filled with good plants. At its heart is an extensive pool, divided by a grassy causeway and fed by a tumbling stream. The slopes above are lavishly planted with trees and shrubs. Several different habitats are provided by the lie of the land, and the wet, mild climate promotes luxurious growth. There is no point in beginning to list plants – almost any gardener will find something unfamiliar here. But this is not just a plant collection for there are all sorts of well planned ornamental schemes and wonderful views over water and hills. A nursery attached to the garden sells a wide range of herbaceous and woody plants of the kind seen growing in the garden.

GREENBANK GARDEN
Strathclyde

Flenders Road, Clarkston,
Glasgow G76 8RB
6m S of city centre
Tel: 0141 639 3281

Owner: The National
Trust for Scotland

Open: Daily 9.30–sunset
(closed 25 and 26 Dec and
1 and 2 Jan). 16 acres

GREENBANK is a very decorative 18th-century house of stucco and stone with a pediment capped with urns. South of the house an old walled kitchen garden, of the same date as the house, is divided into several enclosures with, at its heart, a rondel of clipped yew hedges and a sundial. In other enclosed areas there is that beguiling mixture, so often found in Scottish gardens, of ornamental planting and fruit and vegetables. Old espaliered apple trees rise out of mixed borders which are particularly rich in shrub roses, and orderly vegetable beds spread beneath the walls. A woodland garden threaded with shady walks provides further seclusion. Although the Glasgow suburbs press all around, Greenbank preserves a delicious rural character.

THE HERMITAGE
Tayside

16m N of Perth, 1m W of Dunkeld, signposted off the A9

Owner: The National Trust for Scotland

Open: Daily, dawn–dusk. 37 acres

THERE IS NOT MUCH here for lovers of flower power, but for connoisseurs of dramatic atmosphere few places can beat it. A path winds along the banks of the fast-flowing River Braan through cool coniferous woods; all about are Douglas firs (*Pseudotsuga menziesii*), some of immense size. Soon a vast placid pool is seen, with a mossy stone bridge arching over a narrow ravine, and, on one side, the Hermitage itself. A tremendous roar increases as the visitor enters the building. An open platform reveals the source of the noise – a spectacular broad waterfall whose waters lunge between great boulders lies below the Hermitage on its far side. The Hermitage was built in 1758 by the heir to the 2nd Duke of Atholl, who named it Ossian's Hall; deeper in the woods lies a rustic grotto, Ossian's Cave. Dorothy Wordsworth visited it in its heyday in 1805 and vividly described her admiration for 'the beauties of the place . . . dizzy and alive with waterfalls.'

HILL OF TARVIT HOUSE
Fife

nr Cupar KY15 5PD
2 1/2m S of Cupar by A916
Tel: 01334 653127

Owner: The National Trust for Scotland

Open: Daily 9.30–sunset. 10 acres. House open

ROBERT LORIMER rebuilt the 17th-century mansion at Hill of Tarvit in 1906, and gave it a new formal garden on the slopes below. Here an avenue of sentinel yews, blown sideways by the wind, links yew-hedged terraces which descend to the pastures below. A long border under the first terrace is planted with perennials and annuals and, specially planned for the blind and those with poor sight, has a section of aromatic plants with labels in braille. On one side a lead satyr pipes at the centre of a formal rose garden, and, by the house, a well-head is decorated with a beautiful wrought-iron overthrow designed by Lorimer. Above the house, sweeping along a high wall interrupted by a grand iron gate, a deep border has repeated plantings of kolkwitzia, purple cotinus, philadelphus and *Rosa moyesii* underplanted with anemones, campanulas, geraniums and potentillas. The Edwardian potting shed, heady with compost, is also on view.

Illustration opposite: the waterfall at The Hermitage

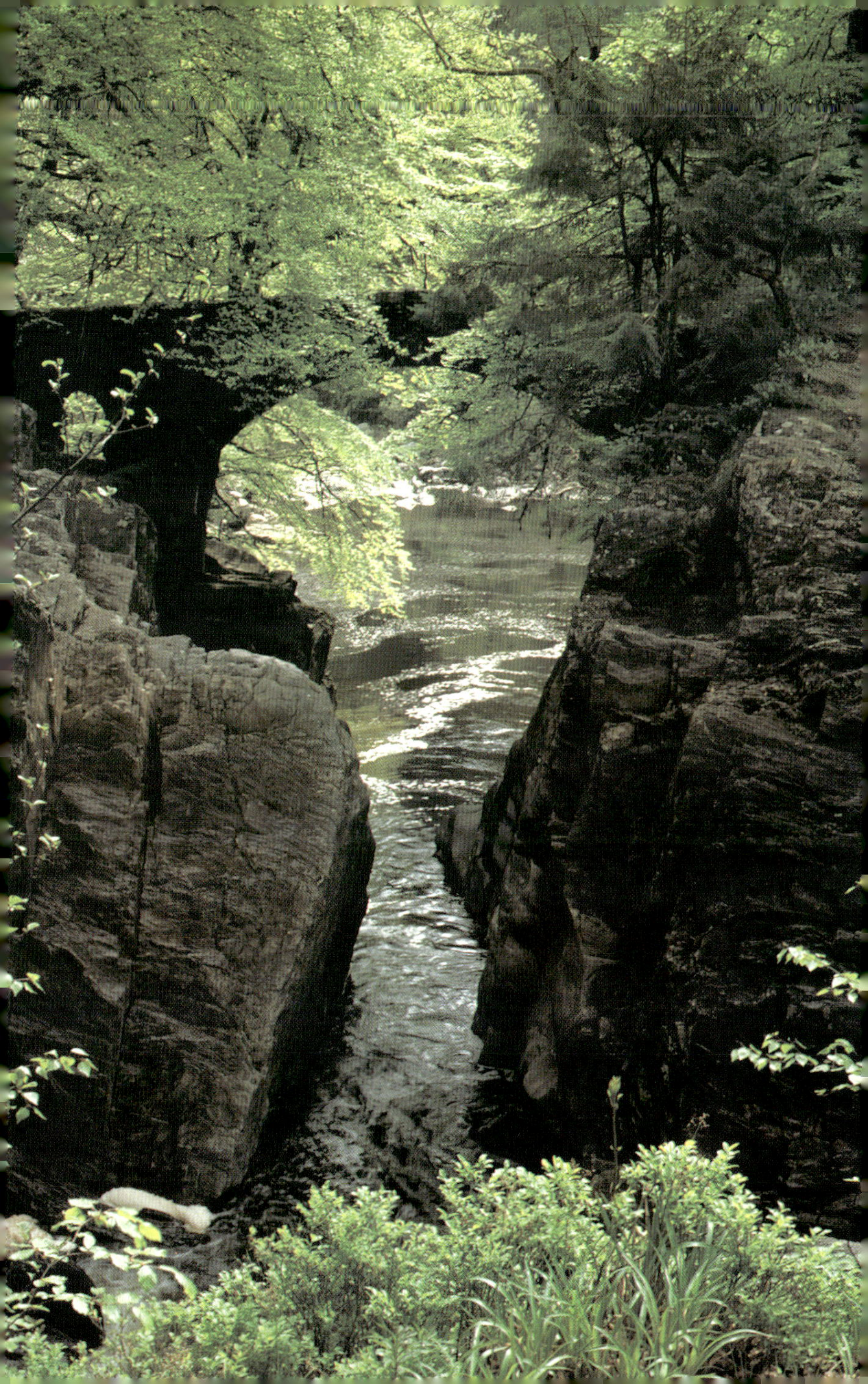

HOUSE OF DUN
Tayside

Angus DD10 9LQ
4m NW of Montrose by A935
Tel: 01674 810264

Owner: The National Trust for Scotland

Open: Daily, 10–sunset. 45 acres

ON GENTLY SLOPING LAND with views of Montrose Basin the House of Dun, a very pretty villa by William Adam, started in 1730, has an enviable position embowered in woodland on the northern slopes. To one side of the house Lady Augusta's Walk follows a tumbling burn through woodland and has an air of agreeable melancholy. In front of the house a long gravel walk, hedged in yew on one side, runs along a wall on which are trained many old varieties of apple and pear, some of which are old Scottish varieties for which these parts were particularly noted. At the end of the walk a restored formal rose garden is sheltered by old stone walls.

HOUSE OF PITMUIES
Tayside

Guthrie, by Forfar
DD8 2SN
7m E of Forfar by A932
Tel: 01241 828245

Owner: Mrs Farquhar Ogilvie

Open: Apr to Oct, daily 10–5. 25 acres

TO THE FRONT of the early Georgian house a gentlemanly atmosphere prevails – fine parkland beyond a ha-ha is framed by old trees, including an exceptional sweet chestnut. The flower garden is behind the house where, in an old walled garden, lavishly planted borders are planned to maintain their flowering interest over a very long season. Colour schemes are fastidiously chosen; a double border, for example, seen from the drawing-room window, has a scheme of blue, cream, white and yellow to go with the colours of the room. Throughout this part of the garden use is made of shrub roses, but abundant other planting, woody and herbaceous, extends the flowering period. The busy-ness of borders is alleviated by occasional simpler schemes – a collection of old delphinium cultivars, a stately walk of *Prunus serrula* with its glistening, peeling bark, hedges of coppiced *Prunus pissardii*, and an airy arch of clipped silver pear. Beyond the walled gardens a riverside walk leads past a castellated dovecote through old woodland of marvellous beeches and oaks underplanted with ornamental shrubs.

INSHRIACH NURSERY
Highland

Aviemore PH22 1QS
4m SW of Aviemore by B970
Tel: 01540 651287

Open: Daily 9–5 (Sat and Sun closes at 4)

AMONG ALPINE plant enthusiasts this is one of the best-known nurseries in Britain. It was founded before World War II by Jack Drake, a former colleague of Will Ingwersen's. A very wide range is carried, and rarities pop up all the time. The exceptionally informative main list (£1.00) also includes plants suitable for wild and bog gardens. Supplementary lists describes rare plants and alpine seeds. A mail order service is provided. The nursery lies in fine birch and juniper woodland, and parts have been beautifully arranged to display the plants.

INVERESK LODGE GARDEN

Lothian

nr Musselburgh EH21 6BQ
6m E of Edinburgh
Tel: 0131 665 7181

Owner: The National Trust for Scotland

Open: Apr to Sept, Mon to Fri 10–4.30, Sat and Sun 2–5; 2 Oct to Mar, Mon to Fri 10–4.30, Sun 2–5.
13 acres

INVERESK is a charming village rich in distinguished houses of the 17th and 18th centuries. Inveresk Lodge belongs to the earlier period, and the unpretentious walled garden with its decorative central sundial complements it well. An excellent rose border was designed by Graham Stuart Thomas; a raised alpine bed is filled with ericaceous plants; good use is made of smaller flowering trees like cherries; and the garden is a model of appropriate and floriferous planting in a modest space.

INVEREWE

Highland

Poolewe IV22 2LQ
6m NE of Gairloch by A832
Tel: 0144 781200

Owner: National Trust for Scotland

Open: Daily 9.30–sunset.
62 acres

FAMOUS GARDENS do not always live up to their reputations but it would be hard to imagine any gardener failing to be excited by Inverewe. In 1862 Osgood Mackenzie came to this very remote corner of the western Highlands – a windswept, bare rocky site at the very edge of a sea-loch. It was 15 years before he got much to grow, but once windbreaks began to be established, the high rainfall and balmy Gulf Stream Drift climate promoted luxuriant growth. Today it is a jungle of mature exotic trees and shrubs laced with winding walks, rising and falling, which give sudden glimpses of shimmering water through foliage. Spring is obviously the showiest season but flowering interest continues throughout the year; in any case, there is immense pleasure to be had at any time in admiring the exotic bark of giant eucalyptus, myrtles and rhododendrons, and much strange and beautiful foliage.

KELLIE CASTLE

Fife

nr Pittenweem KY10 2RF
3m NW of Pittenweem by B9171
Tel: 01333 720271

Owner: The National Trust for Scotland

Open: Daily 9.30–sunset. 1 1/3 acre. Castle open

ON SOUTH-FACING SLOPES to the sea, Kellie Castle, with its crow-steps and turrets, is the perfect Scottish castle. It dates from the 16th to the 17th century but the little walled garden nestling against the castle walls was laid out in 1880 by Robert Lorimer. Here at Kellie, his family home, he made a romantic garden of gravel paths, box-edged beds and rose arbours. His, too, is the gardener's house in the north-west corner with a jaunty carved stone bird on the ridge. Much replanting has recently been done and organic methods used throughout the garden keep it in the pink of good health.

KILDRUMMY CASTLE

Grampian

KILDRUMMY is in the tradition of romantic Victorian gardens where the most important ingredient is the response to the site. Here, in a glen through which flows the burn of Backden, sandstone was quarried in the late middle ages to make

nr Alford AB33 8RA
10m from Alford by A944
Tel: 01975 571277/571203

Owner: Kildrummy Castle Garden Trust

Open: Apr to Oct, daily 10–5

Kildrummy Castle whose ruins rise above the old silver firs and beeches that clothe the glen. The estate was bought in 1898 by Colonel James Ogston, a soap tycoon, who developed the garden, making excellent use of the old quarry, the linked pools of the burn, and its wooded banks. He commissioned a rock garden from the famous Yorkshire firm of Backhouse, and this today has a good collection of alpine plants. A copy of a bridge in Aberdeen – the Brig o' Balgownie – spans the burn, and paths wind along its banks giving views of rhododendrons and other flowering shrubs.

KINROSS HOUSE
Tayside

Kinross KY13 7ET
In the centre of Kinross

Owner: Sir David Montgomery

Open: May to Sept, daily 10–7. 4 acres

DECORATIVE GATE-PIERS mark the entrance to Kinross House, and an avenue of limes leads straight as an arrow to the house itself – long, low and with a distinct whiff of something French. It was designed in the 1680s by Sir William Bruce for his own use and he also designed the garden that goes with it. The entrance avenue forms a central axis which continues on the far side of the house to a gate with a beautifully carved stone surround through which are glimpsed the ruins of Loch Leven castle. Romantically sited on an island, this is where Mary Queen of Scots was imprisoned in 1567. The garden between the house and the loch descends in gentle terraces with grassy walks and herbaceous borders. A deep border runs along the far wall which is finely decorated with piers and heraldic animals. There is nothing like Kinross, it has unique character.

LEITH HALL
Grampian

Kennethmont, by Huntly
AB54 4QQ
6m S of Huntly by B9002,
1m N of Kennethmont
Tel: 01464 831269

Owner: The National
Trust for Scotland

Open: Daily 9.30–sunset

THE HALL is a handsome mid 17th-century mansion, the ancestral home of the Leith and Leith-Hay family. Although there are traces of an early 18th-century layout the present garden is an almost entirely 20th-century creation, chiefly by Charles and Henrietta Leith-Hay before World War I. Here are ebullient borders flourishing as they flourish nowhere better than in Scotland. A 1920s rock garden has been replanted by the Scottish Rock Garden Club and everywhere there are excellent plants to admire. The fine beech woods are full of wood anemones and views of the Coreen Hills and the surrounding rural landscape make a beautiful backdrop.

LOCHSIDE ALPINE NURSERY
Highland

Illustration:
Campanula carpatica

Ulbster KW2 6AA
7m S of Wick by A9
Tel: 01955 651320

Open: Mar to Oct, daily
10–6; also by appointment

TERRY AND JANE Clarke's nursery is almost certainly the northernmost supplier of good plants in Britain – and possibly in Europe; it is about the same latitude as Stockholm. It is so remote that the Clarkes offer its visitors bed and breakfast hospitality which is an arrangement that makes even more sense now that they no longer provide a mail order service. Their stock is chiefly herbaceous and full of good things at exceptionally reasonable prices: campanulas in variety, cyclamen, outstanding gentians, many phlox, a long list of primulas and wonderful saxifrages. It is never possible for them to list everything that is for sale at the nursery, so a visit is to be recommended.

LOGAN BOTANIC GARDEN
Dumfries and Galloway

Port Logan, Stranraer
DG9 9ND
14m S of Stranraer by A716
Tel: 01776 860231

Owner: Royal Botanic
Garden Edinburgh

Open: 15 Mar to 31 Oct,
daily 10–6. 10 1/2 acres

PORT LOGAN lies in the middle of a narrow spit of land, the Mull of Galloway, which juts out into the sea in the extreme south-west of Scotland. A grove of Chusan palms immediately announces the character of this place – sub-tropical plants flourish here and provide some rare and beautiful sights. The garden was started by the McDouall family who lived here for 800 years, and since 1969 it has been in the care of the Royal Botanic Garden at Edinburgh. But this is not just a botanic garden, for it is beautifully laid out, particularly in the walled garden which has fine terraces and well planned borders under an avenue of cabbage palms (*Cordyline australis*). The climate is exceptionally mild, and several different habitats provide conditions for a huge range of tender plants. A small selection of plants is offered for sale.

MALLENY HOUSE GARDEN
Lothian

Balerno EH14 7AF
In Balerno, 7m SW of
Edinburgh by A70
Tel: 0131 449 2283

Owner: The National
Trust for Scotland

Open: Daily 9.30–dusk.
2 acres

THE HOUSE at Malleny is an ornamental riddle, with features of the 17th and 18th centuries and hints of something much older. Its tower and conical roof on the garden side contribute much to the atmosphere of the place. A walled enclosure divided by a yew hedge lies at the heart of the garden, with a splendid quartet of ancient yew trees clipped into the shape of pointed mushrooms. Roses are everywhere, and Malleny has a National Collection of 19th-century shrub roses which are mingled with other plants in handsome mixed borders on two sides of the walled garden. There is, in addition, a separate collection of modern roses. In a corner of the garden behind the greenhouse is displayed a collection of bonsai arranged by the Scottish Bonsai Society. Despite being in the suburbs of Edinburgh, Malleny has a rare quality – the remote and soothing atmosphere of an old-fashioned garden in the depths of the country.

MELLERSTAIN
Borders

nr Gordon TD3 6LG
7m NW of Kelso by A6089
Tel: 01573 410225

Owner: The Earl of Haddington

Open: Easter weekend 12.30–5; May, Jun and Sept, Wed, Thur and Sun 12.30–5; Jul and Aug, daily except Sat 12.30–5

THE GREAT EARLY 18TH-CENTURY house at Mellerstain, designed by William Adam and later added to by his son Robert, originally had a formal garden that was removed in the 18th-century landscape gardening craze. In the early 20th century, however, a version of it was reinstated by the architect Sir Reginald Blomfield. A row of clipped cones of yew runs across the back of the house, and terraces descend in stately progression – starting with a splendid double staircase – ornamented with parterres of modern roses, lavender, clipped shapes of box and generous lawns. All this provides a decorative foreground for the curvaceous lake set in woodland below – with idyllic views of the Cheviot Hills in the distance.

THE MURREL GARDENS
Fife

Aberdour KY3 0RN
1m N of Aberdour on B157
Tel: 01383 860156
Fax: 01383 860157

Owner: Mrs J. Milne

Open: Apr to Oct, daily except Sun 10–5. 7 1/2 acres

HIDDEN IN A FOLD of land facing south towards the Firth of Forth, The Murrel has a rare site. Designed in 1908 by Frank Deas in the Arts and Crafts style the house and garden have been excellently restored since 1984 by a new owner. To one side of the house, on south-facing slopes, a walled garden gives protection to many tender plants, such as *Buddleja crispa* and *Pittosporum tobira,* rarely seen out-of-doors in these parts. Below the walled garden a formal sunken garden with rose beds leads to a water garden overhung with old rhododendrons and ornamental trees. A ravine-like wild garden, still being replanted but already exquisitely beautiful, leads back up the hill where, to the west of the house, a large rock garden is laid out with scree beds. An excellent range of plants, some unusual and propagated in the garden, is for sale.

THE PINEAPPLE

Central

Dunmore, nr Stirling
On the Dunmore Estate
(enter by East Lodge) 6m
SE of Stirling by A905
Tel: 01628 825925

Owner: The National Trust for Scotland

Open: Daily, 10–sunset

THE PINEAPPLE IS a wonderful survival, a banqueting house of lovely eccentricity. Built in 1761 in the great kitchen garden of Dunmore Castle, it was given to the National Trust for Scotland who leased it to The Landmark Trust who have beautifully restored it. No architect is known but the craftsmanship is superb – the pineapple leaves are exquisitely carved in stone, and curvaceous gothic windows ornament the second floor. The former kitchen garden has been replanted as a formal orchard with rows of fruit-trees planted in turf. Visitors may not enter the Pineapple's interior; it may, however, be rented as a holiday house from The Landmark Trust (Shottesbrooke, Maidenhead, Berkshire SL6 3SW. Tel: 01628 825925).

PITMEDDEN

Grampian

IN THIS REMOTE CORNER of Aberdeenshire is one of the most beguiling gardens you could hope to see. There was a garden here in the 17th century but in 1818 the house was burnt down, the estate changed hands and the original garden disappeared. However,

nr Pitmedden, Ellon
AB4 0PD
14m N of Aberdeen by
A920 and B999
Tel: 01651 842352

Owner: The National
Trust for Scotland

Open: May to Sept, daily
10–5.30. 4 3/4 acres

the garden walls, elegant pavilions, garden steps and gate-piers all survive, and in 1954 the National Trust planted immense formal parterres with a central avenue of clipped yew pyramids and a fountain. The parterres are edged in intricately shaped box hedges with compartments filled with coloured chippings and arrangements of annuals, blocks of a single colour, different every year. Looking down from the surrounding terraces with their beautiful gazebos, the effect is marvellous. Running along the south- and east-facing walls are a pair of excellent borders and above the walled garden a tunnel of old varieties of apples leads to a formal herb garden. Pitmedden has an enchanting atmosphere, unlike any other garden.

POLLOK HOUSE

Glasgow

ALTHOUGH NOW ENGULFED by urban sprawl the Pollok House estate, for 800 years the property of the Maxwell family, preserves the beautiful character of old parkland. The dashing grey stone house was built in the mid 18th century and has pretty formal gardens spreading out below the house. From box-edged parterres and a gravel walk a double

2060 Pollokshaws Road,
G43 1AT
3m SW of the city centre
by A77 and B762
Tel: 0141 632 0274

Owner: City of Glasgow
District Council

Open: Daily except
Christmas and New Year's
Day, Mon to Sat 10–5, Sun
11–5. 361 acres

staircase leads to a lower terrace with lovely views of the parkland on the far side of the river. Elegant ogee-roofed pavilions overlook the terrace, and to one side a path leads up to grassy walk between beds planted with Himalayan birches underplanted with hostas and backed by rhododendrons. Nearby, through the woods, is the famous Burrell Collection.

POYNTZFIELD HERB NURSERY
Highland

Poyntzfield, Black Isle, by
Dingwall IV7 8LX
5m W of Cromarty on
B9163
Tel: 01381 610352

Open: Mar to Oct, Mon to
Sat 1–5

THIS IS ONE of the northernmost nurseries in Britain, which gives it a special interest. It specialises in herbs and, over the years, a collection of clones has been built up that are hardy in this severe climate. Thus, anyone buying plants here may be confident that they are acquiring pretty tough customers. Over 300 varieties are stocked, all organically grown, and there is a particularly attractive collection of culinary and medicinal plants native to Scotland. An excellent catalogue (three 1st-class stamps and s.a.e.) is produced, the only one I know of that gives common names in Gaelic, where they exist. A mail order service is provided.

ROYAL BOTANIC GARDEN
Edinburgh

ONE OF THE OLDEST botanic gardens in Britain, it was founded in 1670 and moved to its present site in 1820. Today, from the gardener's point of view, it is an exciting place. There are areas of specific habitats – an unforgettable rock garden, a

Inverleith Row, EH3 5LR
1m N of the centre of
Edinburgh
Tel: 0131 552 7171
Fax: 0131 5520382

Owner: Trustees of the
Royal Botanic Garden
Edinburgh

Open: Nov to Feb, daily
10–4 (closed 25 Dec and 1
Jan); Mar to April, daily
10–6; May to August, daily
10–8; Sept to Oct, daily
10–6. 67 acres

woodland garden and a peat garden; collections of rhododendrons, heaths and alpines; several magnificent glasshouses; marvellous trees everywhere; and excellent demonstration gardens. These are ingredients found in dozens of botanic gardens, but at Edinburgh the beauty of the setting – high, undulating land with sweeping views of the city to the south and the hills beyond the Firth of Forth to the north – the exemplary standards of upkeep, and the liveliness of it all make it exceptional. Also, unlike other botanic gardens, Edinburgh seems to have the interests of the ordinary gardener close to heart. For its size it has a remarkably diverse collection, so one plant or another will be flowering at any time of the year. Places like this set standards from which all gardeners may learn.

THREAVE SCHOOL OF HORTICULTURE
Dumfries and Galloway

Stewartry, Castle Douglas
DG7 1RX
1m W of Castle Douglas by
A75
Tel: 01556 502575

Owner: The National
Trust for Scotland

Open: Daily 9.30–sunset.
65 acres

THE NATIONAL TRUST FOR SCOTLAND has its own school of horticulture here, and the gardens, largely created by the students since the school started in 1960, are of great interest. Mature woodland of beech, conifers and oak forms the background to a large collection of shrub roses, sweeping mixed borders, many dwarf heathers and conifers, peat and rock gardens, a collection of over 200 narcissi and a youthful arboretum that is already showing its paces. A walled kitchen garden has splendidly blowsy borders and superbly maintained glasshouses. Threave holds a National Collection of penstemons.

YOUNGER BOTANIC GARDEN BENMORE
Strathclyde

Illustration:
Rhododendron morii

Benmore, Dunoon
PA23 8QU
7m N of Dunoon by A815
Tel: 01369 706261
Fax: 01369 706369

Owner: Trustees of the Royal Botanic Garden Edinburgh

Open: 15 Mar to 31 Oct, daily 10–6. 120 acres

THE YOUNGER BOTANIC GARDEN BENMORE is a country annexe of the Royal Botanic Garden in Edinburgh. Its history starts in the 1820s with the first plantings of conifers, and today, superb old specimens of Douglas firs, larch, Scots pine and a splendid avenue of Wellingtonias (*Sequioadendron giganteum*) make a wonderful background to later collections of ornamental shrubs and trees. The mild climate and very high rainfall promotes spectacular growth in conifers, and some of the specimens here are among the largest in the British Isles. The climate also makes this an ideal place for rhododendrons and today there are about 250 different species, 100 subspecies and forms and a further 300 hybrids and cultivars. There are excellent specimens, too, of deciduous trees such as southern beeches (*Nothofagus* species) and *Davidia involucrata*, and autumn is brilliant with the foliage of azaleas, cercidiphyllums, enkianthus and maples.

Stickey Wicket Garden 138
Stillingfleet Lodge
   Nurseries 270
Stourhead 91
Stone House Cottage 177
Stowe Landscape Gardens
   92
Stratford-upon-Avon
   Gardens 207
Studley Royal 271
Sudeley Castle 178
Sulgrave Manor 208
Sutton Park 271
Swiss Garden, The 245
Syon Park and Gardens 54

Tapeley Park 139
Tatton Park 178
Thorp Perrow Arboretum
   272
Threave School of
   Horticulture 305
Tile Barn Nursery 55
Tintinhull House 140
Trebah 140
Trengwainton Garden 140
Tresco Abbey 141
Tretower Court 179
Trewithen 142
Tudor House Garden 93

Upton House 209

Valley Clematis 246
Valley Garden 49

Waddesdon Manor 93
Wadham College 88
Wakehurst Place Garden 55
Wallington 272
Warwick Castle 209
Washfield Nursery 56
Waterwheel Nursery 181
Wentworth Castle
   Gardens 272
West Dean Gardens 56
Westbury Court Garden
   181
Westonbirt Arboretum 181
Wetheriggs Country
   Pottery 274
Whichford Pottery 209
Gilbert White's House 94

Wightwick Manor 210
Wimpole Hall 246
Wisley Garden 58
Wollerton Old Hall 182
Wolterton Park 247
Wootten's Plants 247
Wrest Park 248

Yalding Organic Gardens
   58
Younger Botanic Garden
   Benmore 306

Lochside Alpine Nursery 299
Logan Botanic Garden 300
Longstock Water Gardens 83
Lower Severalls Herb Nursery 127
Luton Hoo 233
Lyme Park 163
Lyte's Cary Manor 128

Magdalen College 88
Malleny House 300
Mallet Court Nursery 128
Mannington Hall 234
Manor House, The, Walton-in-Gordano 128
Manor House, The, Upton Grey 84
Mapperton Garden 129
Patricia Marrow 129
Marwood Hill Gardens 130
Mead Nursery, The 85
Melbourne Hall 201
Melford Hall 235
Mellerstain 301
Menagerie, The 131
Merrimens Gardens 37
Milton Lodge 131
Minterne 131
Misarden Park 164
Monksilver Nursery 235
Monocot Nursery, The 131
Montacute House 132
Moseley Old Hall 203
Mottisfont Abbey Garden 85
Mount Edgcumbe 133
Mount Stewart 309
Muncaster Castle 264
Murrel Gardens, The 301
Museum of Garden History 38

Ness Gardens 164
New College 88
New Place 208
Newby Hall 265
Newnham College 219
Norden Alpines 266
Norfolk Lavender 236
Northbourne Court 38
Notcutts Nurseries Ltd 236

Nymans Garden 40

Old Court Nurseries Ltd 165
Old Rectory, The, Burghfield 86
Osterley Park 41
Overbecks Garden 133
Oxburgh Hall 237
Oxford Botanic Garden 87
Oxford College Gardens 88

Packwood House 204
Padlock Croft 238
Painshill Park 41
Painswick Rococo Garden 165
Pantiles Nurseries 42
Paradise Centre 238
Parham House 43
Park Green Nurseries 239
Parnham House 134
Pashley Manor 42
Peckover House 239
Pencarrow House 135
Penjerrick 135
Penpergwm Lodge 166
Penrhyn Castle 166
Penshurst Place 44
Perhill Nurseries 168
Perry's Plants 266
Perryhill Nurseries 44
Petworth House 45
Pineapple, The 302
Pitmedden 302
Plas Brondanw 168
Plas Newydd 169
Plas-yn-Rhiw 170
Polesden Lacey 45
Pollok House 303
Port Lympne Gardens 46
Portmeirion 171
Pots and Pithoi 47
Potterton & Martin 240
Pound Hill House 88
Powis Castle 171
Poyntzfield Herb Nursery 304
Prior Park Landscape Garden 136
Priory, The 172

Raveningham Hall 241

Reads Nursery 241
Renishaw Hall 204
G. Reuthe Ltd 47
Rievaulx Terrace 267
Roche Court Sculpture Garden 89
Rodmarton Manor 173
Romantic Garden Nursery, The 242
Roof Gardens, The 48
Rookhope Nurseries 267
Rosemoor Garden 136
Rousham House 90
Rowallane Garden 310
Rowden Gardens 137
Royal Botanic Garden, Edinburgh 304
Royal Botanic Gardens, Kew 48
Rushfields of Ledbury 173
Ryton Organic Gardens 206

St John's College (Cambridge) 219
St John's College (Oxford) 88
Saling Hall 242
Saltram 137
Sandringham House 244
Savill Garden 49
Scotney Castle 50
Scotts Nurseries Ltd 138
Seaton Delaval Hall 268
Sellet Hall Gardens 268
Sezincote 173
Shakespeare's Birthplace 207
Sheffield Park 51
Sheringham Park 244
Shugborough 206
Sissinghurst Castle Garden 51
Sizergh Castle 270
Snowshill Manor 174
Somerleyton Hall 245
Spetchley Park 175
Spinners 91
Standen 52
Stanway House 176
Stapeley Water Gardens 177
Starborough Nursery 54

Dunham Massey 153
Dunrobin Castle 288
Dunster Castle 114

East Lambrook Manor 114
Eastgrove Cottage Garden 154
Edmondsham House 116
Edrom Nurseries 288
Edzell Castle 289
Emmetts Garden 23
Erddig 154
Euston Hall 222
Exbury Gardens 71

Fairhaven Garden Trust, The 223
Falkland Palace 289
Farnborough Hall 196
Felbrigg Hall 224
Fenton House 23
Fibrex Nurseries Ltd 197
Fishbourne Roman Palace Garden 24
Fisks Clematis Nursery 224
Forde Abbey 117
Foxgrove Plants 73
Furzey Gardens 73

Gannock Growers 225
Garden House 117
Gardens of the Rose, The 225
Gawsworth Hall 155
Gibside 256
Glebe Cottage Plants 118
Glendurgan Garden 118
Glenwhan Garden 290
Gnome Reserve, The 119
Godinton Park 24
Goodnestone Park 25
Gravetye Manor 26
Great Comp 26
Great Dixter 27
Greatham Mill 74
Green Farm Plants 75
Greenbank Garden 291
Greencombe 120
Greys Court 75
Grizedale 256
Groombridge Place Gardens 28
Gunby Hall 226

Hackfall Wood 257
Haddon Hall 197
Haddonstone Ltd 198
Hadspen Gardens 120
Halecat Garden Nurseries 258
Hall Farm Nursery 155
Hall's Croft 207
Ham House 28
Hampton Court 29
Hanbury Hall 156
Hannays of Bath, The 122
Hardwick Hall 198
Hardy's Cottage Garden Plants 76
Hare Lane Pottery 122
Harewood House 259
R. Harkness & Co Ltd 226
Harlow Carr Botanical Gardens 259
Hartshall Nursery Stock 227
Hatfield House 227
Anne Hathaway's Cottage 208
Haughley Park 228
Hawkstone Park 156
Hazeldene Nursery 30
Headland 122
Heale Garden 76
Heligan 123
Helmingham Hall 228
Herb and Heather Centre 260
Hergest Croft 156
Hermitage, The 292
Herterton House Gardens 260
Hestercombe 124
Hever Castle 30
Hexham Herbs 260
Hidcote Manor Garden 158
High Beeches, The 32
Highdown 33
Hiley Nursery 33
Hill of Tarvit House 292
Hillier Gardens and Arboretum, The 78
Hillier's Nurseries Ltd 78
Hinton Ampner 79
Hodges Barn 159
Hodnet Hall 159
Hoecroft Plants 230

Holden Clough Nursery 261
Holdenby House Gardens 199
Holehird Gardens 262
Holker Hall 262
Hollington Nurseries 79
Hopleys Plants 231
House of Dun 294
House of Pitmuies 294
How Caple Court Gardens 160
Howick Hall 263
Hyde Hall 231

Ickworth 232
Iden Croft Herbs 34
Iford Manor 80
W.E.Th. Ingwersen Ltd 34
Inshriach Nursery 295
Inveresk Lodge Garden 296
Inverewe 296

Jenkyn Place 80

Kedleston Hall 200
Kellie Castle 297
Kelmscott Manor 81
Kelways Nurseries 125
Kiftsgate Court 161
Kildrummy Castle 297
Killerton 125
Kingston Maurward Gardens 125
Kingstone Cottages 162
Kinross House 298
Kirby Hall 200
Knebworth 233
Knightshayes Court 126
Kyoto Garden 35

Langley Boxwood Nursery 82
Lanhydrock 127
Lea Gardens 201
Leeds Castle 36
Leith Hall 299
Leonardslee Gardens 36
Levens Hall 264
Lindisfarne Castle 264
Little Cottage, The 82
Little Moreton Hall 162

INDEX

Abbey Dore Court Garden 145
Abbotsbury Sub-Tropical Gardens 98
Abriachan Nurseries 277
Achamore 277
Alfriston Clergy House 12
Alton Towers 185
Jacques Amand 12
Anglesey Abbey 213
Antony House 98
Antony Woodland Garden and Woods 99
Apple Court 61
Arbigland 278
Architectural Heritage 145
Architectural Plants 13
Ardfearn Nursery 278
Ardtornish 279
Arduaine 280
Arley Hall 146
Arlington Court 99
Ascott 61
Ashtree Cottage 62
Athelhampton 100
Audley End 213
David Austin 185
Avon Bulbs 101

B. & H.M. Baker 214
Barnsley House Garden 146
Barrington Court 102
Barton Manor 62
Bateman's 13
Bath Botanical Gardens 102
Batsford Arboretum 147
John Beach Ltd 186
Peter Beales Roses 214
Bedgebury National Pinetum 14
Belsay Hall 251
Belton House 215
Benington Lordship 216
Bernwode Plants 64
Berrington Hall 148
Bicton College of Agriculture 103
Bicton Park Gardens 103
Biddulph Grange 186

Birmingham Botanical Gardens 187
Blackmore & Langdon Ltd 104
Blackthorn Nursery 64
Blaise Castle 104
Blenheim Palace 65
Blickling Hall 216
Blooms of Bressingham 217
Bluebell Nursery 188
Bodnant 148
Borde Hill 14
Bosvigo House 105
Botanic Nursery, The 65
Boughton House Park 188
Bowood 67
Bramham Park 251
Branklyn Garden 280
Bressingham Gardens 218
Bridgemere Garden World 150
Broadleigh Gardens 106
Brodick Castle 280
Brodsworth Hall Gardens 252
Brogdale 15
Broughton Castle 68
Burncoose & South Down Nurseries 106
Buscot Park 69

Caddick's Clematis Nurseries 150
Caerhays Castle 107
Calke Abbey 189
Cally Gardens 281
Cambridge Botanic Garden 218
Cambridge College Gardens 218
Canons Ashby House 190
Capel Manor 15
Castle Ashby Gardens 190
Castle Bromwich Hall Gardens 191
Castle Drogo 107
Castle Howard 252
Castle Kennedy 282
Castlewellan National Arboretum 308
Cawdor Castle 282
Charlecote Park 191
Charleston Farmhouse 16

Chatsworth 192
Beth Chatto Gardens 220
Chelsea Physic Garden 16
Chenies Manor 69
Chiffchaffs 108
Chilstone Garden Ornaments 18
Chirk Castle 151
Chiswick House 19
Church Hill Cottage Gardens 19
Clandon Park 20
Clare College 219
Claremont Landscape Garden 20
Claverton Manor 109
Dorothy Clive Garden, The 151
Cliveden 70
Cluny House Gardens 283
Coghurst Nursery 21
Coleton Fishacre Garden 109
Compton Acres 110
Cotehele 111
Coton Manor 193
Cottage Garden Roses 194
Cottesbrooke Hall 194
Courts, The 71
Cragside House 253
Craigieburn Classic Plants 283
Cranborne Manor Gardens 112
Crarae Gardens 284
Crathes Castle 285
Crossing House 220
Crowther of Syon Lodge 21
Crûg Farm Plants 152
Culross Palace 286
Culzean Castle 285

Dalemain 253
Dartington Hall 112
Deacons Nursery 71
Denmans 22
Docton Mill 113
Docwra's Manor 221
Doddington Hall 222
Drummond Castle 287
Duchy of Cornwall Nursery 114
Duncombe Park 254

317

erythroniums
    Greencombe
euphorbias
    Abbey Dore Court
    Bernwode Plants
    Oxford Botanic Garden
ferns (hardy)
    Savill and Valley Gardens
ferns (polystichum)
    Greencombe
    Holehird Gardens
figs
    Reads Nursery
foxgloves
    Botanic Nursery
fritillaries (European species)
    Cambridge Botanic Garden
geraniums
    Cambridge Botanic Garden
    East Lambrook Manor
galeobdolon
    Monksilver Nursery
hollies
    Rosemoor
    Valley Garden
hostas
    Apple Court
    Harewood House
hydrangeas
    Holehird Gardens
ivy
    Erddig
junipers
    Bedgebury National Pinetum
kniphofias
    Barton Manor
lamium
    Monksilver Nursery
lavender
    Norfolk Lavender
Lawson cypresses
    Bedgebury National Pinetum
magnolias
    Bodnant
    Valley Garden
mahonias
    Valley Garden

maples (excluding Acer japonicum *and* A. palmatum *cultivars)*
    Hergest Croft (Acer japonicum)
    Westonbirt Arboretum
meconopsis
    Craigieburn Classic Plants
Michaelmas daisies
    Old Court Nurseries
mints
    Iden Croft
oaks
    The Hillier Garden and Arboretum
origanums
    Iden Croft
penstemons
    Kingston Maurward Gardens
    Rowallane
peonies
    Branklyn Garden
periwinkles
    Monksilver Nursery
pieris
    The High Beeches
    Valley Garden
pinks (old garden varieties)
    Kingstone Cottages
pittosporum
    Bicton College
polygonums
    Rowden Gardens
primulas (Asiatic species)
    Cluny House
pulmonarias
    Stillingfleet Lodge Nurseries
rhododendrons (falconera group)
    Wentworth Castle Gardens
rhododendrons (species)
    Valley Garden
roses (pre 1900)
    Mottisfont Abbey
roses (19th-century)
    Malleny House
santolina
    Herb and Heather Centre

saxifrages (European species)
    Cambridge Botanic Gardens
snowdrops
    Wisley Garden
stewartias
    The High Beeches
styracaceae
    Holker Hall
thymes
    Hexham Herbs
tulips (species and primary hybrids)
    Cambridge Botanic Garden
viburnums
    Hyde Hall
willows (lowland species)
    Westonbirt Arboretum

Thomas Mawson
(1861–1933)
Wightwick Manor

W.A. Nesfield
(1793–1881)
Castle Howard
Harewood House

Russell Page
(1906–85)
Leeds Castle
Port Lympne

Sir Joseph Paxton
(1803–65)
Chatsworth
Somerleyton
Tatton Park

Harold Peto
(1854–1933)
Buscot Park
Heale House
Iford Manor
West Dean Gardens

Humphry Repton
(1752–1818)
Antony House
Blaise Castle
Bowood
Hatchlands
Plas Newydd
Sheffield Park
Sheringham Park
Tatton Park
Wimpole Hall

William Robinson
(1838–1935)
Emmetts
Gravetye Manor
Killerton House
Nymans

Lanning Roper
(1912–83)
Claverton Manor
Penshurst Place
Scotney Castle

Edward Weir Schultz
(1860–1951)
Cottesbrooke Hall

F. Inigo Thomas
(1866–1950)
Athelhampton

Sir John Vanbrugh
(1644–1726)
Blenheim Palace
Claremont
Seaton Delaval Hall

Sir Clough Williams-Ellis
(1883-1978)
Plas Brodanw
Portmeirion

NATIONAL COLLECTIONS OF PLANTS

The National Council for the Protection of Plants and Gardens (NCCPG) has set up National Collections of groups of plants, most of which are not normally accessible to the public. However, some of particular interest to gardeners are held by gardens and nurseries described in this book. They are as follows:

agapanthus
   Bicton College
apples
   Brogdale
astilbes
   Holehird Gardens
   Marwood Hill Gardens
begonias
   Stapeley Water Gardens
bromeliads
   Stapeley Water Gardens
campanulas
   Padlock Croft
cistus
   Chelsea Physic Garden
clematis
   Burford House Gardens
colchicums
   Felbrigg Hall
crab-apples
   Hyde Hall
crocosmias
   Lanhydrock
daylilies
   Antony House
dianthus (old garden pinks)
   Kingstone Cottages
dogwoods
   Sir Harold Hillier Garden
   Newby Hall
   Rosemoor

Scotts Nurseries Ltd
Sudeley Castle

Shrubs
Bluebell Nursery
Burncoose & Southdown
Duchy of Cornwall
  Nursery
Hillier's Nurseries Ltd
Hopley's Plants
Notcutt's Nurseries Ltd
Spinners
Waterwheel Nursery

Snowdrops
Avon Bulbs
Foxgrove Plants

Trees
Bluebell Nursery
Hillier's Nurseries Ltd
Mallet Court Nursery
Notcutt's Nurseries Ltd
Pantiles Nurseries
Scotts Nurseries Ltd
Spinners

Tulips
Jacques Amand
Broadleigh Gardens
W.E.Th. Ingwersen

Violas and Pansies
Hazeldene
W.E.Th. Ingwersen
Norden Alpines

Water Lilies
Stapeley Water Gardens

GARDENS BY FAMOUS DESIGNERS

Sir Reginald Blomfield
(1856–1942)
Godinton Park
Mellerstain
Sulgrave Manor

Charles Bridgeman
(d.1738)
Claremont
Rousham Hall
Stowe
Wimpole Hall
Wolterton Park

Lancelot 'Capability' Brown
(1716–83)
Audley End
Berrington Hall
Blenheim Palace
Bowood
Castle Ashby
Chatsworth
Claremont
Euston Hall
Harewood House
Ickworth
Luton Hoo
Petworth
Sheffield Park
Stowe
Warwick Castle
Wimpole Hall
Wrest Park

Percy Cane
(1881–1976)
Dartington Hall
Falkland Palace

Dame Sylvia Crowe
(1901–)
Cottesbrooke Hall
Oxford Botanic Garden

William Emes
(1730–1803)
Belton House
Erddig

Beatrix Farrand
(1872–1959)
Dartington Hall

W.S. Gilpin
(1762–1843)
Audley End
Scotney Castle

Gertrude Jekyll
(1843–1932)
Broughton Castle
Hestercombe
Knebworth
Lindisfarne Castle
Manor House, Upton Grey

Sir Geoffrey Jellicoe
(1900–)
Cliveden
Cottesbrooke Hall
Mottisfont Abbey

William Kent
(1685–1748)
Claremont
Euston Hall
Rousham House
Stowe

George London
(d. 1714)
Chatsworth
Hanbury Hall
Petworth

Sir Robert Lorimer
(1864–1929)
Hill of Tarvit
Kellie Castle

Sir Edwin Lutyens
(1869–1944)
Castle Drogo
Hestercombe
Knebworth

Clematis
John Beach Ltd
Caddick's Clematis Nursery
Fisk's Clematis Nursery
Great Dixter
Valley Clematis

Colchicums
Broadleigh Gardens
W.E.Th. Ingwersen
The Monocot Nursery

Conifers
Blooms of Bressingham
Duchy of Cornwall Nursery
Hartshall Nursery Stock
Hilliers Nurseries Ltd

Daylilies
Apple Court

Delphiniums
Blackmore & Langdon Ltd

Ferns
Fibrex Nurseries
Spinners

Fruit Trees
Bernwode
Brogdale
Deacons Nursery
Hilliers Nurseries Ltd
Reads Nursery
Scotts Nurseries Ltd

Fuchsias
B. and H.M. Baker

Geraniums
Bernwode Plants
Crûg Farm Plants
East Lambrook Manor
Glebe Cottage Plants
Hall Farm Nursery
Rushfields of Ledbury

Grasses
Apple Court
Hoecroft Plants
Rushfields of Ledbury

Hellebores
Avon Bulbs
Blackthorn Nursery
Fibrex Nurseries Ltd
Washfield Nursery

Herbaceous Perennials
Blackthorn Nursery
Blooms of Bressingham
Bosvigo House
Bernwode Plants
Cally Garden
Beth Chatto Garden
Church Hill Cottage Garden
Craigieburn Classic Plants
Crûg Farm Plants
East Lambrook Manor
Eastgrove Cottage Gardens
Foxgrove Plants
Gannock Growers
Green Farm Plants
Hadspen Garden
Hall Farm Nursery
The Hannays of Bath
W. & L. Harley
Merriments Gardens
Monksilver Nursery
Old Court Nurseries Ltd
Perhill Nurseries
Perry's Plants
Rowden Gardens
Rushfields of Ledbury
Stillingfleet Lodge Nursery
Washfield Nursery
Waterwheel Nursery
Wootten's Plants

Herbs
Herb and Heather Centre
Hollington Nurseries
Iden Croft
Lower Severalls Herb Nursery
Poyntzfield Herb Nursery

Hostas
Apple Court
Hadspen Garden
Park Green Nurseries

Ivy
Fibrex Nurseries Ltd

Magnolias
Burncoose & Southdown Nurseries
Spinners
Starborough Nursery

Maples
Mallet Court Nursery
Spinners
Starborough Nursery

Meconopsis
Craigieburn Classic Plants

Pelargoniums
Fibrex Nurseries Ltd
Wootten's Plants

Peonies
Kelways Nurseries

Pinks
Bernwode Plants
Glebe Cottage Plants
W.E.Th. Ingwersen
Kingstone Cottages

Primulas
Abriachan Nurseries
Cluny House
Edrom Nurseries
Glebe Cottage
W.E.Th. Ingwersen
Inshriach Nursery
Monksilver Nursery
Norden Alpines
Paradise Centre
Rowden Gardens

Rhododendrons
Burncoose & Southdown
Lea Gardens
G. Reuthe
Spinners
Starborough

Roses
David Austin
Peter Beales Roses
Cottage Garden Roses
Cranborne Manor
R. Harkness & Co Ltd
Perryhill Nurseries

Luton Hoo
The Murrel
Newby Hall
Newstead Abbey
Royal Botanic Garden, Edinburgh
Sizergh Castle
Wisley Garden

Rose Gardens
Broughton Castle
Castle Howard
Cliveden
The Gardens of the Rose
Haddon Hall
Helmingham Hall
Hodges Barn
Hyde Hall
Kiftsgate Court
Malleny House
Mannington Hall
Mottisfont Abbey
Polesden Lacey
Renishaw Hall
Sissinghurst Castle
Sudeley Castle
Warwick Castle

Water and Bog Gardens
Buscot Park
Beth Chatto Gardens
Coleton Fishacre
Docton Mill
Forde Abbey
Hermitage, The
Hodnet Hall
Longstock Water Gardens
Marwood Hill Gardens
Minterne
Sezincote
Stapeley Water Gardens
Westbury Court

Woodland Gardens
Abbotsbury Sub-tropical Gardens
Achamore
Antony Woodland Garden
Arbigland
Ardtornish
Arduaine
Bodnant
Borde Hill

Brodick Castle
Brodsworth Hall Gardens
Caerhays Castle
The Dorothy Clive Garden
Castle Howard
Cotehele
Cragside House
Craigieburn Classic Plants
Crarae Garden
Exbury Gardens
Fairhaven Garden Trust
Furzey Gardens
Glendurgan Garden
Gravetye Manor
Great Comp
Greencombe
Grizedale
Groombridge Place Gardens
The High Beeches
Holker Hall
Howick Hall
Inverewe
Killerton House
Knightshayes Court
Leonardslee
Minterne
Muncaster Castle
Nymans
Penjerrick
Rowallane
Saltram House
Savill Garden
Scotney Castle
Sheffield Park
Thorp Perrow
Trebah
Trengwainton
Trewithen

NURSERIES FOR SPECIFIC KINDS OF PLANTS

Alpines
Abriachan Nurseries
Ardfearn Nursery
Edrom Nursery
Holden Clough Nursery
W.E.Th. Ingwersen
Inshriach Nursery
Lochside Alpine Nursery
Norden Alpines
Old Court Nurseries
Padlock Croft
Perhill Nurseries
Potterton & Martin
Rookhope Nurseries

Aquatic Plants
Rowden Gardens
Stapeley Water Gardens

Box
Langley Boxwood Nursery

Bulbs
Jacques Amand
Avon Bulbs
Broadleigh Gardens
The Monocot Nursery
Paradise Centre

Camellias
Burncoose & Southdown
Coghurst Nursery
Marwood Hill Garden
Starborough Nursery

Campanulas
Bernwode Plants
Padlock Croft
W. E. Th. Ingwersen
Norden Alpines
Wootten's Plants

Citrus Fruit
Reads Nursery

TYPES OF GARDENS AND GARDEN FEATURES

Arboreta
Batsford Arboretum
Bedgebury National Pinetum
Borde Hill
Castlewellan National Arboretum
Exbury Gardens
Hergest Croft
The Hillier Garden and Arboretum
Milton Lodge
Ness Garden
Royal Botanic Garden, Edinburgh
Royal Botanic Garden, Kew
Saling Hall
Savill Garden
Thorp Perrow
Valley Garden
Wakehurst Place
Westonbirt

Especially Good Borders
Anglesey Abbey
Arley Hall
Barnsley House
Benington Lordship
Blickling Hall
Clare College
Cottesbrooke Hall
Crathes Castle
Falkland Palace
Great Dixter
Hardwick Hall
Helmingham Hall
House of Pitmuies
Kellie Castle
Knightshayes Court
Leith Hall
Manor House, Upton Grey
Mount Stewart
Newby Hall
Oxburgh Hall
Parham House
Powis Castle
The Priory
Tintinhull House
Upton House

Botanic Gardens
Cambridge Botanic Garden
Chelsea Physic Garden
Harlow Carr Botanical Gardens
Logan Botanic Garden
Oxford Botanic Garden
Royal Botanic Garden, Edinburgh
Royal Botanic Garden, Kew
Younger Botanic Garden Benmore

Demonstration Gardens
Capel Manor
Harlow Carr
Rosemoor
Ryton Organic Gardens
Wisley Garden
Yalding

Herb Gardens
Gunby Hall
Hardwick Hall
Herb and Heather Centre
Hexham Herbs
Holdenby Hall Gardens
Hollington Nurseries
Iden Croft
Lower Severalls Herb Nursery
Pitmedden
Poyntzfield Herb Nursery
Scotney Castle
Sissinghurst Castle

Japanese Gardens
Capel Manor
Compton Acres
Heale House
Kyoto Garden
Newstead Abbey
Saling Hall
Tatton Park

Kitchen Gardens
Barnsley House
Barrington Court
Calke Abbey
Edmondsham House
Felbrigg Hall
Greys Court
Gunby Hall
Harlow Carr
Helmingham Hall
Tintinhull House
Upton House
West Dean
Wisley Garden

Landscape Gardens
Antony House
Audley End
Blaise Castle
Blenheim Palace
Boughton House Park
Bowood
Chatsworth
Claremont
Duncombe Park
Euston Hall
Farnborough Hall
Gibside
Hackfall Wood
Hawkstone Park
Hermitage, The
Mount Edgcumbe
Osterley Park
Painshill
Painswick Rococo Garden
Petworth
Prior Park
Rievaulx Terrace
Royal Botanic Garden, Kew
Scotney Castle
Sheffield Park
Sheringham Park
Shugborough
Stourhead
Stowe
Studley Royal
Wolterton Park
Wrest Park

Rock Gardens
Cragside House
Killerton House

Curious statues of monkeys and other animals decorate the enclosing walls and a menagerie of creatures lurks in the undergrowth. On the far side of the house woodland, with many rhododendrons and ornamental trees, presses in on a lake whose banks are planted with drifts of iris, crocosmia or kniphofia. Mount Stewart is nothing if not bold, but Lady Londonderry's strong sense of design holds it brilliantly together and makes it one of the finest gardens in Britain.

ROWALLANE GARDEN
County Down

Illustration: Penstemon *'George Home'*

Saintfield, Ballynahinch
BT24 7LH
11m SE of Belfast by A7
Tel: 01238 510131

Owner:
The National Trust

Open: Apr to Oct daily 10.30–6 (weekends 2–6). 20 acres

THE DRIVE leading up to Rowallane passes through dense woodland with mossy rocks pressing in on either side. The garden was chiefly made by Hugh Armytage Moore who came here in 1903. He was particularly interested in woody plants, especially rhododendrons which he planted in the handsomely undulating site in bold clumps and belts, as though they were the ingredients of a landscape garden. Many of his plantings were raised from seed collected by the great plant hunters of the early 20th century – such as Wilson, Forrest and Kingdon-Ward. The microclimate is very benign, as the many species from the southern hemisphere show – olearias from Australia, the orange-flowered *Desfontainea spinosa* from Chile and *Pseudowintera colorata*, with curiously variegated foliage, from New Zealand. The character of the garden is essentially informal but beds in the walled garden have excellent shrub roses and flowering shrubs, and the National Collection of large-flowered penstemons.

MOUNT STEWART
County Down

Newtownards BT22 2AD
15m E of Belfast by A20
Tel: 012477 88387/88487

Owner:
The National Trust

Open: Apr to Sept, daily
10.30–6; Oct, Sat and Sun
10.30–6. 78 acres. House
open

GOOD GARDENS often bear the stamp of one exceptional creator, but few so firmly as Mount Stewart. Edith, Marchioness of Londonderry came to Mount Stewart as a young wife in 1921 and plunged into the making of the garden; today, restored by the National Trust, it is still very much as she made it. The climate at Mount Stewart is exceptionally mild, with high humidity from the sea. This allows an exceptional range of tender plants: huge eucalyptus, an avenue of the New Zealand cabbage palm (*Cordyline australis*) and tender conifers such as *Cupressus cashmiriana*. To the west of the house a sunken garden is surrounded on three sides by a pergola with roses, vines and the rare *Billardiera longiflora* with brilliant blue berries in autumn. Beds in the centre are brilliant in spring with orange azaleas, and in summer with a rich mixture of herbaceous plants. Behind the house the Italian garden is a giant parterre in which the beds – edged with purple berberis or golden thuya – have artful but ebullient colour schemes: grey, white and blue to the west, and orange, yellow and scarlet to the east.

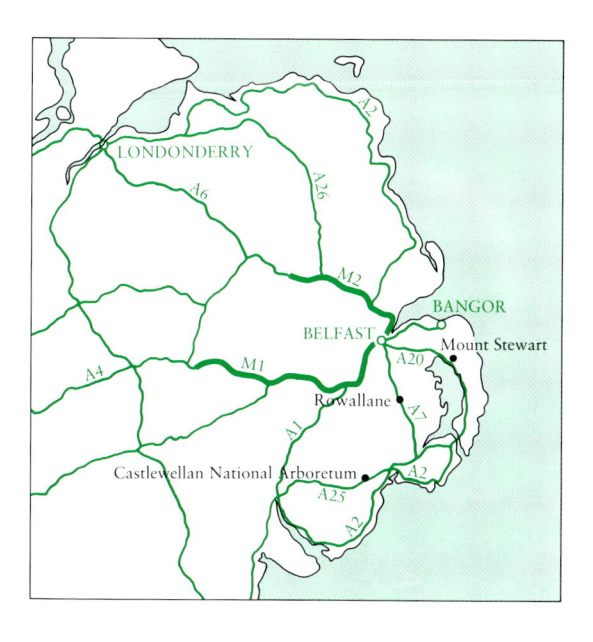

CASTLEWELLAN NATIONAL ARBORETUM
County Down

Castlewellan BT31 9BW
30m S of Belfast by A24
and minor roads
Tel: 013967 78664

Owner: Department of Agriculture (Northern Ireland)

Open: Daily, 10–dusk. 108 acres

THE ANNESLEY FAMILY started this great arboretum and plant collection in the 1870s. It benefits from a fine site, with a curving lake, in the foothills of the Mourne Mountains near the coast of southern County Down. The original 12 1/2-acre walled arboretum, now called the Annesley Garden, has fine borders, and exceptional flowering shrubs and ornamental trees, many of them rare and tender species from the southern hemisphere such as the evergreen *Carpodetus serratus* from New Zealand and *Pilgerodendron uviferum* from the Andes. North of the walled garden, azaleas, camellias and rhododendrons thrive under the canopy of beech and oak. An area of woodland by the lake is planted with deciduous trees chosen for especially brilliant autumn colouring. Throughout the arboretum there are outstanding specimens of trees, several of which date from the original 19th-century plantings, giving great character to the place.

NORTHERN
IRELAND